IMAGES
of Modern America

NORAD
and Cheyenne Mountain AFS

On the Front Cover: Clockwise from the top:
Comet Hale-Bopp over Cheyenne Mountain (Courtesy of John Rising), entrance to Cheyenne Mountain Complex (Courtesy of the US Air Force), Building 2, NORAD and US Northern Command Headquarters, Peterson Air Force Base (AFB), September 11, 2013 (Author's collection), US Air Force F-15 shadows a Soviet Tu-95 Bear Bomber (Courtesy of the US Air Force), first explosion breaking ground at Cheyenne Mountain AFS (Courtesy of the US Air Force)

On the Back Cover: From left to right
US Air Force E-3 AWACS (Courtesy of the US Air Force), girder fragment from the World Trade Center, 9/11 Memorial, Headquarters, NORAD-USNORTHCOM, Peterson AFB (Author's collection), 1980s command center inside Cheyenne Mountain Complex (Courtesy of the US Air Force)

IMAGES
of Modern America

NORAD AND CHEYENNE MOUNTAIN AFS

J. Brian "Bear" Lihani

ARCADIA PUBLISHING

ISBN 978-1-4671-3330-2

Published by Arcadia Publishing
Charleston, South Carolina

Printed in the United States of America

Library of Congress Control Number: 2014959800

For all general information, please contact Arcadia Publishing:
Telephone 843-853-2070
Fax 843-853-0044
E-mail sales@arcadiapublishing.com
For customer service and orders:
Toll-Free 1-888-313-2665

Visit us on the Internet at www.arcadiapublishing.com

Dedicated to the men and women of NORAD and CMAFS past and present, and for my wife, Christina; son, Jason; and Mom and Dad

Contents

ACKNOWLEDGMENTS

When I began my Air Force career the one Air Force command that I felt was the one I wanted to be a part of was the North American Air Defense Command (NORAD). I thought that defending my homeland and family and friends was the greatest calling that could be accomplished. Having the honor to be a part of the NORAD mission for the majority of my Air Force career were some of the most satisfying and fulfilling of those many years. I always enjoy talking about NORAD and the mission and am proud to have compiled this book.

I thank the NORAD command historians, Dr. Lance Blyth and Dr. Brian Laslie. They provided the majority of the photographs and opened their archives in assisting in putting this book together. I also thank Maj. Jamie Humphries from the NORAD-USNORTHCOM Public Affairs office in reviewing the manuscript and his coordinating assistance. Unless noted, all images are US Air Force photographs and courtesy of the US Air Force.

And my biggest thanks goes to my wonderful wife, Christina Lihani, for her proofreading and suggestions and her patience and strong support. You are the wind beneath my wings.

LEGEND

BMEWS Ballistic Missile Early Warning System – Provided NORAD with immediate indications of missile launches anywhere in the world that could be a threat to North America.

COC Combat Operations Center – The main operational center for NORAD. This is where key decisions are made by senior leaders regarding potential threats to North America.

CONAD Continental Air Defense – The military command charged with the air defense of the United States. Operational after World War II, it was the precursor to NORAD.

DEW Line Distant Early Warning Line – Located in the far Arctic regions of Canada and Alaska, this line of long range and short range radars look over the North Pole and Arctic region for any airborne threats that would be coming that way. Spanning from the western part of Alaska to the eastern coast of Canada, this radar network is a key system to NORADs mission.

NWS North Warning System – This is the modern system that replaced the DEW Line in the 1980s and provides more reliable data in the Arctic region.

SAGE Semi-Automated Ground Environment – This was the computer system used at the air defense squadrons in the US and Canada. This state of the art system filled an entire basement of a huge concrete block house until it was replaced by two computers the size of soda vending machines in the mid-1980s.

Introduction

Before World War II began for the United States, the US War Department informed the public that the Air Defense Command (ADC) was being created to "further the development of means and methods for defense against air attacks." It was 1939, and the airplane was only 36 years old, but it had proven itself as a formidable war machine in World War I. Although never threatened, the War Department realized the potential danger of enemy aircraft. The ADC was formed in 1940, but it was not until 1946 that it became a military command of the Army. That year, Gen. Carl "Tooey" Spaatz, commanding general, Army Air Forces, testified to Congress on a need for a US Army Air Defense Command. General Spaatz stated, "In view of the possibility of air attack in any future war, we feel that the air defense of the United States cannot be left to chance. There must be a commander responsible for it. We must be properly organized so there cannot possibly be an air surprise such as occurred at Pearl Harbor. We hope and expect we will have enough appropriation to provide equipment and personnel to maintain radar stations open 24 hours a day . . . The Air Defense Command is established for this purpose."

The Joint Chiefs of Staff established Continental Air Defense Command (CONAD) on September 1, 1954, and its mission was to defend the continental United States against air attacks. The US Army Air Defense Command became a component of CONAD, and in 1956, the Secretary of Defense signed the plan that reorganized CONAD (separating it from the US Air Force Air Defense Command) and also added Alaska as part of its responsibilities. This new structure also gave CONAD the ability to assist Canada and Mexico in air defense. Because of this structure and new responsibilities, the Joint Chiefs of Staff and Canadian Chiefs of Staff Committee were introducing the potential integration of operational control of the air defense forces of both Canada and the United States. The study was assigned to the Joint Canadian–United States Military Study Group for review, which they completed in 1956 with the recommendation that the two countries' air defense forces integrate. Both countries' leadership reviewed the proposal, and in August 1957 the two governments formally announced the approval of the establishment of an integrated Canadian and American air defense command. Gen. Earle E. Partridge, CONAD commander, proposed that operational control of Canadian and US air defense forces be assumed by an integrated headquarters in Colorado Springs, Colorado. General Partridge also recommended the title North American Air Defense Command (NORAD) for the newly formed force. Formal approval of the location and name was given on September 6, 1957, thereby establishing NORAD. Ent Air Force Base in Colorado Springs was selected as headquarters, and the Air Operations Center there became responsible for operational control of NORAD air defense forces.

The formal agreement establishing NORAD was signed on May 12, 1958. This agreement proposed principles that included the appointment of a Commander in Chief North American Air Defense Command (CINCNORAD) and a deputy (DCINCNORAD), who would not be from the same country. The military chiefs developed, and approved, terms of reference for NORAD, effective June 10, 1958. These terms gave NORAD the mission of defending the United States, Canada, and Alaska (not yet a state) against air attacks. On August 5, 1958, NORAD issued an order that established NORAD regions and divisions in the United States, Canada, and Alaska.

As time passed, General Partridge felt the current location of the NORAD Air Operations Center was too vulnerable to an attack. With the new requirement for a ballistic missile defense system display, the need for a new command post was evident. In a letter to the military leaders of both countries, General Partridge stated, "It has been recognized for several years that the facilities at Ent Air Force Base are quite inadequate both from a point of view of availability of floor space as well as security. The combat operations center is a concrete block building of extremely light construction and is exposed to the traffic on the adjacent street so that a man with a bazooka passing in a car could put the establishment out of commission."

As a result of this letter, the USAF asked NORAD for a recommendation of a new location. NORAD replied that it preferred a location for a new combat operations center underground in the Colorado Springs area. General Partridge asserted that the new facility had to be a hardened facility capable of withstanding the overpressure, and earth shock, of a thermonuclear blast. Additionally, the location should be away from other prime targets and convenient to multiple and diverse communications routes. A study of potential locations was performed along the Rockies, and it was determined the best location was the Colorado Springs area. It was recommended that the combat operations center be built inside a granite mountain with headquarters located in the general vicinity—either the Air Force Academy or Fort Carson. Two granite mountain areas were evaluated, one north of Colorado Springs and the other south of the city. Before a final choice was made, a detailed survey of the rock formations had to be undertaken. Extensive drilling operations on the mountain and valley floor provided geological information on rock and soil composition. The US Army Corps of Engineers reviewed many factors in the final site selection, and when all details were compared, Cheyenne Mountain was chosen. Three key criteria were used for the selection of Cheyenne Mountain—geographically centered in North America, area of low seismic activity, and an already established military presence in Colorado Springs. In 1959, the decision was made to carve out a cavern in the 100 million-year-old Cheyenne Mountain as the new location of the NORAD Command Center. Two years of extensive planning and blueprints ensured proper excavation. On May 18, 1961, the excavation began, with the official ground breaking held at the construction site on June 19, 1961, when Gen. Robert M. Lee (Air Defense Command commander) and Gen. Laurence Kuter (CINCNORAD) simultaneously set off symbolic dynamite charges. It took the construction team a little over a year to complete the excavation of Cheyenne Mountain. Hard rock miners used over one million pounds of explosives to remove nearly 700,000 tons of granite, which formed nearly three miles of tunnel and chambers.

As the mountain facilities were completed, NORAD was evolving as a major military command charged with the air defense of North America. Featured in major motion pictures, television shows, documentaries, and even game shows, NORAD and Cheyenne Mountain have become part of America's heritage and lore. Many people mistakenly refer to Cheyenne Mountain as "NORAD," and although it was built as a direct result of NORAD requiring a hardened facility for its new command center, NORAD was never headquartered at Cheyenne Mountain. The 721st Mission Support Group (721st MSG) operates and maintains a survivable, reliable, and secure installation for Cheyenne Mountain. The 721st MSG falls under the 21st Space Wing at Peterson AFB, the "landlords" of Cheyenne Mountain Air Force Station (CMAFS).

For over 50 years, NORAD has watched the skies of North America to prevent any attacks. From the Cold War to the War on Terrorism and beyond, NORAD and the Cheyenne Mountain Air Force Station continue to maintain a presence in guarding the United States and Canada. The two nations will always work to protect the sovereignty of its skies by keeping watch on aircraft, missiles, and space systems that could be a threat. The future is unknown as to the dangers that could face the two countries, but evolving technology will help in deterring any enemy. The men and women of NORAD and CMAFS remain vigilant in protecting the United States and Canada.

One

AIR DEFENSE

THE EARLY YEARS

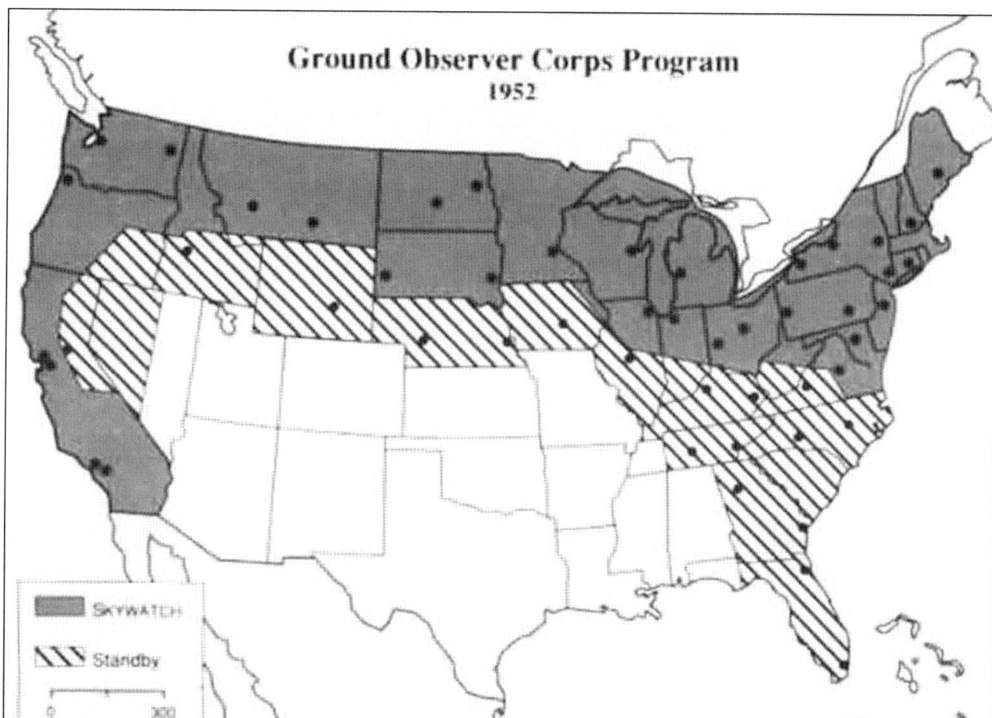

The Ground Observer Corps (GOC) began in World War II, when nearly 1.5 million civilian volunteers were enrolled by the Army Air Forces to man 14,000 observation posts. Positioned along both coasts, the GOC's mission was to visually search the skies for enemy aircraft attempting to penetrate American airspace.

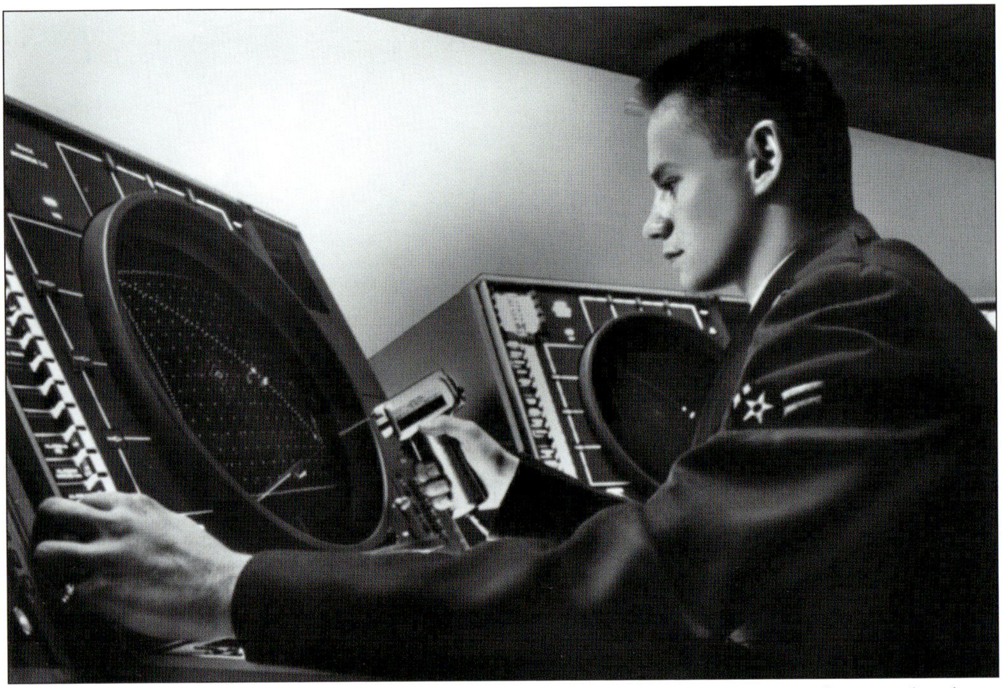

In the early 1950s, a US Air Force airman first class uses a light gun to acquire data on the then-modern radar scope at an air defense unit. The light gun was the precursor to the computer mouse and enabled the console operator to select necessary information on specific radar data.

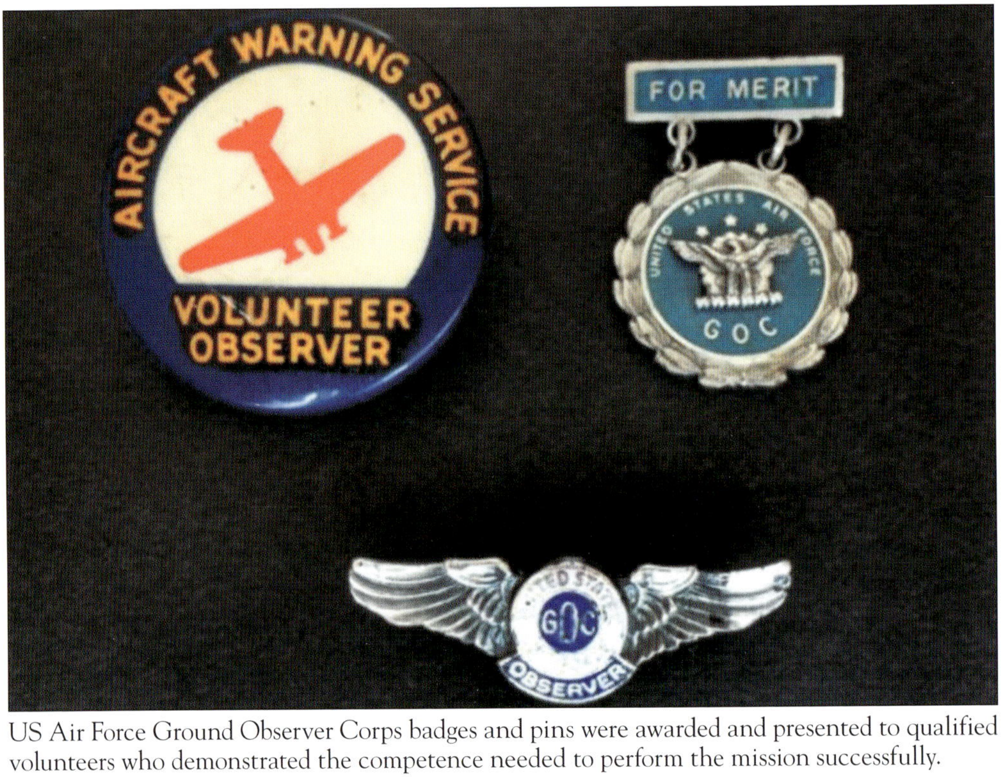

US Air Force Ground Observer Corps badges and pins were awarded and presented to qualified volunteers who demonstrated the competence needed to perform the mission successfully.

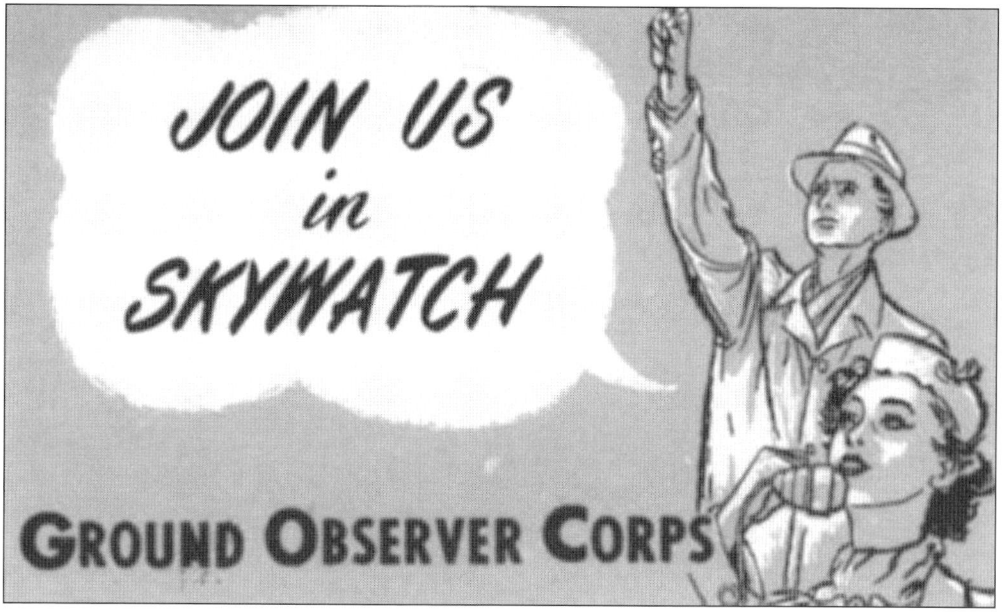

The Ground Observer Corps (GOC) was a major factor in the early air defense of the United States and Canada. There was much advertising for the GOC, and this stamp is one example. Other items used to spread the word included billboards, fliers, interviews, etc. Operation Skywatch was a revised GOC program to garner many more volunteers. Eventually, more than 800,000 volunteers stood watch at over 16,000 posts.

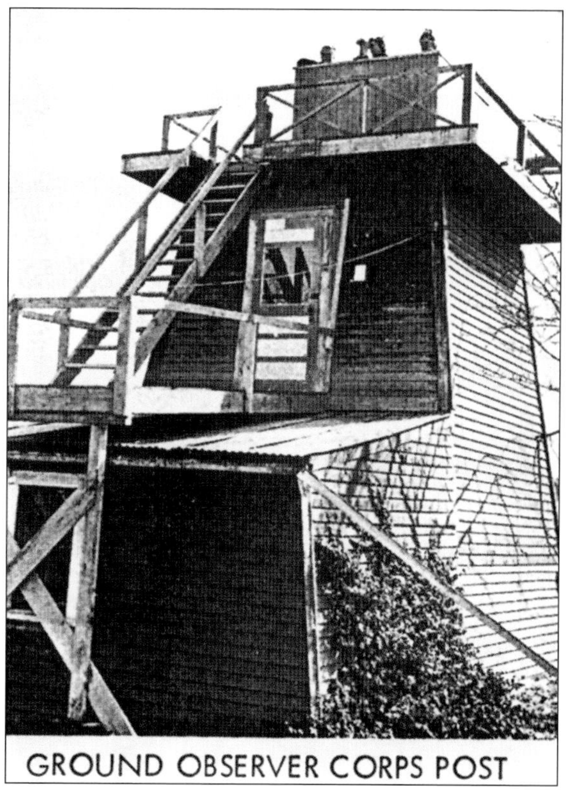

GROUND OBSERVER CORPS POST

This ground observer post design was used by volunteers around the United States and Canada. Each post had aircraft silhouette charts and binoculars to help identify aircraft, and during the Korean War, many posts were manned 24 hours a day in order to fill low-altitude radar gaps.

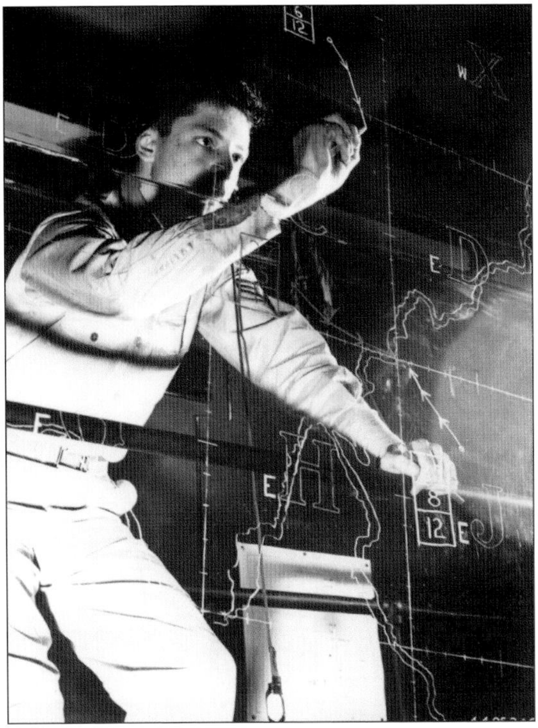

In the early 1950s, the Air Defense Command moved to Colorado Springs' Ent Air Force Base. This Air Force technician is plotting positions on the Plexiglas board in the combat operations center.

Pictured here is an aerial view of Ent Air Force Base, located in downtown Colorado Springs, Colorado. By virtue of its location near the center of the country, Colorado Springs was deemed an imminently secure area for the United States' critical air defense headquarters.

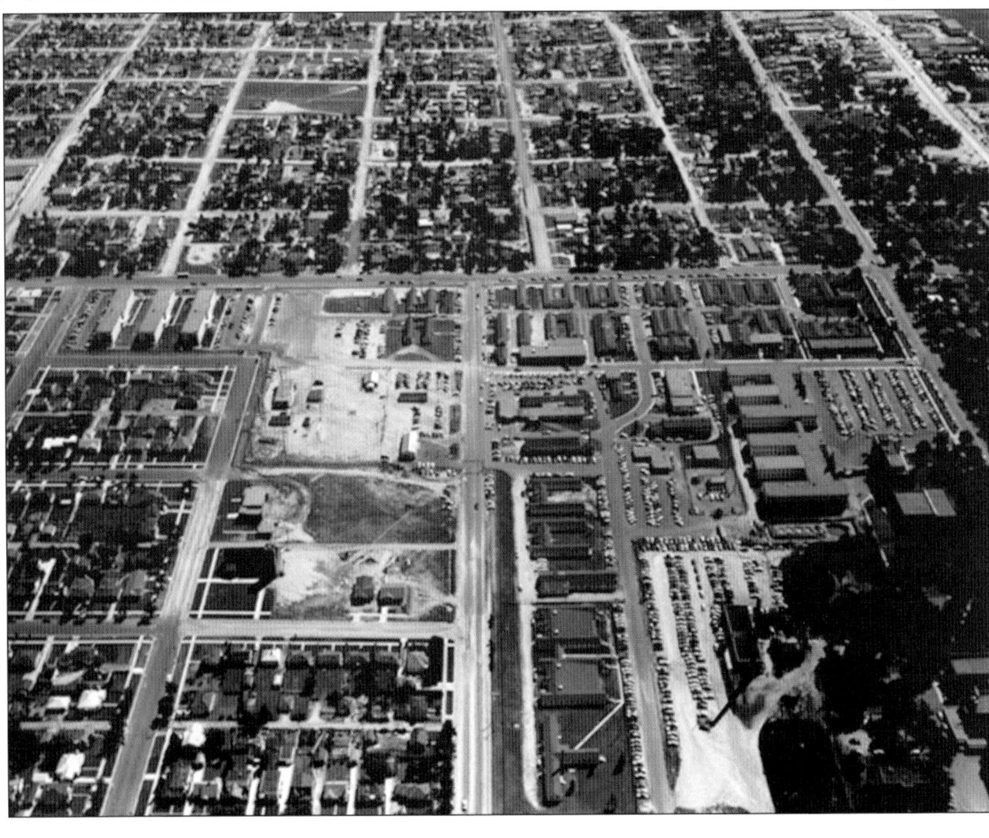

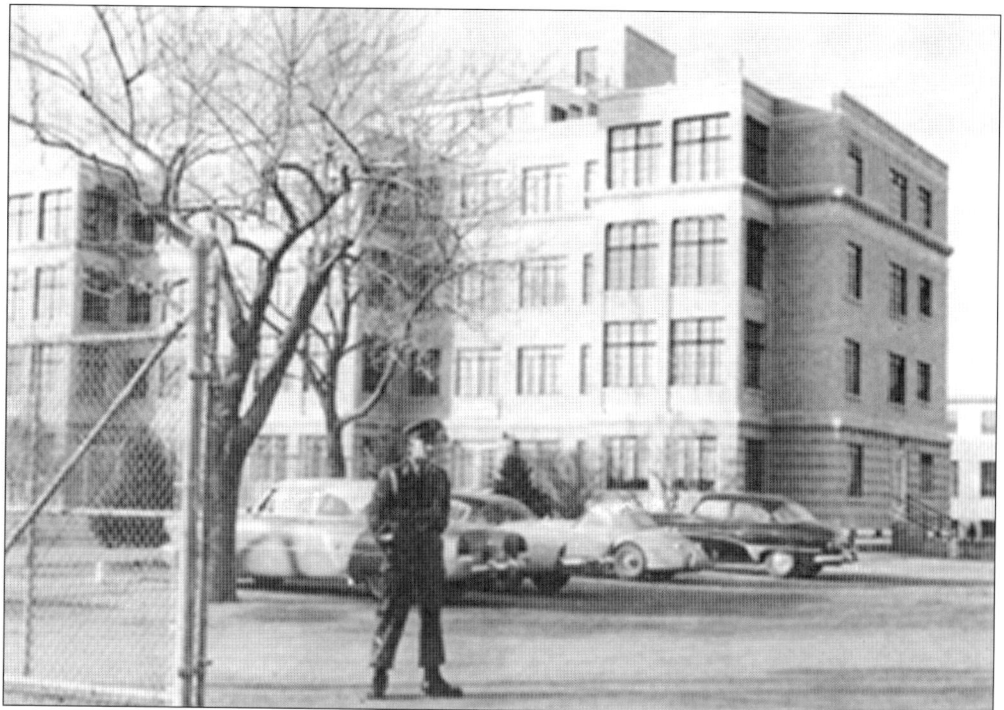

This is the Continental Air Defense (CONAD) headquarters at Ent AFB, the early air defense headquarters prior to moving to other facilities. As the years progressed and the danger of an enemy air attack increased, headquarter buildings were made more secure and in safer locales.

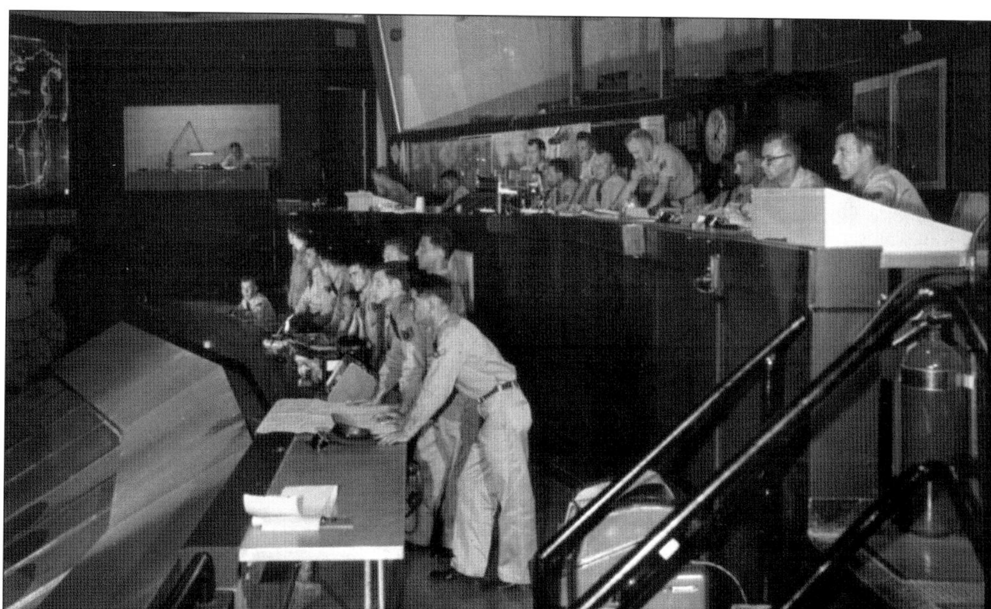

The combat operations center inside the headquarters building at Ent Air Force Base was the nerve center for air defense operations. Utilizing 1950s state-of-the-art technology, the center was manned around the clock.

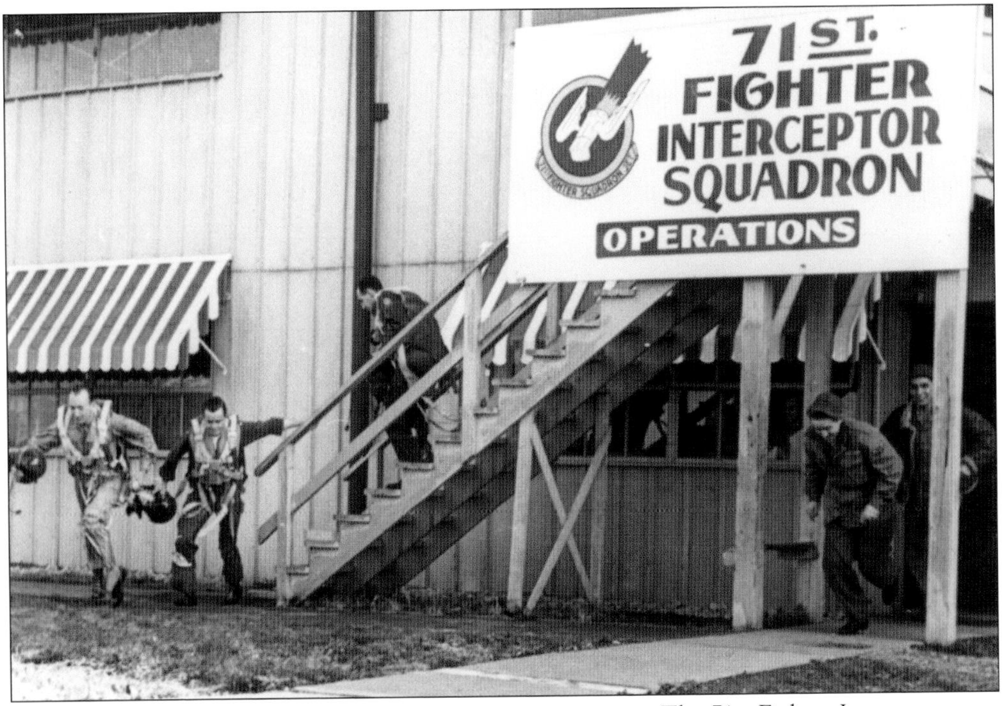

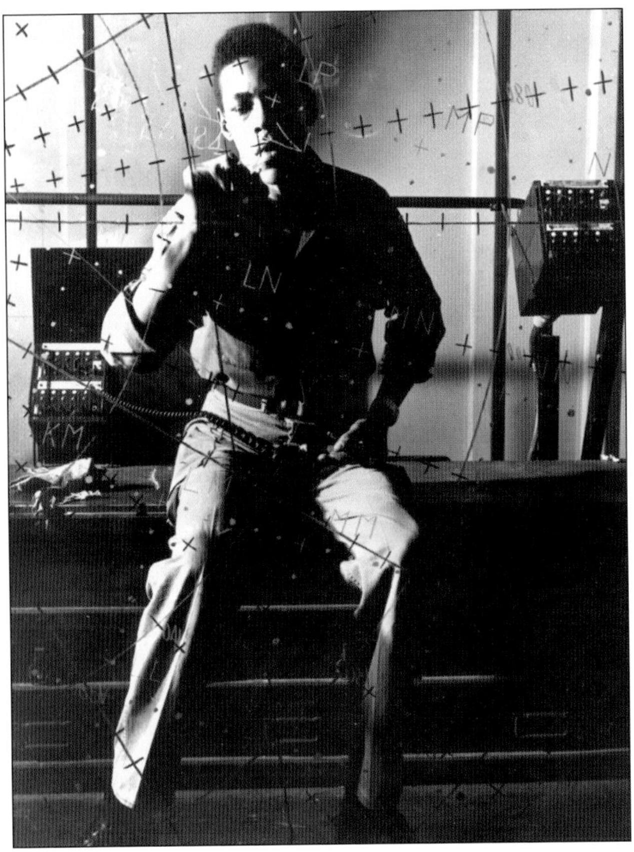

The 71st Fighter Interceptor Squadron based at Griffiss Air Force Base in Rome, New York, flew the F-102 Delta Dagger aircraft. It was one of many alert facilities providing immediate response if an enemy aircraft penetrated US airspace.

The plotting board inside the ADC Combat Operations Center at Ent Air Force Base was a precursor of automated boards that provide the crews with the latest information on unknown and unidentified aircraft movement and status of air defense forces.

HEADQUARTERS
NORTH AMERICAN AIR DEFENSE COMMAND
ENT AIR FORCE BASE
COLORADO SPRINGS, COLORADO

GENERAL ORDERS)
NUMBER 1)

12 September 1957

ESTABLISHMENT OF NORTH AMERICAN AIR DEFENSE COMMAND

Announcement is made of the establishment of the North American Air Defense Command (abbreviation NORAD), effective 12 September 1957 as a Combined Command for the air defense of the continental United States, Canada, Alaska, and the Northeast Area, with headquarters at Ent Air Force Base, Colorado Springs, Colorado.

E. E. PARTRIDGE
General, USAF
Commander-in-Chief

DISTRIBUTION:
A, B, C, D, E, F

On September 12, 1957, General Partridge signed the official stand-up order establishing the North American Air Defense Command (NORAD). This order also delineated NORAD's area of operations, which includes the United States, Canada, Alaska, and the Northeast Area.

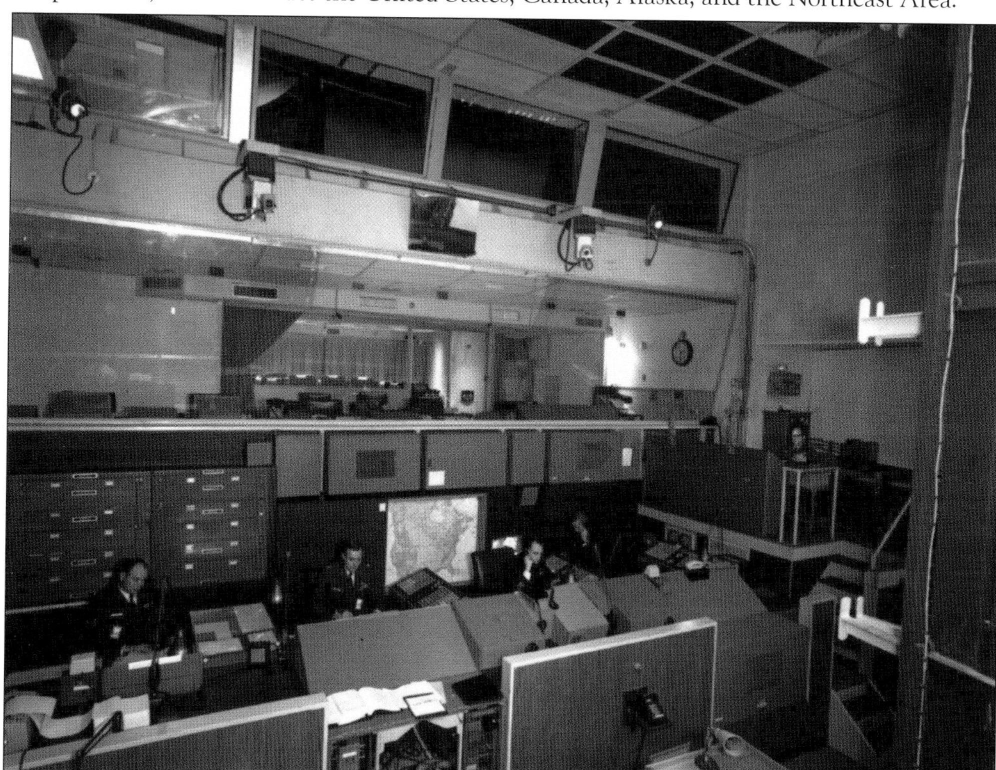

This is an overall view of the combat operations center inside ADC headquarters at Ent Air Force Base. The general and his staff would form on the tier areas for the best view of the many positions in the center.

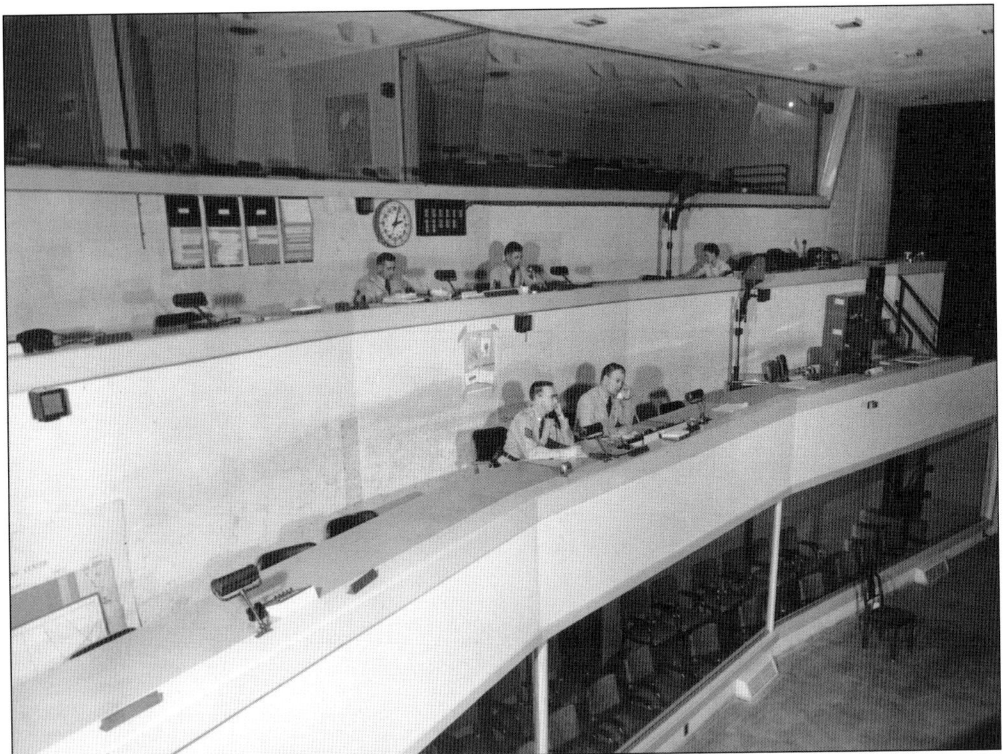

Featured here is another view of the combat operations center inside the hardened facility at Ent Air Force Base. The tiered seating area is where the NORAD leadership would sit during exercises and real-world contingencies. This arrangement allowed the decision-making senior leaders a full view of all staff members.

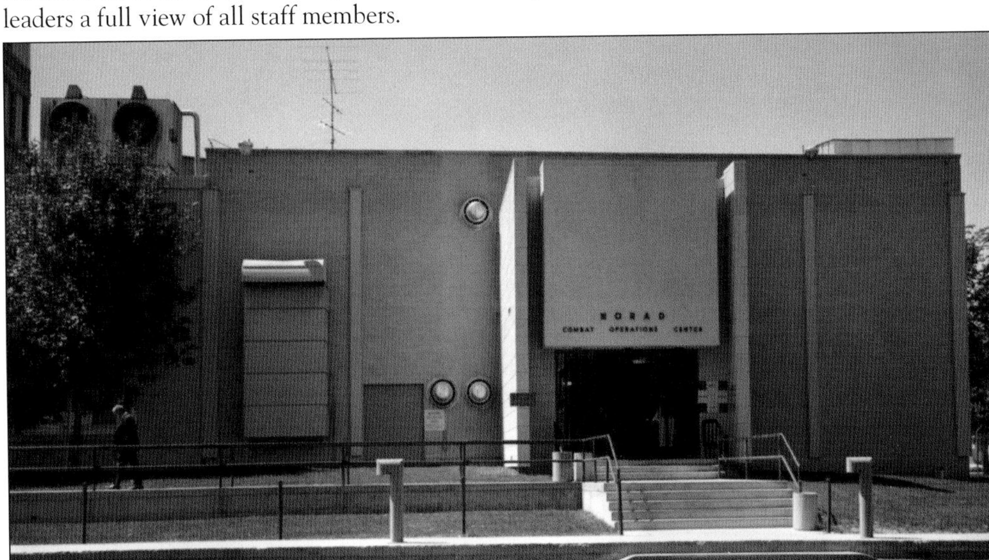

The entrance to the NORAD Combat Operations Center is pictured here, the building that housed the nerve center for NORAD's air defense operations at Ent Air Force Base. Service members from both the United States and Canada ensured air sovereignty was maintained for North America from this building.

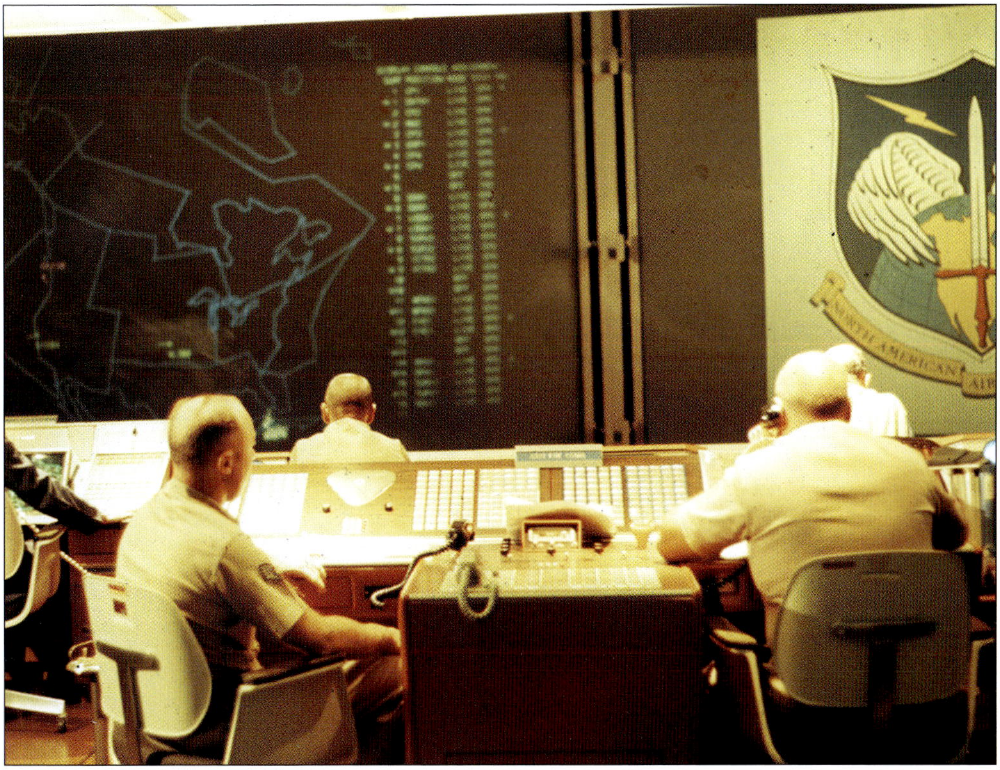

The City of Colorado Springs was proud to be the home of NORAD and the combat operations center. Service members are pictured here at work inside the operations center; note the NORAD emblem on the right.

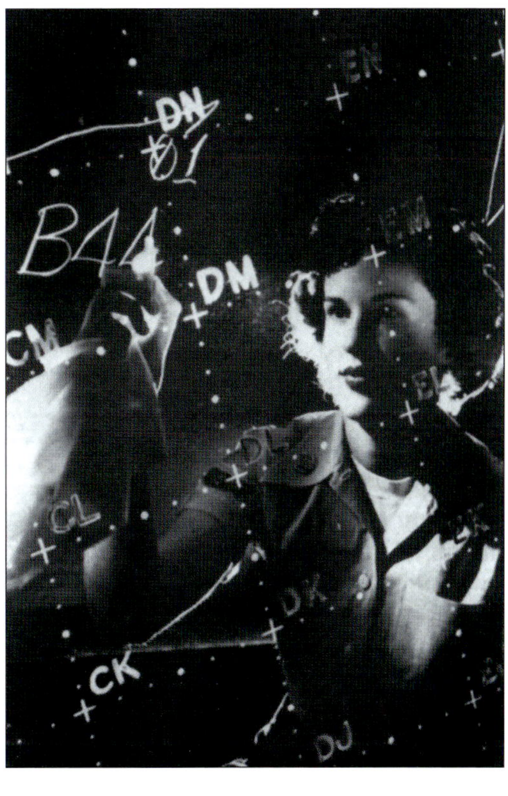

An enlisted board plotter uses a grease pencil to plot a location on the massive Plexiglas board. A grease pencil was used because its marks could be easily removed with a rag and new updates quickly made.

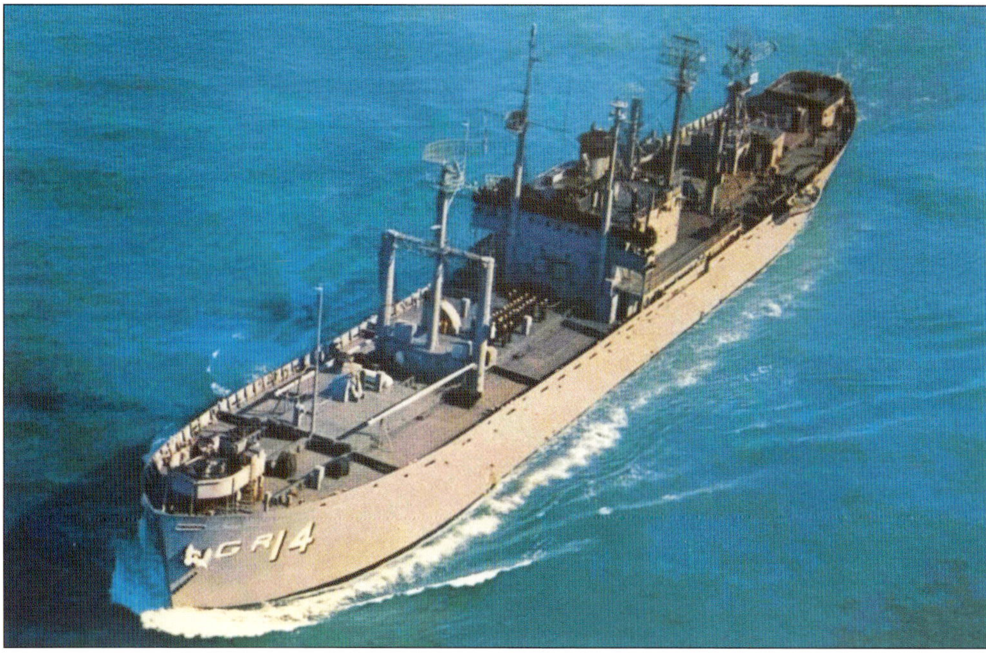

In 1952, US Naval Forces Continental Air Defense Command picket ships were placed on around-the-clock duty off the East Coast (1955 for West Coast). These ships had radars that provided information to the air defense units and patrolled both coasts until spring 1960. They were a part of the Distant Early Warning Line (DEW Line) during that time.

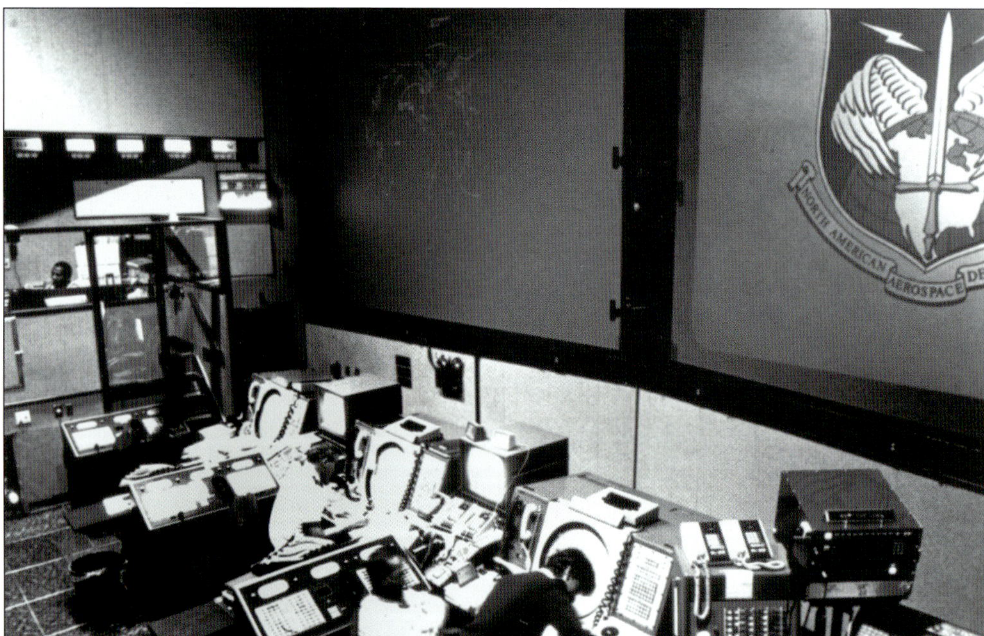

This photograph conveys the enormity of the plotting boards used to show the locations of items of interest to the commander in chief of NORAD. The on-duty general officer was CINCNORAD's representative in making key decisions in the air defense mission when time was of the essence.

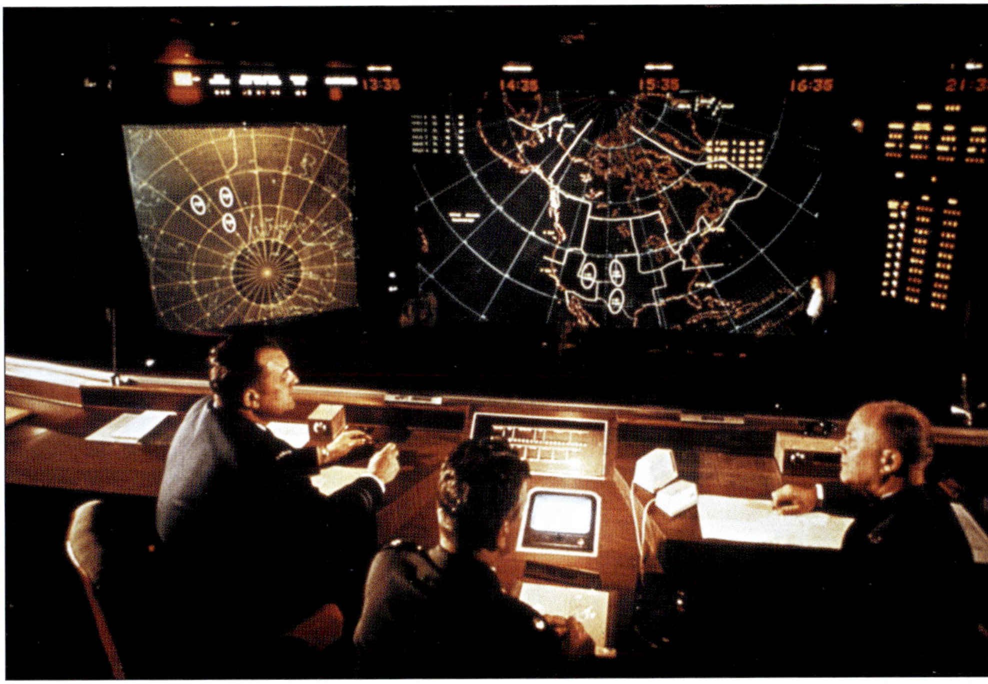

The command director was a flag officer (brigadier general) who was on duty in the combat operations center during every shift. The officer's leadership was needed during potentially hostile situations, and the command director was the senior representative for CINCNORAD.

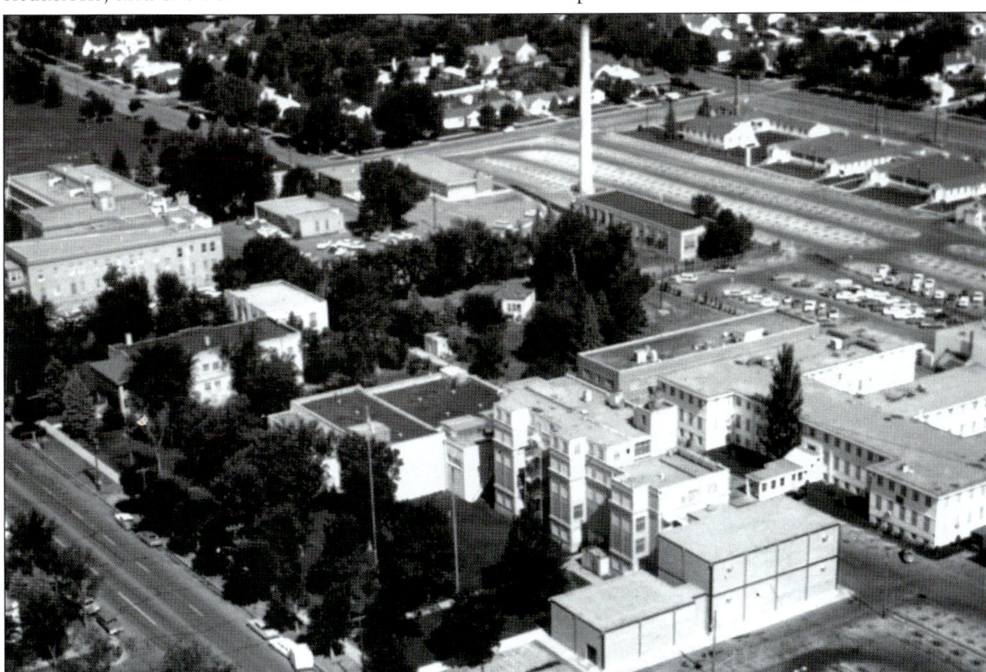
This is an aerial view of Ent Air Force Base in downtown Colorado Springs, Colorado. The large white building in the center of the photograph is NORAD headquarters, which also housed the combat operations center.

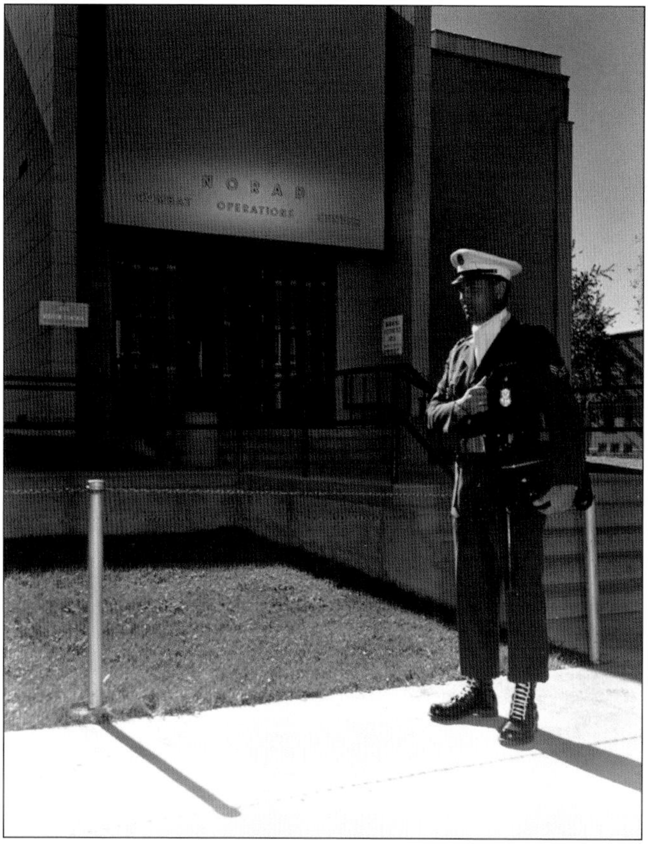

The entrance to the NORAD Combat Operations Center was guarded by an air policeman, who ensured that only properly credentialed people were granted access to the center. This entrance was located in the NORAD Headquarters at Ent Air Force Base.

Pictured here is the NORAD Headquarters sign at Ent Air Force Base. As the sign indicates, this building also housed offices of organizations that provided forces or services to the NORAD mission.

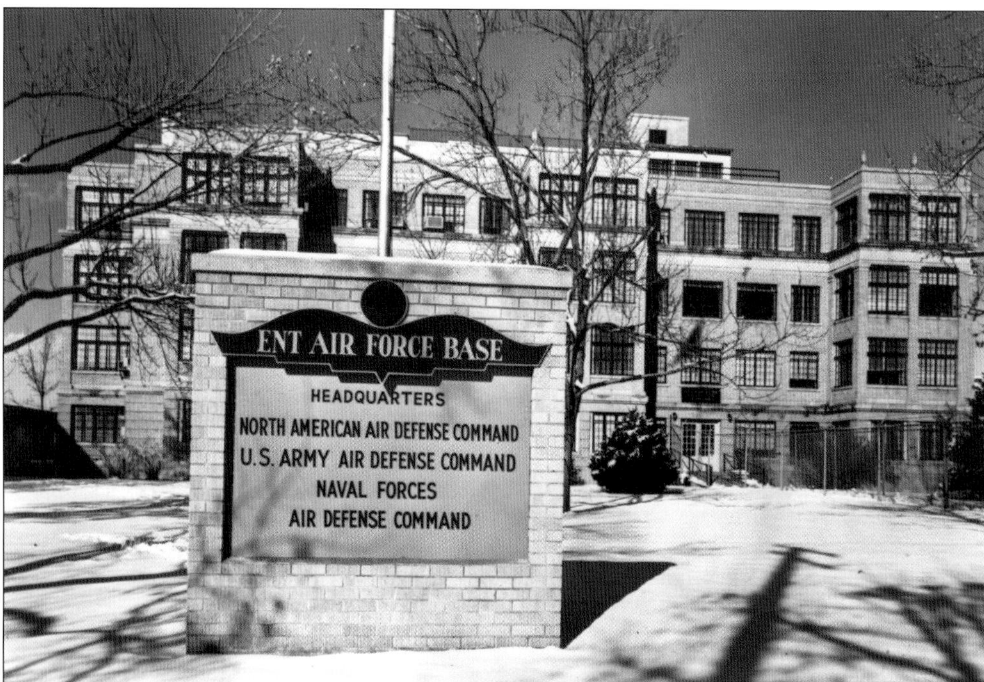

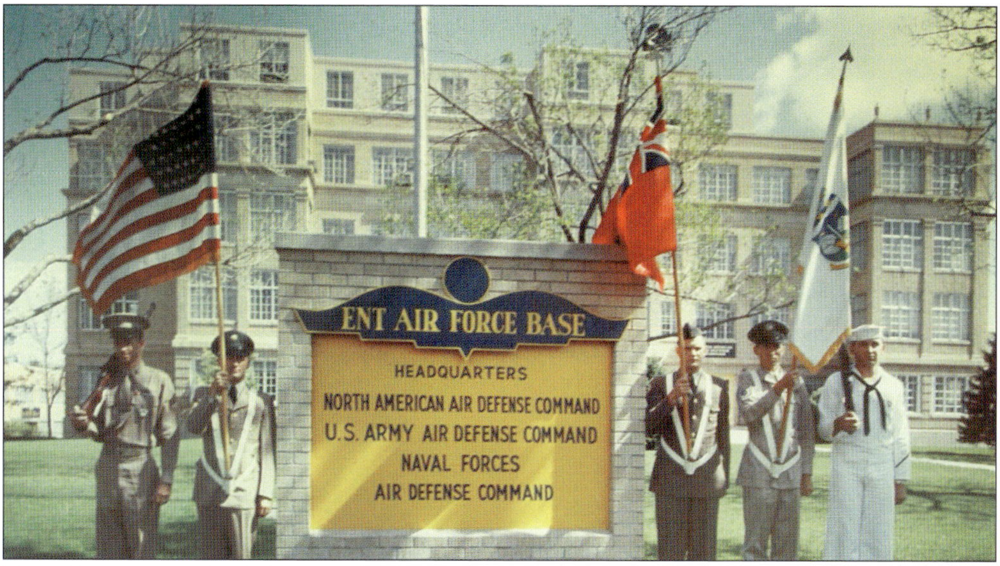

The official NORAD Color Guard was a multiservice and binational color guard. Comprised of members of the US Air Force, Navy, Army, and Marines as well as the Royal Canadian Air Force, the color guard performed at numerous military and civic affairs in the local area.

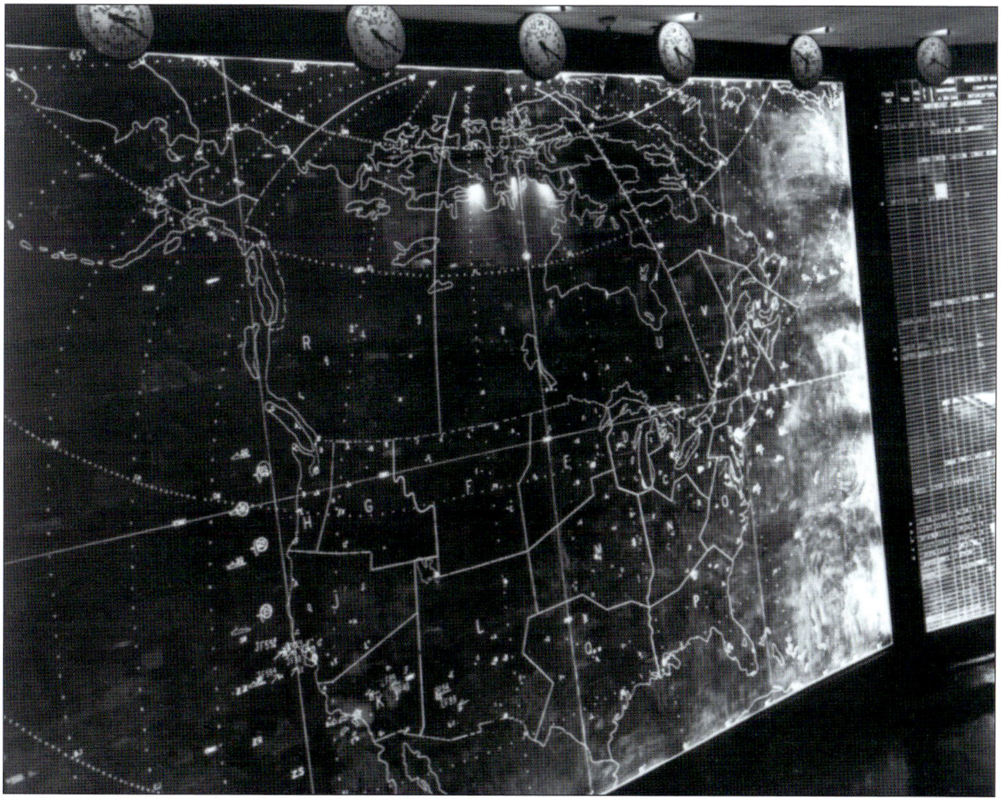

The large plotting board inside the NORAD Combat Operations Center was used to keep leadership informed about the movements of alert fighters and unknown aircraft. It also provided information on surveillance outages that could affect the ability to track unknown aircraft.

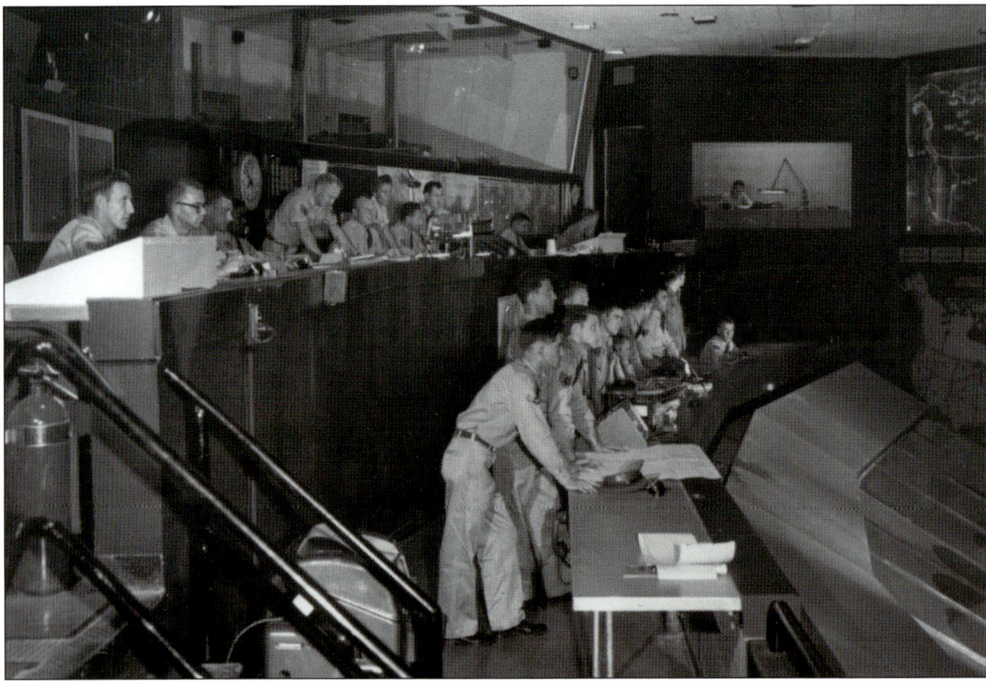

Manning the combat operations center was a 24-hour operation, 365 days a year, and included crews that normally worked eight-hour shifts. Crews consisted of experts who provided the command center with necessary data on a wide variety of critical subjects.

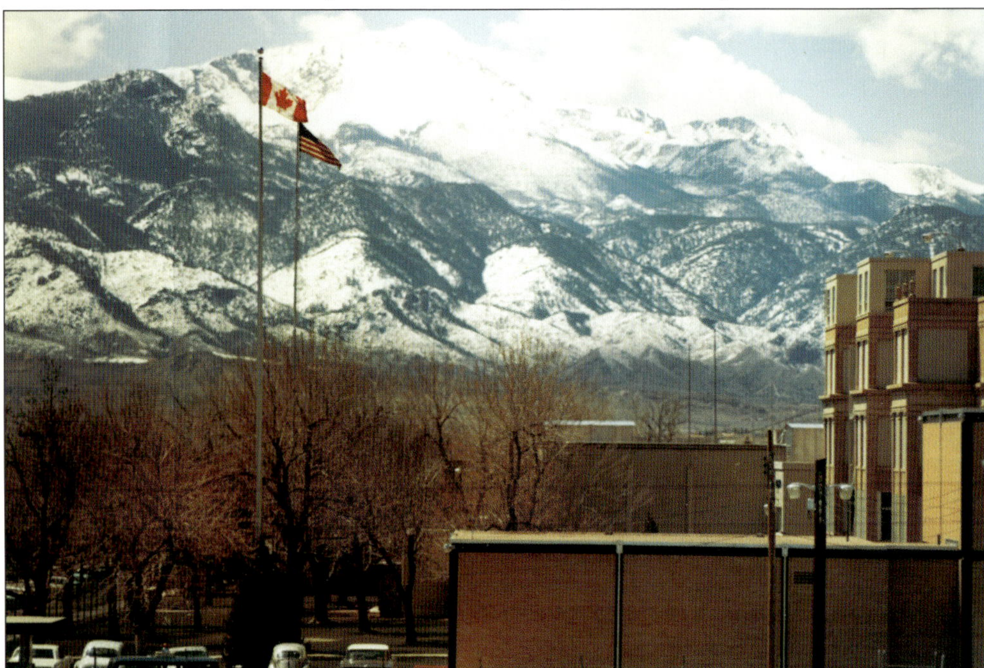

Ent Air Force Base was located in the heart of Colorado Springs, Colorado, with Pikes Peak looming in the distance. Although in a superb location, the security of the facility was questioned, and thus the search for a hardened facility that would provide protection from enemies began.

Two

Cheyenne Mountain AFS

Construction & the Early Years

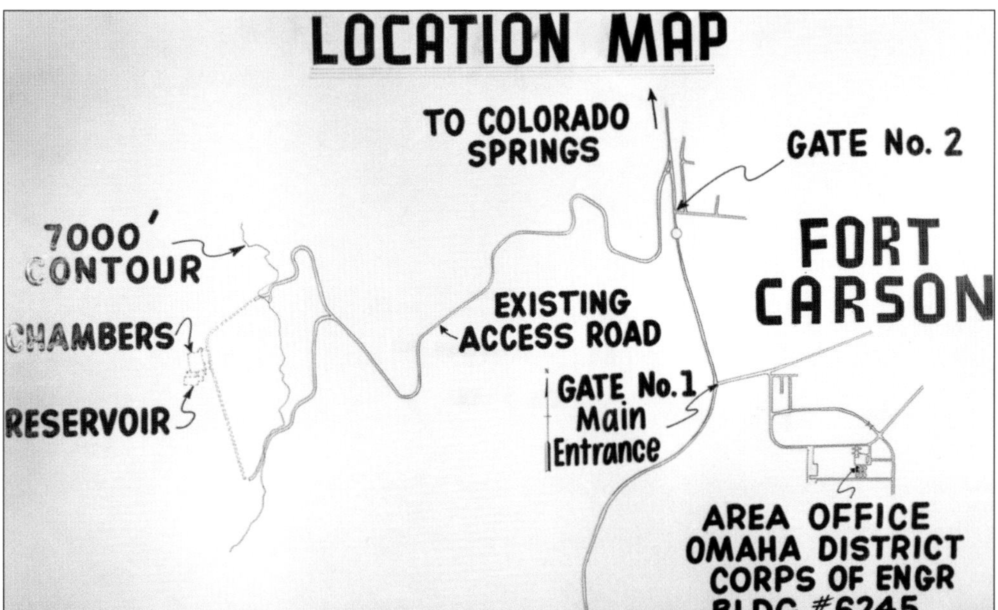

This drawing is the presentation slide showing the location of the planned Cheyenne Mountain Combat Operations Center. Designers proposed and detailed the planned excavation and removal of tons of granite to make room for the center.

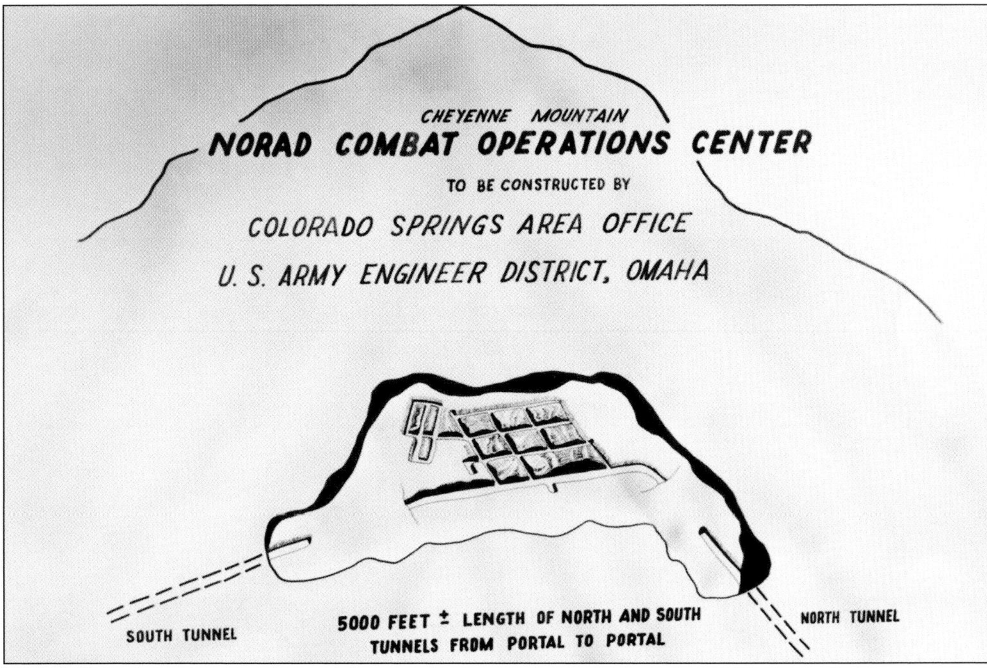

The massive undertaking of the excavation of Cheyenne Mountain was accomplished by the Army Corps of Engineers from Omaha, Nebraska, and their selected teams.

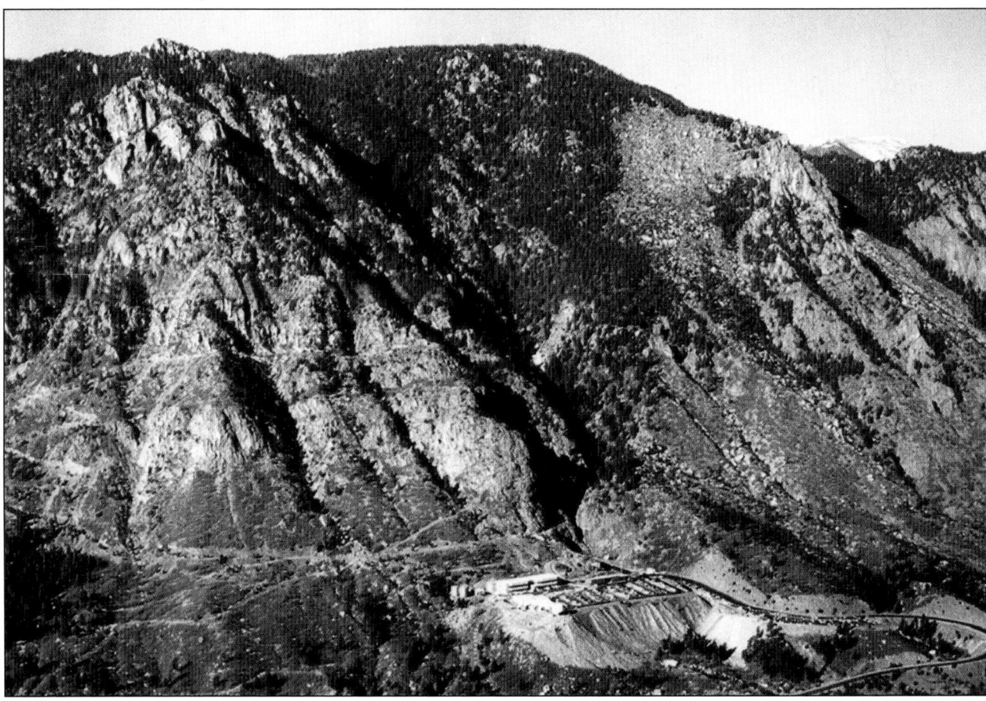

Cheyenne Mountain is located approximately 10 miles south of the city center of Colorado Springs, directly across from Fort Carson Army Post. This 100-million-year-old mountain was selected for its natural location and geological composition, which make it able to withstand an earthquake and nuclear explosion.

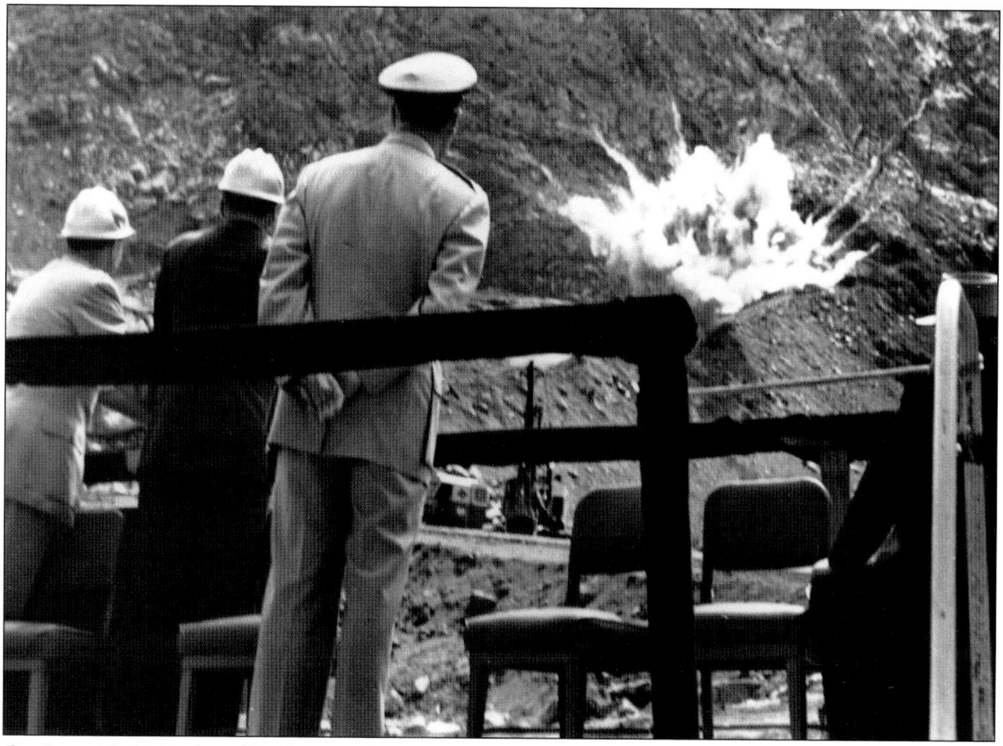

On June 16, 1961, the official ground-breaking ceremony of the new NORAD Combat Operations Center took place at the Cheyenne Mountain construction site. General Lee (Air Defense Command) and General Kuter (NORAD) simultaneously set off symbolic detonations to begin the construction with the press of a little button.

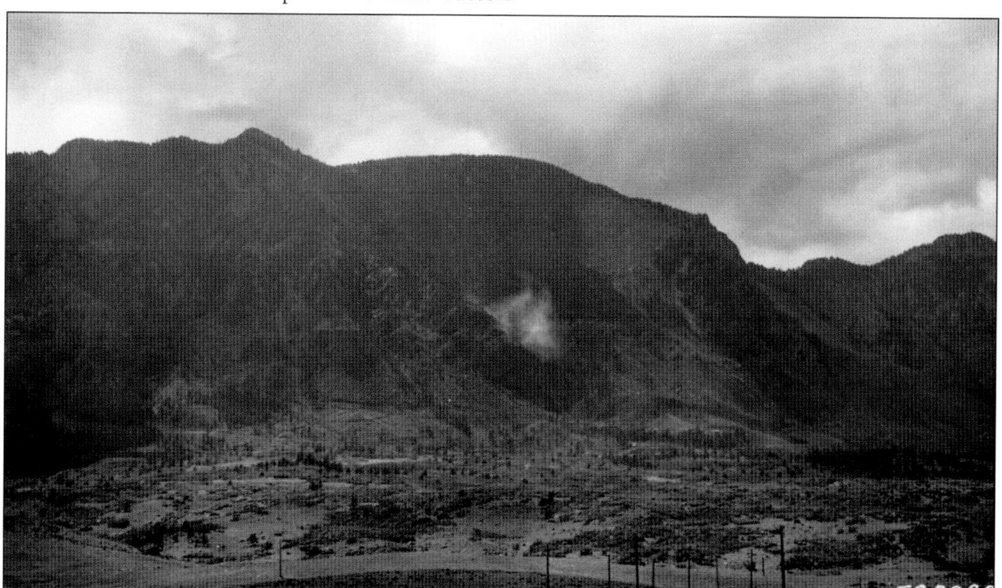

Pictured here is another view of the initial dynamite explosion that began the construction of the Cheyenne Mountain Air Force Station. Attended by dignitaries and military members from the area, the ground breaking marked the start of one of America's most impressive military projects.

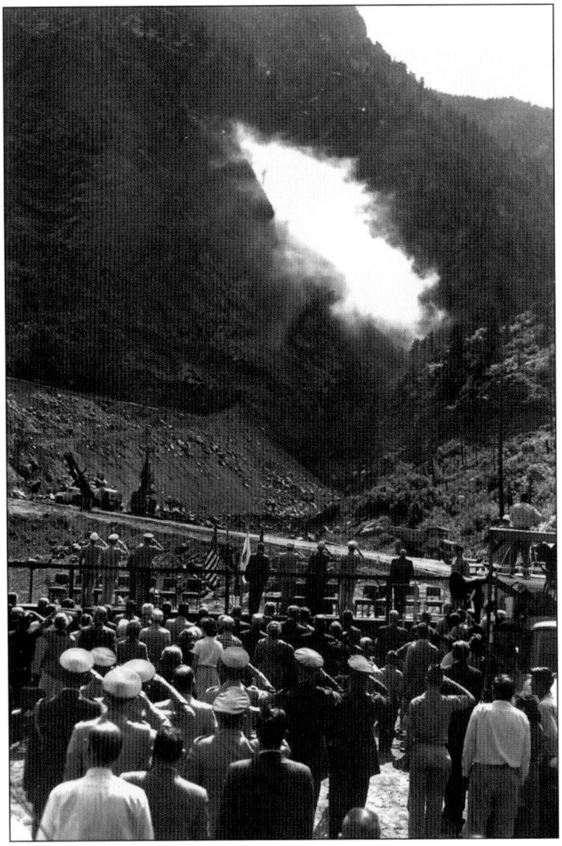

A well-attended crowd of Colorado Springs city dignitaries, military leaders, and civilians viewed the initial explosions that began clearing the area of the entrance to Cheyenne Mountain Air Force Station.

This sign indicates the area of the construction site for the new combat operations center. The entrance to the new center is several hundred feet above the base of the mountain, and the Utah Construction & Mining Company performed the excavation portion of the project.

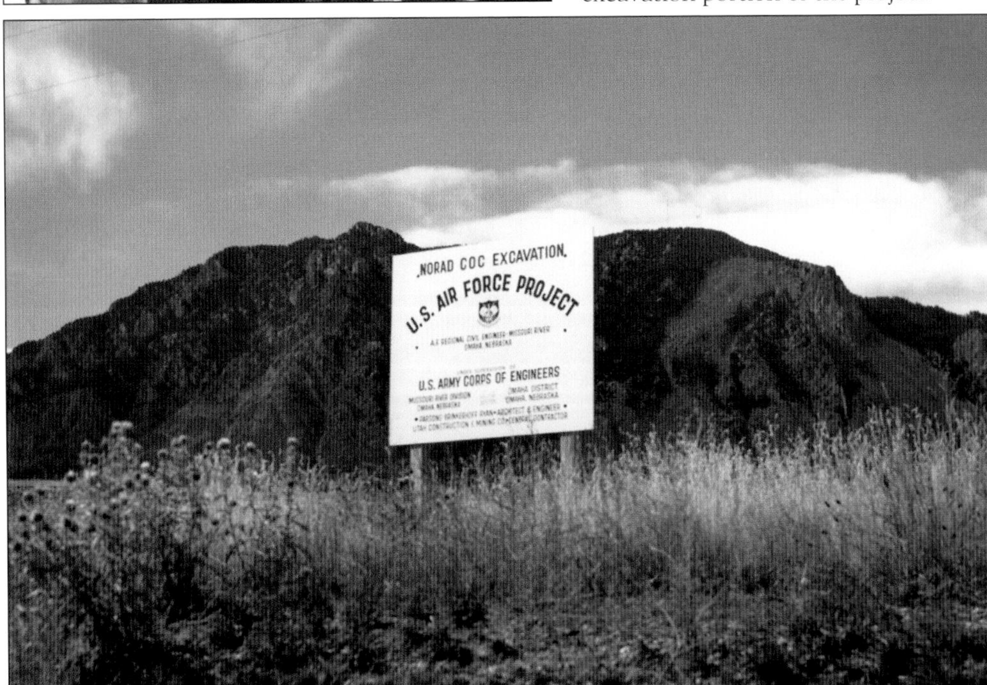

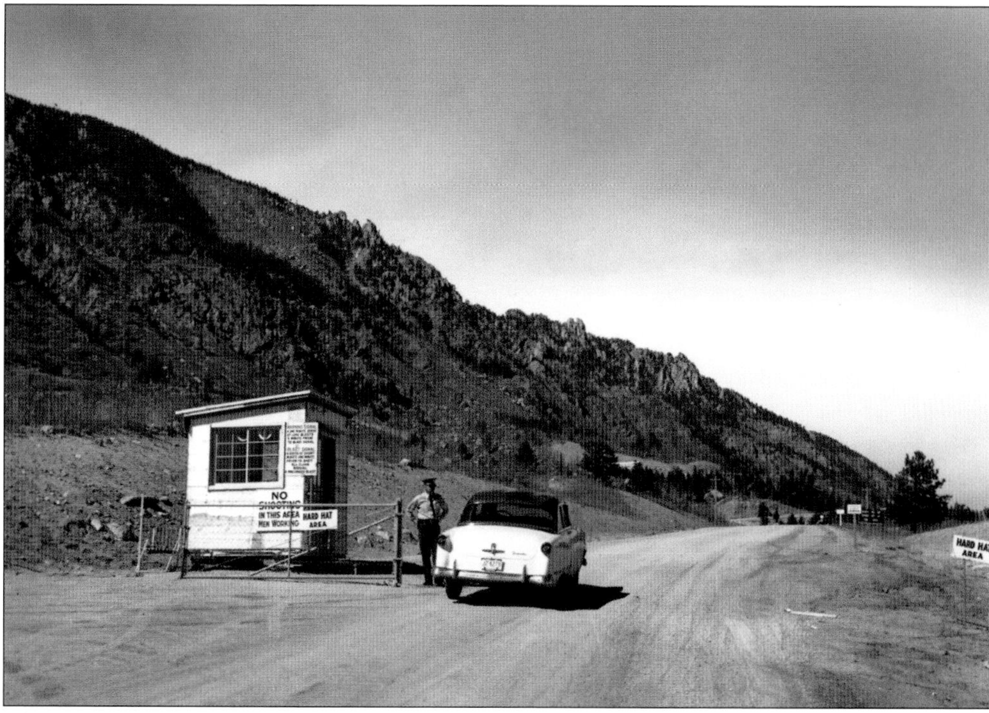

Checkpoints for entrance into the construction site were monitored so that only authorized construction crews and visitors were allowed. This top secret facility required security procedures from the onset.

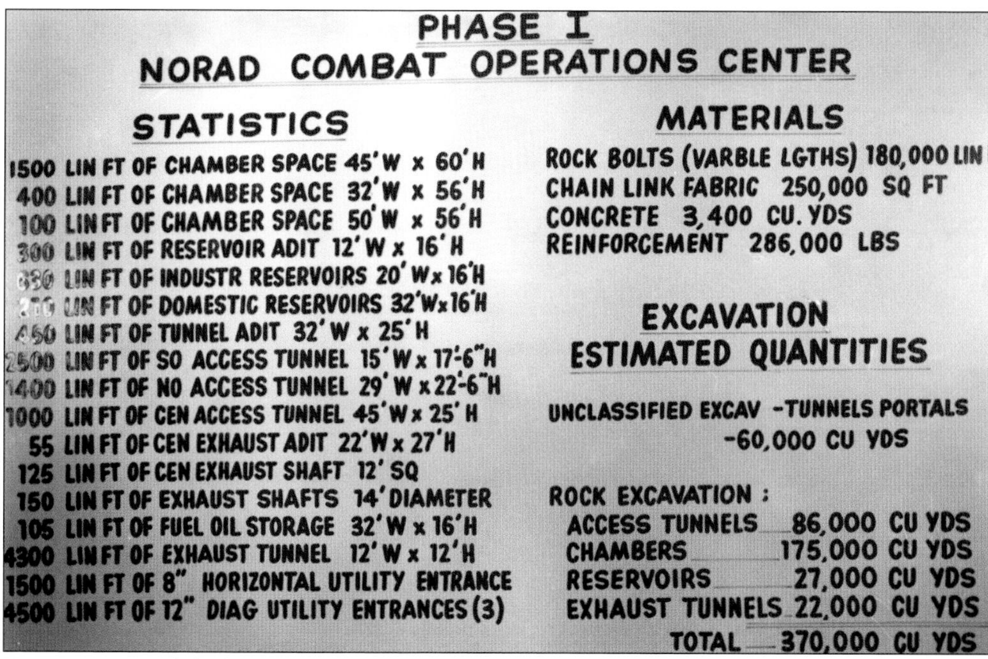

A presentation slide shows all the statistics and materials estimated for the massive undertaking. It was approximated that 370,000 cubic yards of granite would need to be removed from all the tunnels, chambers, and reservoirs.

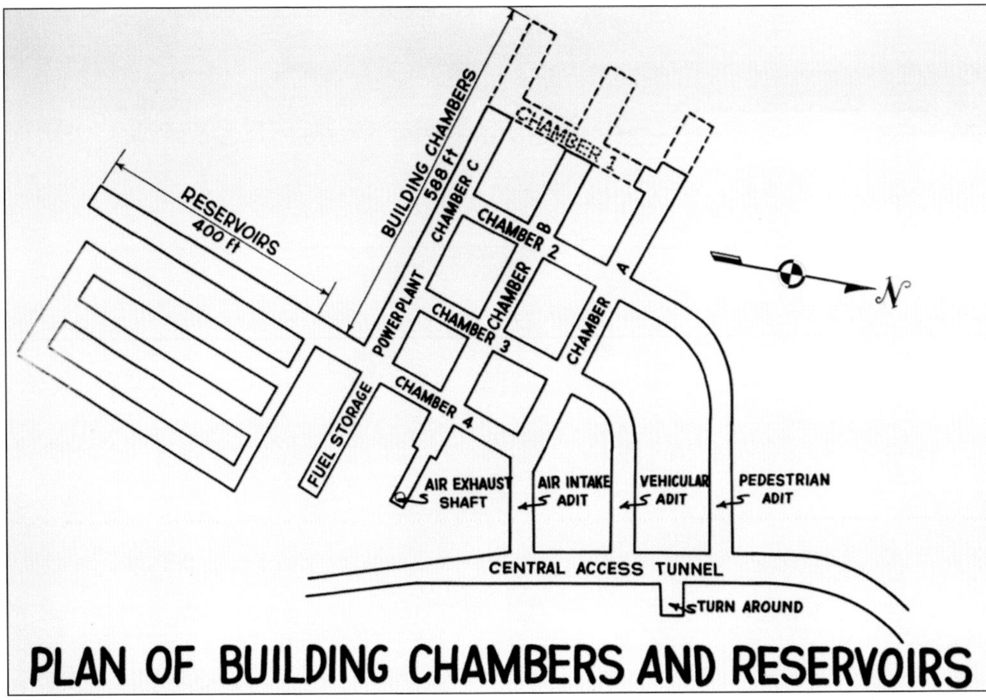

This slide depicts the planned tunnels, chambers, and reservoirs inside Cheyenne Mountain Air Force Station. Although there were some modifications made to the final layout, this is a fairly accurate representation of the actual design.

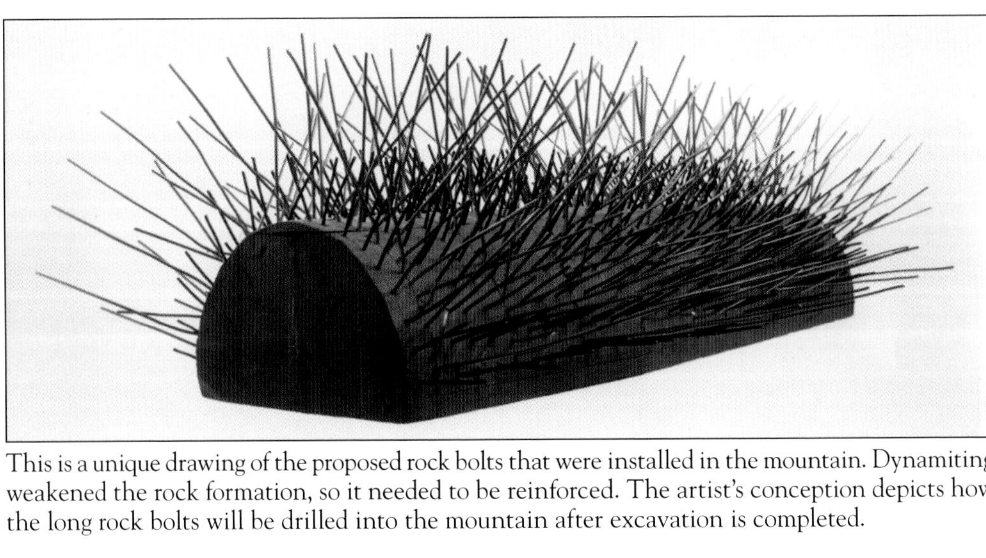

This is a unique drawing of the proposed rock bolts that were installed in the mountain. Dynamiting weakened the rock formation, so it needed to be reinforced. The artist's conception depicts how the long rock bolts will be drilled into the mountain after excavation is completed.

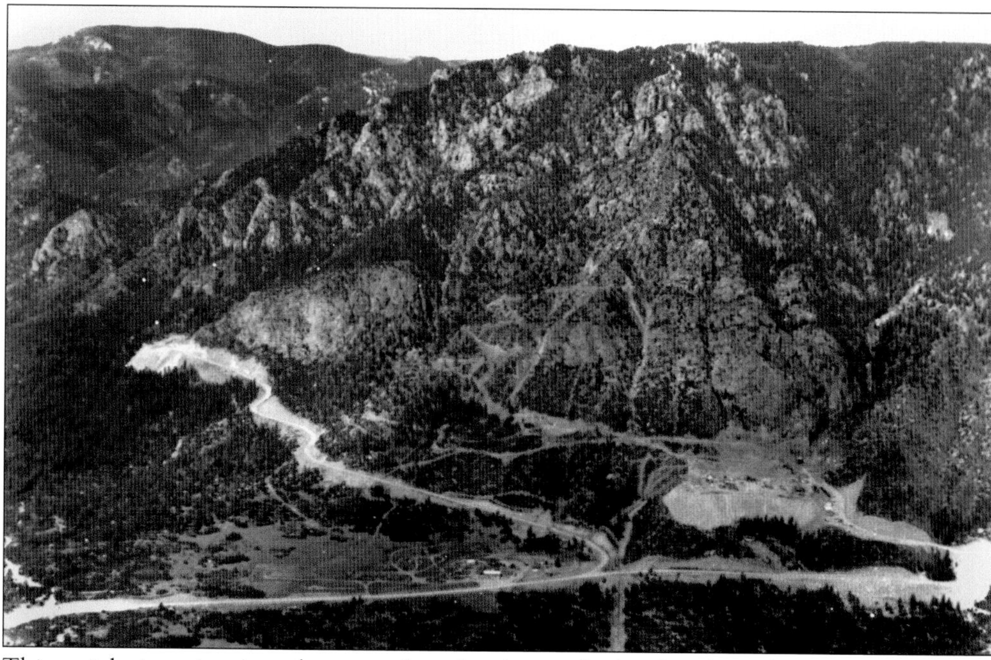

This aerial view pinpoints the area selected to house the hardened combat operations center. From the Utah Construction & Mining Company's base camp, the main access road branches out, circles the mountain toward the north and south portals, bores through a mile of solid granite, and meets again 1,000 feet under the earth's surface.

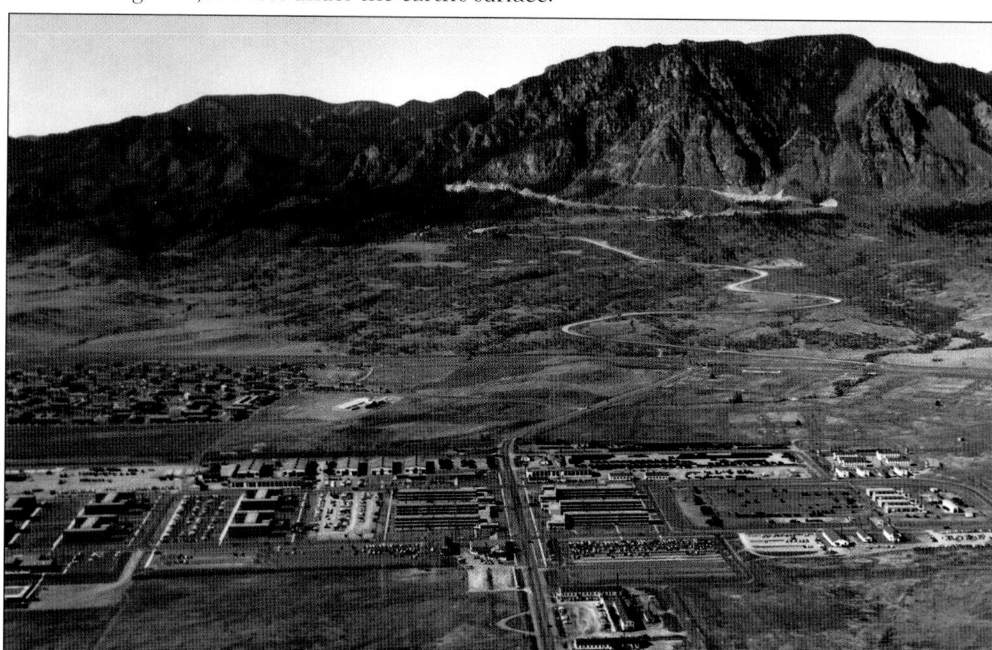

Cheyenne Mountain Air Force Station is located across Colorado State Route 115 from the US Army's Fort Carson. Fort Carson is pictured here in the foreground with Cheyenne Mountain behind. The station's close proximity to Fort Carson provides an added security measure to the top secret facility.

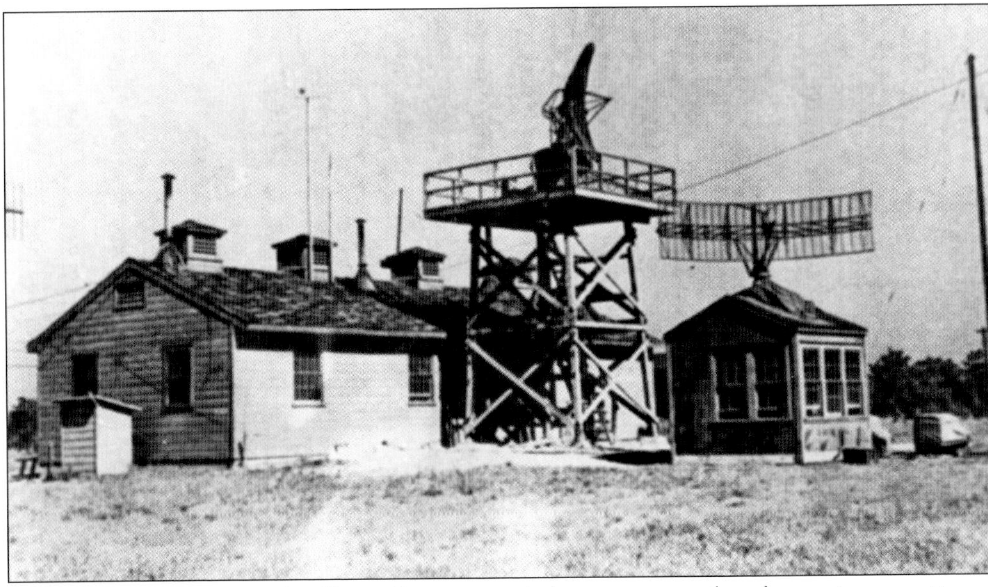

As Cheyenne Mountain Air Force Station was being constructed, radar stations continued to provide data to combat operations center at Ent AFB. This unnamed radar station has the height-finder system (vertical radar), which provided the altitude of suspect aircraft, as well as the surveillance radar, which gave the location of the aircraft.

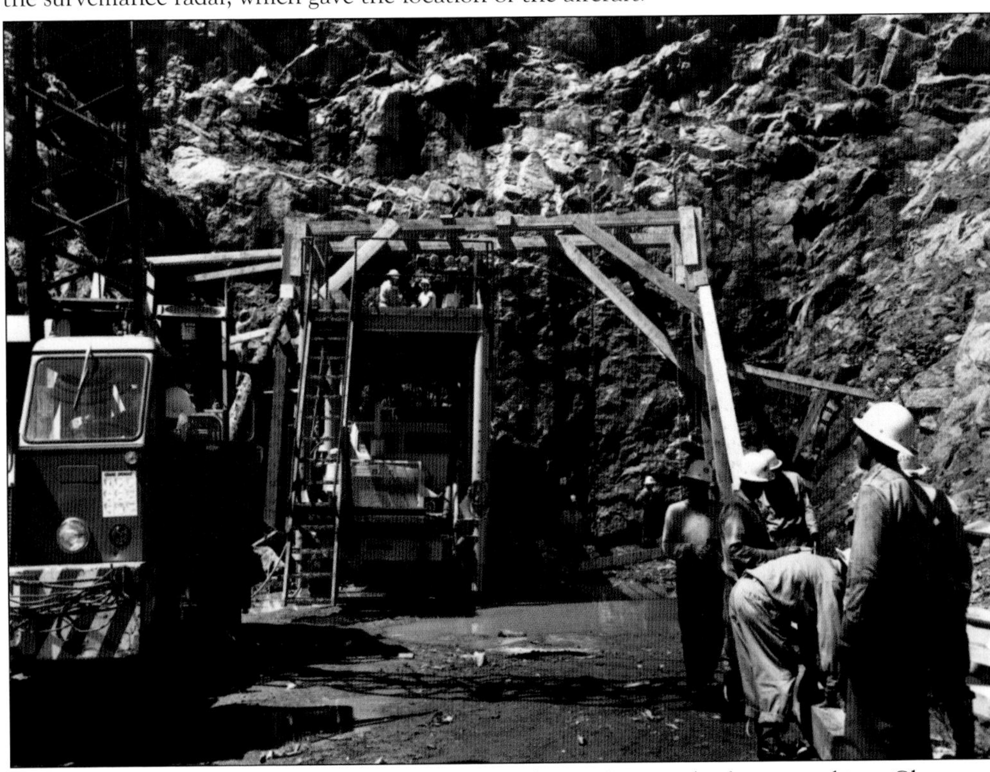

Utah Construction & Mining Company engineers begin shaping the first tunnel into Cheyenne Mountain. The entrance to the mountain was the beginning of one of America's most ambitious military construction projects.

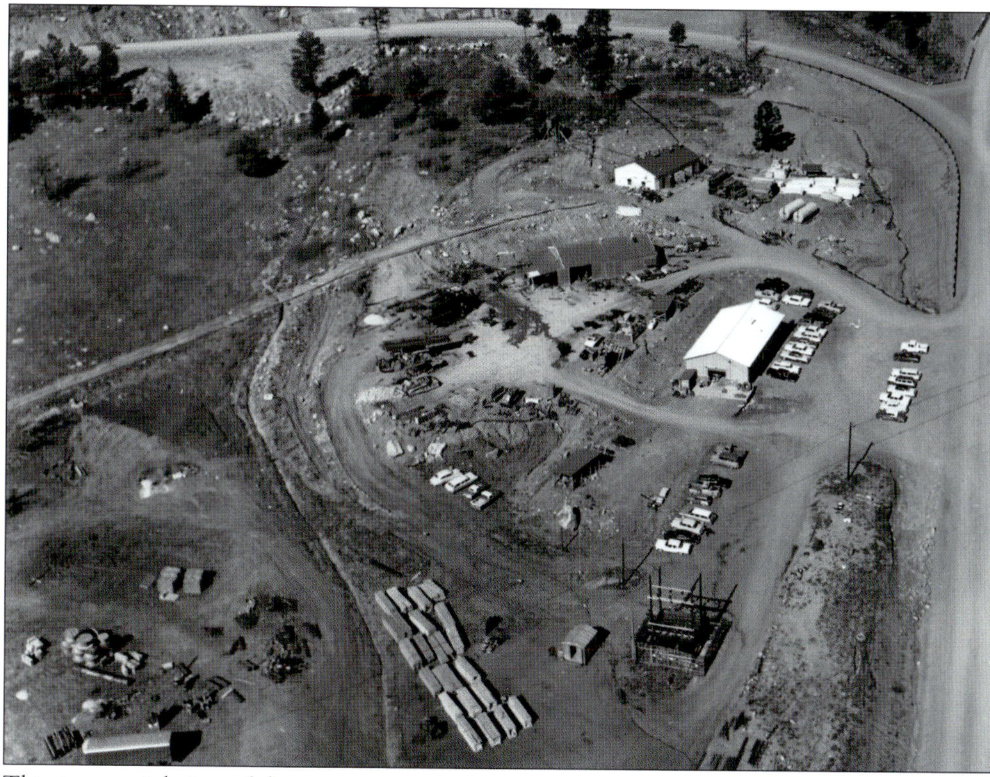

This is an aerial view of the staging area for the construction company's equipment. Located near the entrance, this area provided the crews with easy access to heavy equipment and tools needed to excavate the mountain.

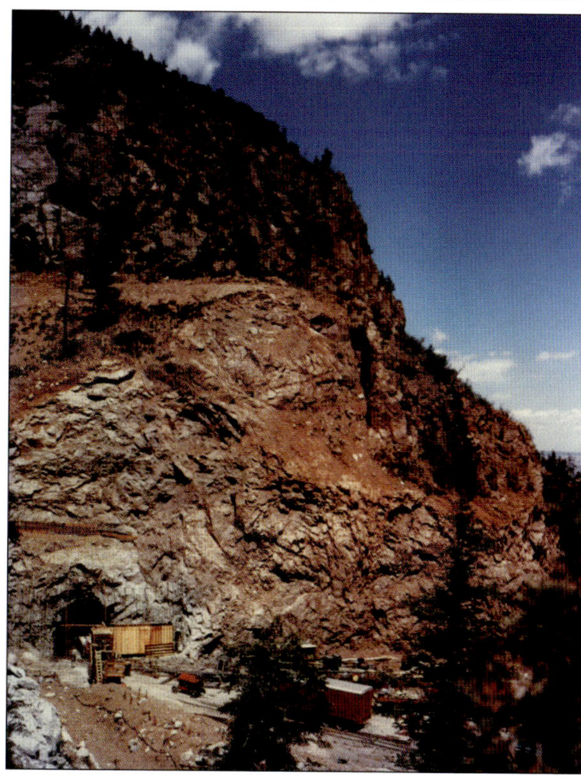

Excavation of the main entrance to Cheyenne Mountain is underway in this aerial photograph. Known as the north portal, this is the main entrance for personnel entering the Cheyenne Mountain Operations Center.

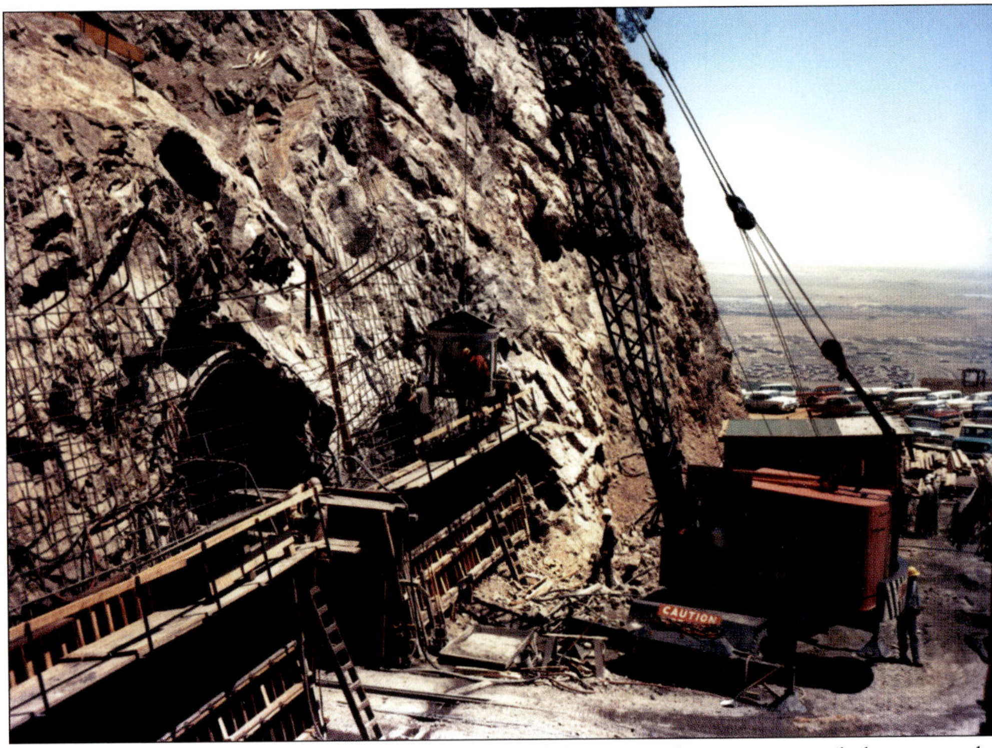

Due to the enormity of the excavation project, much heavy machinery was needed to move the tons of granite and metal needed to erect the infrastructure. Here, a large crane is pouring cement through a hopper for the entrance to the mountain tunnel.

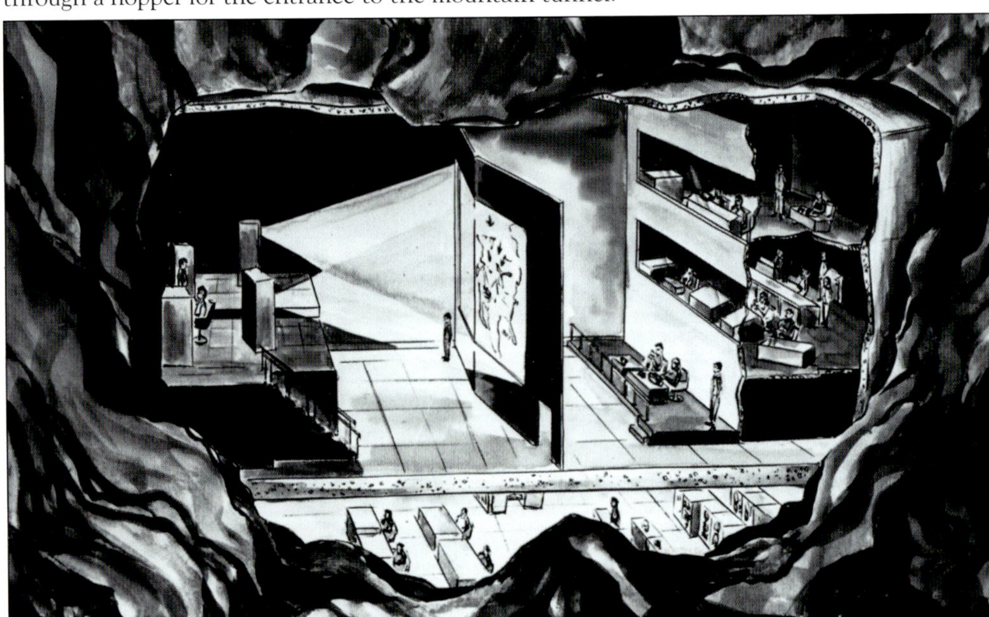

This is an artist's conception of the combat operations center under construction inside Cheyenne Mountain. This state-of-the-art technology replaces the older grease pencil–marked status board at the command center at Ent AFB.

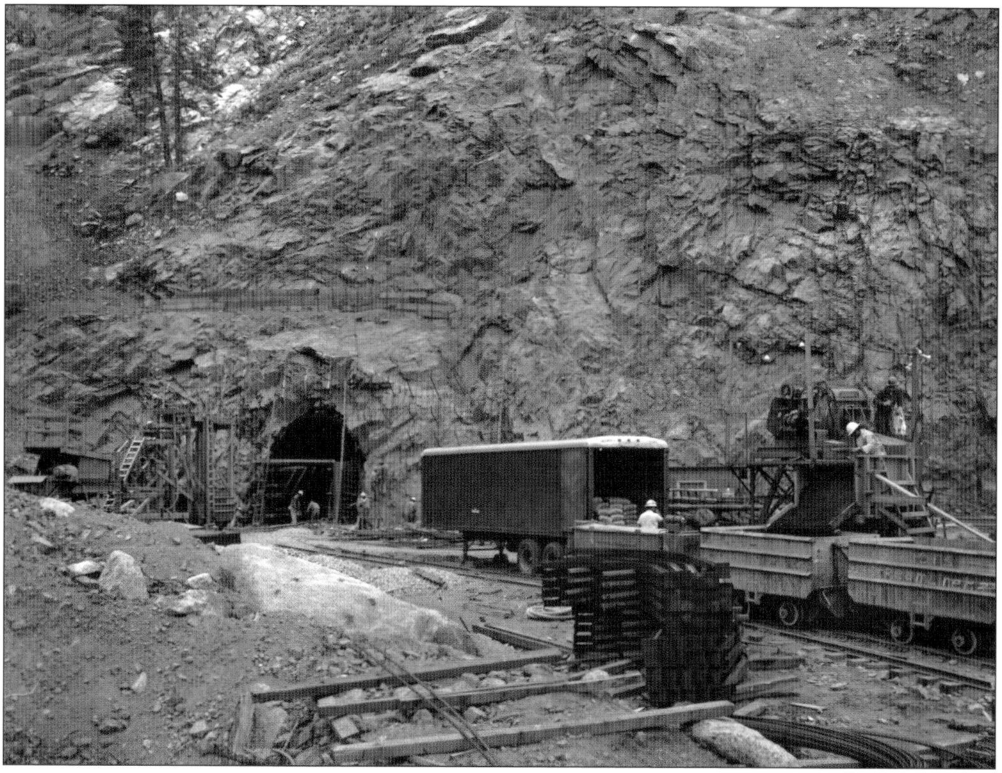

The complexity of the excavation required a company with mining experience, and the Utah Construction & Mining Company was well equipped, as evidenced by the use of small mining cars to move materials into the mountain as well as remove granite being excavated.

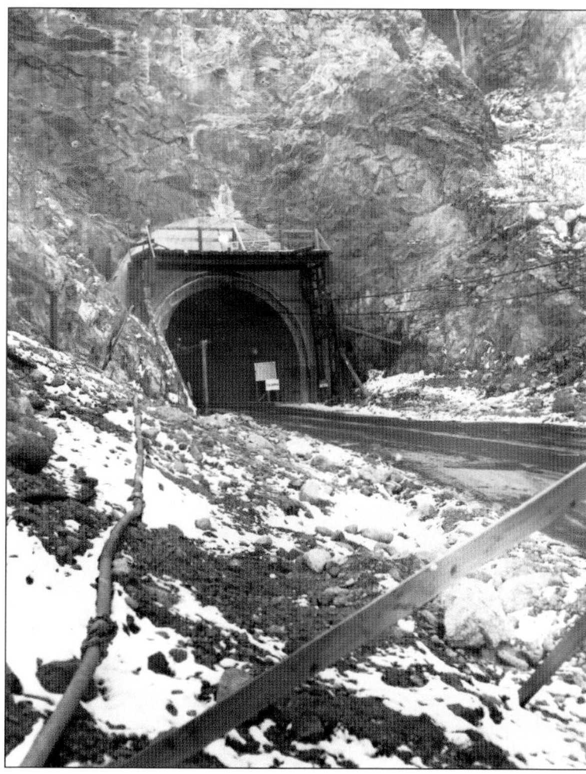

The tunnel entrance is taking shape in this wintery photograph. The construction crew formed the main tunnel entrance out of steel and concrete. As one enters the tunnel after the main entry, the raw, excavated tunnel is the main passageway inside.

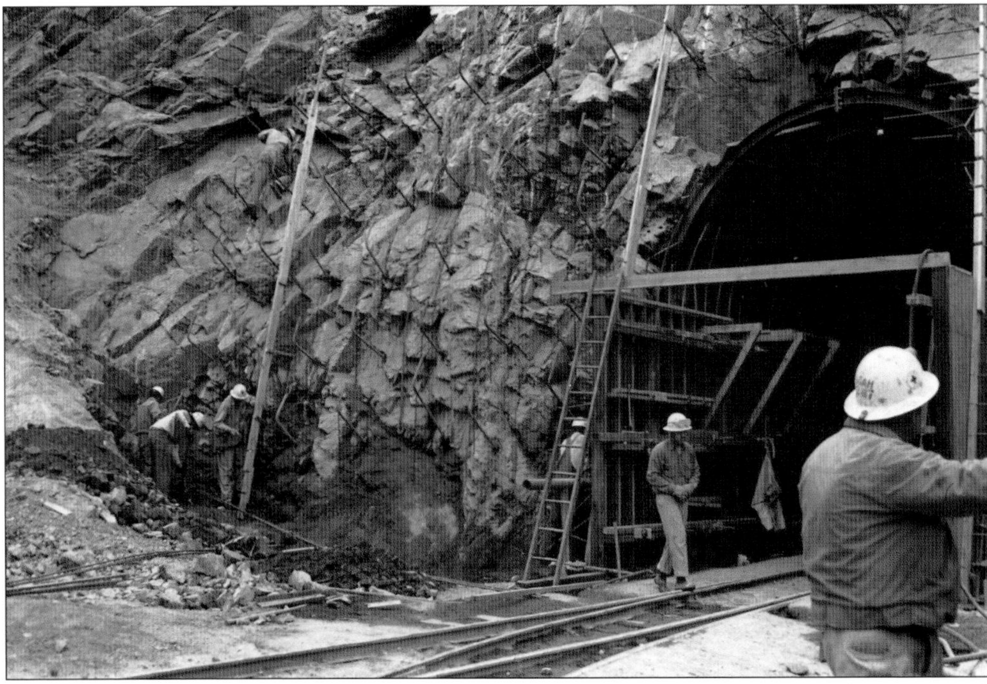

Pictured here is another view of the construction crew working on the entry to the main north portal tunnel to the mountain. This entrance is nearly 23 feet high and 29 feet wide, and it is the primary artery for traffic, both vehicular and pedestrian.

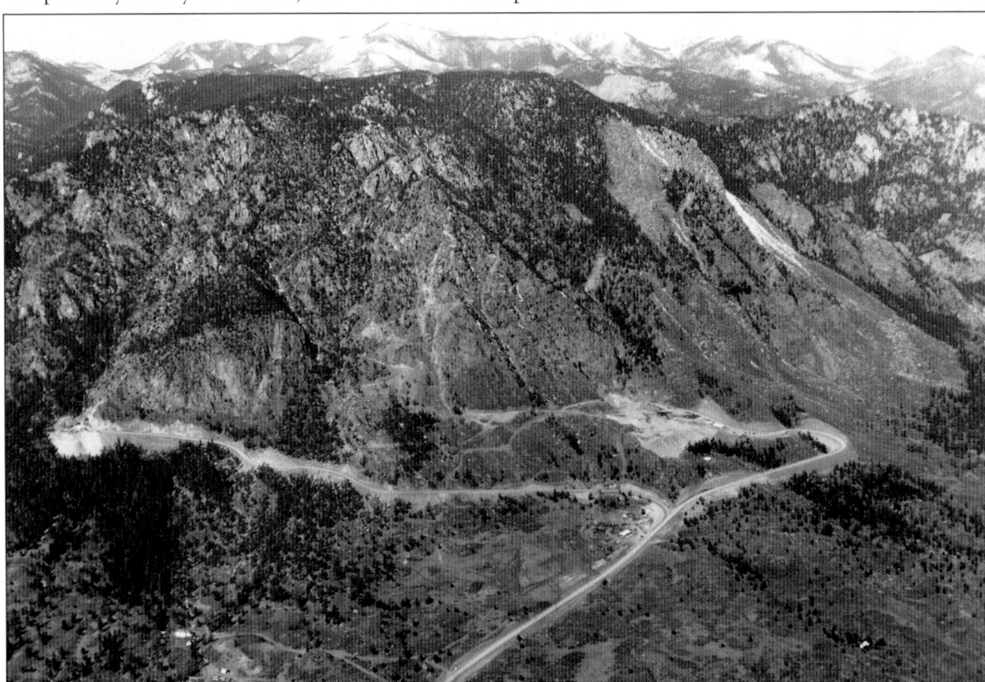

This aerial view shows the two main pathways to the entrances into the mountain. The right fork leads to the north portal (main entrance) and the left fork leads to the south portal.

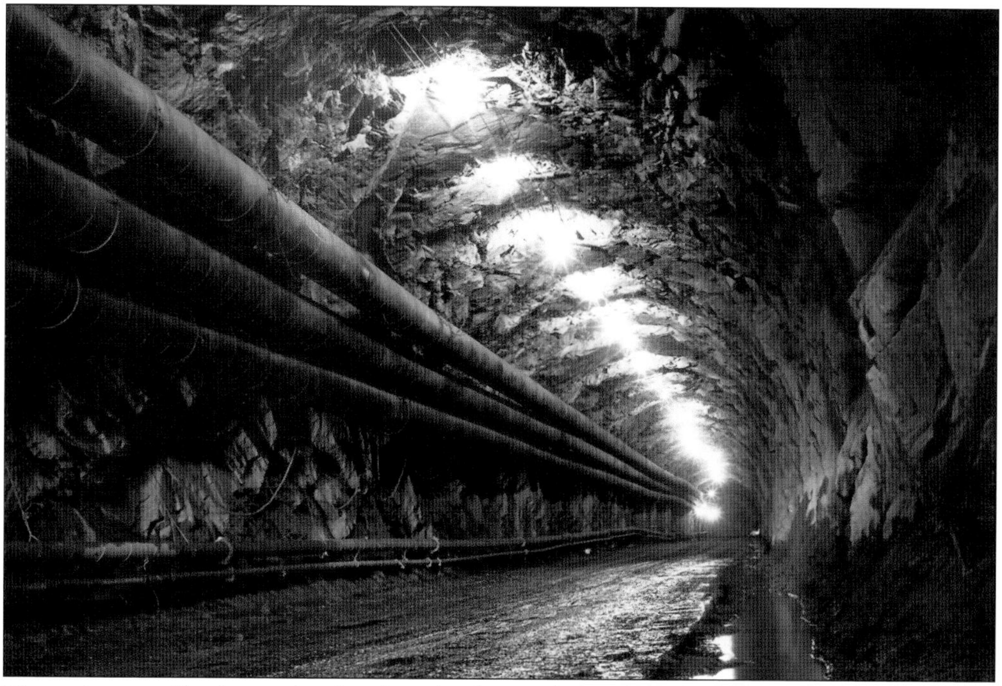

The main tunnel leads into the chambers that house the combat operations center, and the piping is feeding the construction area with water and cables for electricity. These were repositioned after construction was completed, although they are still inside the mountain.

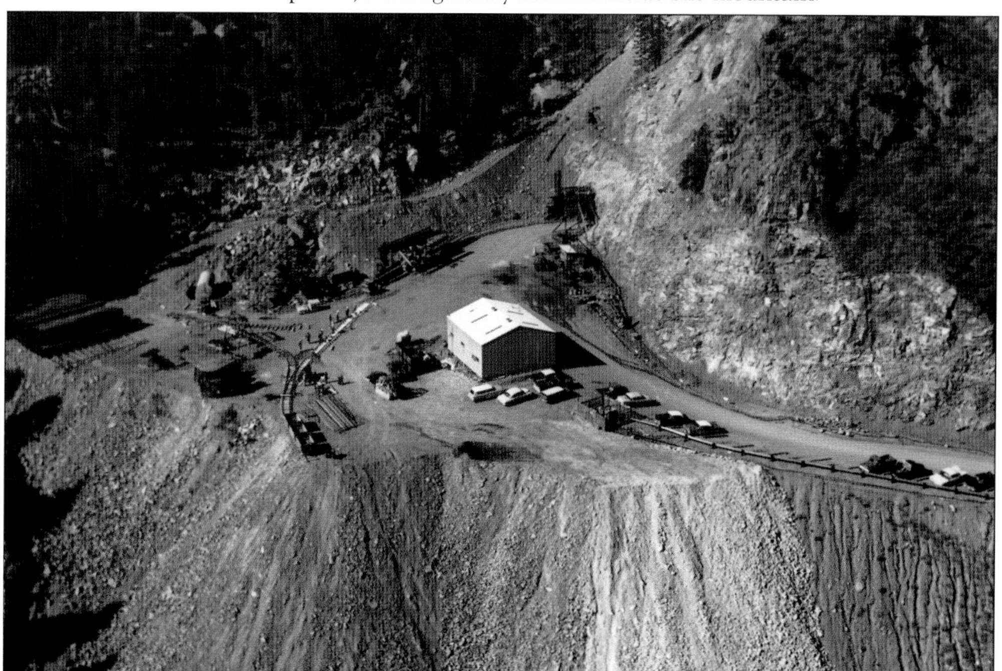

This aerial view shows the main equipment staging area for the construction crews. The road on the right is the main road leading up the mountain, and to the left of the building is where the parking lot was created, using the many tons of granite excavated from the interior of the mountain.

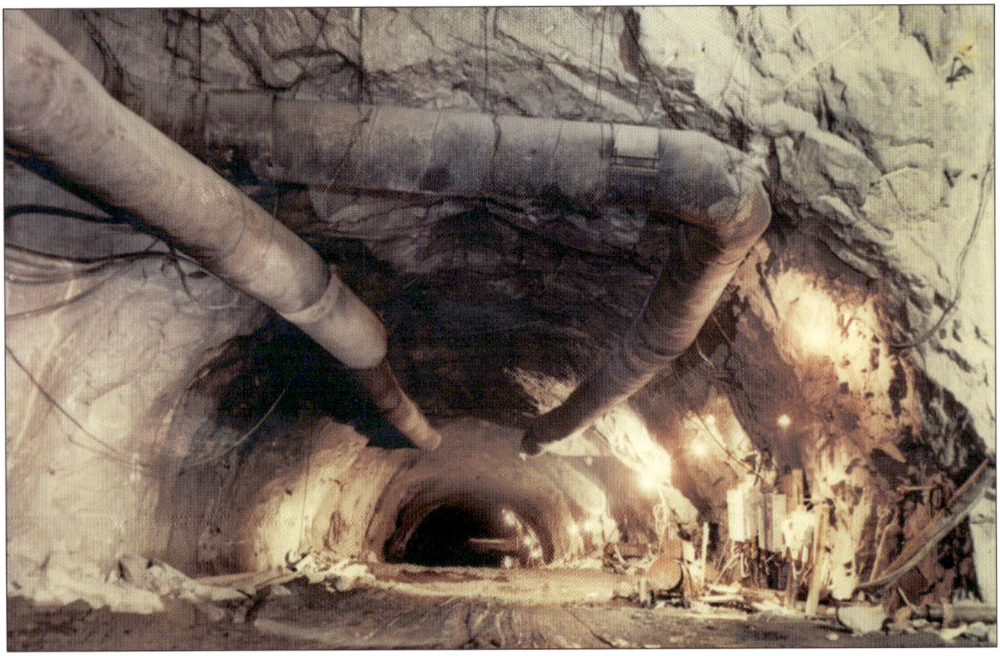

Pictured here is the main tunnel into the complex. Looking inside from the north portal, this view reveals the incredible amount of granite that had to be excavated to make such a large tunnel. The rock was removed and dumped into the canyon outside the north portal, later to be used for the parking lot.

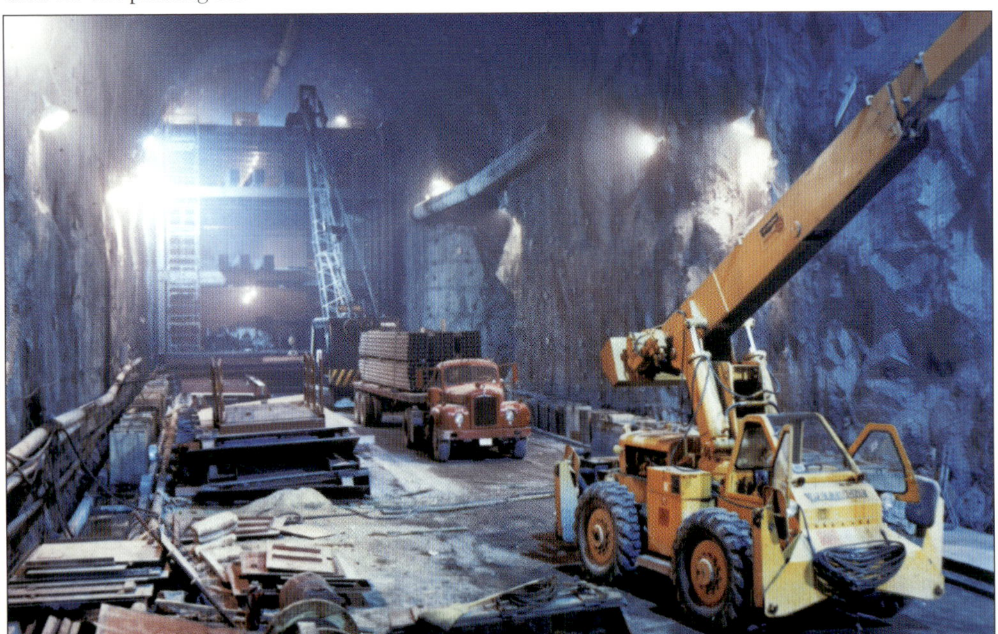

The US Navy was called in to construct the buildings inside the mountain. The Navy was experienced in making the most out of tight quarters because of the ships and submarines they build, and the Navy influence is evident in the center's construction. This three-story building is the main structure for the entrance to the combat operations center.

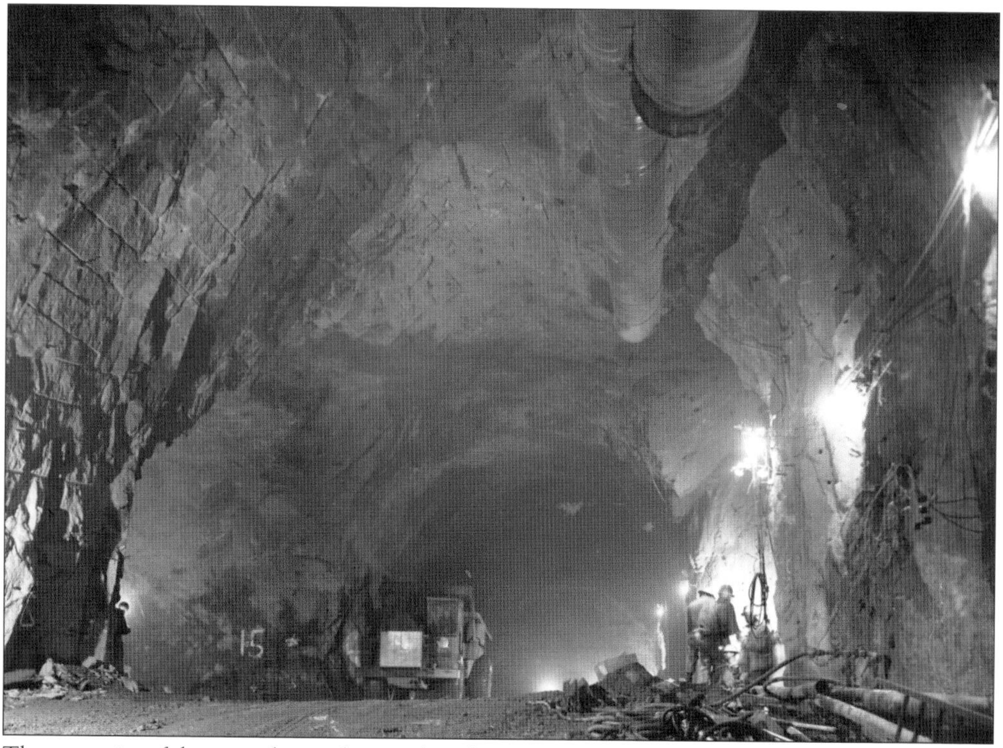

The enormity of the tunnel is evident in this photograph, which captures an earthmover trundling through the tunnel with much room to spare. The cavern is as high as 60.5 feet in some places.

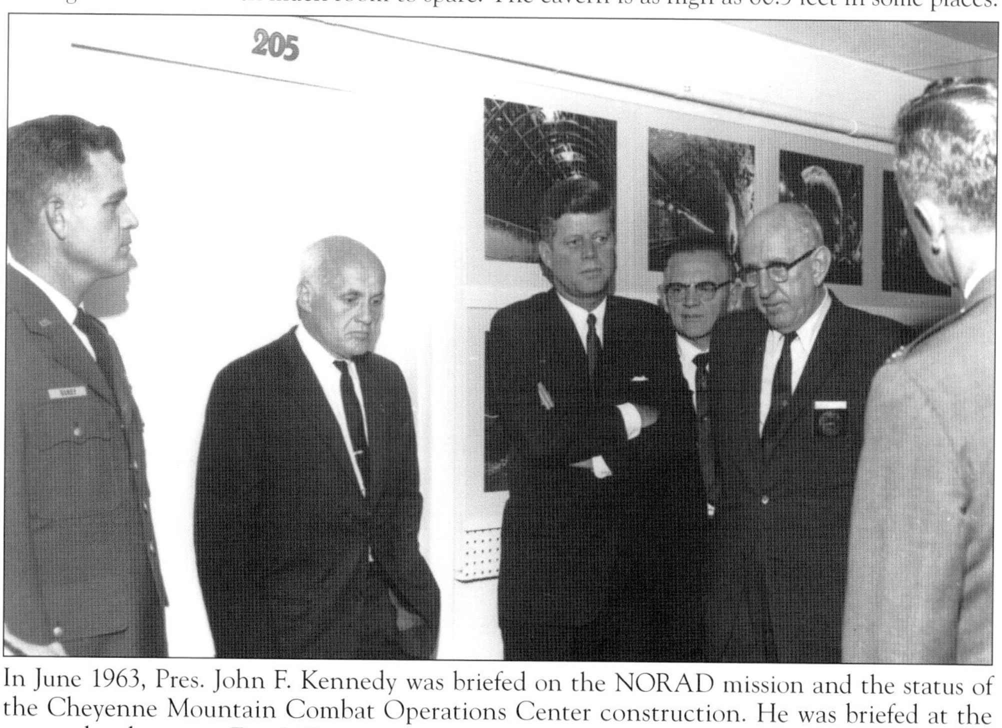

In June 1963, Pres. John F. Kennedy was briefed on the NORAD mission and the status of the Cheyenne Mountain Combat Operations Center construction. He was briefed at the current headquarters, Ent AFB.

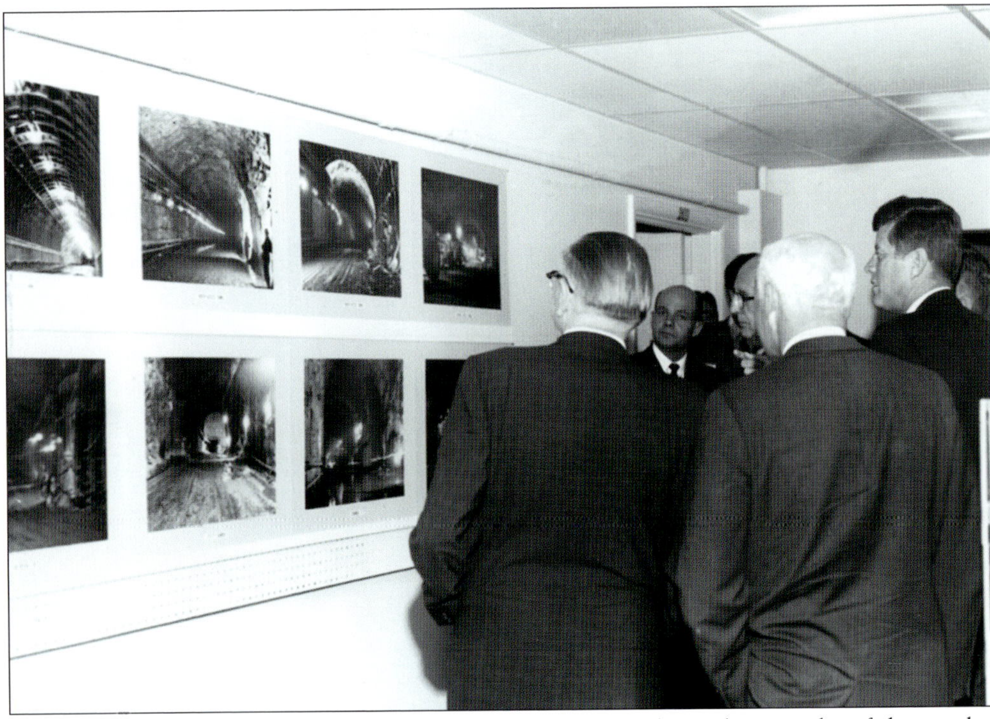

President Kennedy is pictured here looking at construction phase photographs of the combat operations center. Although Kennedy was briefed on the construction status, he did not actually tour the facility.

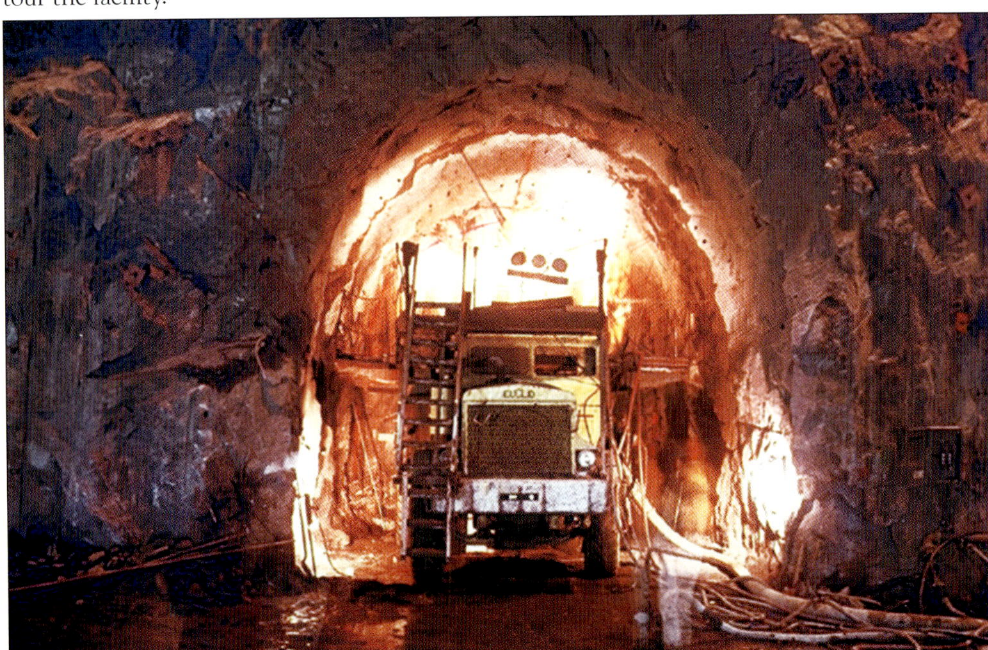

Construction continues in one of the passageway tunnels. Large semi-trailer trucks had to be carefully maneuvered inside the mountain to ensure they were able to get out easily. Many times spotters were used to guide them.

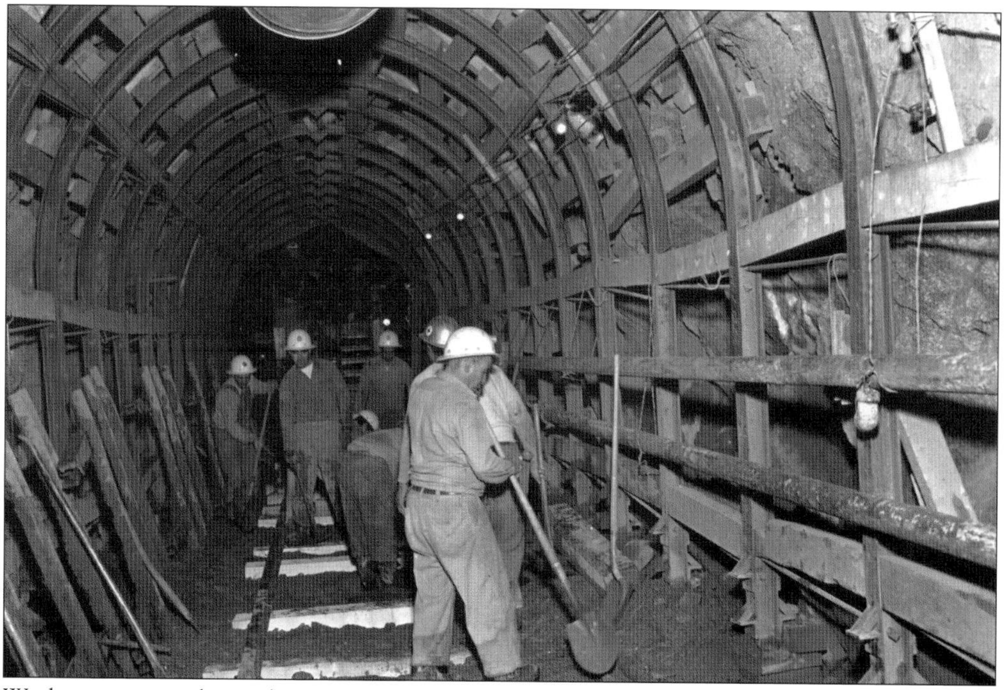

Workers excavate dirt and granite from one of the many side tunnels leading to the 15 buildings inside the mountain. This tunnel is being prepared with railroad tracks for easier movement of loads via mining-style railcars.

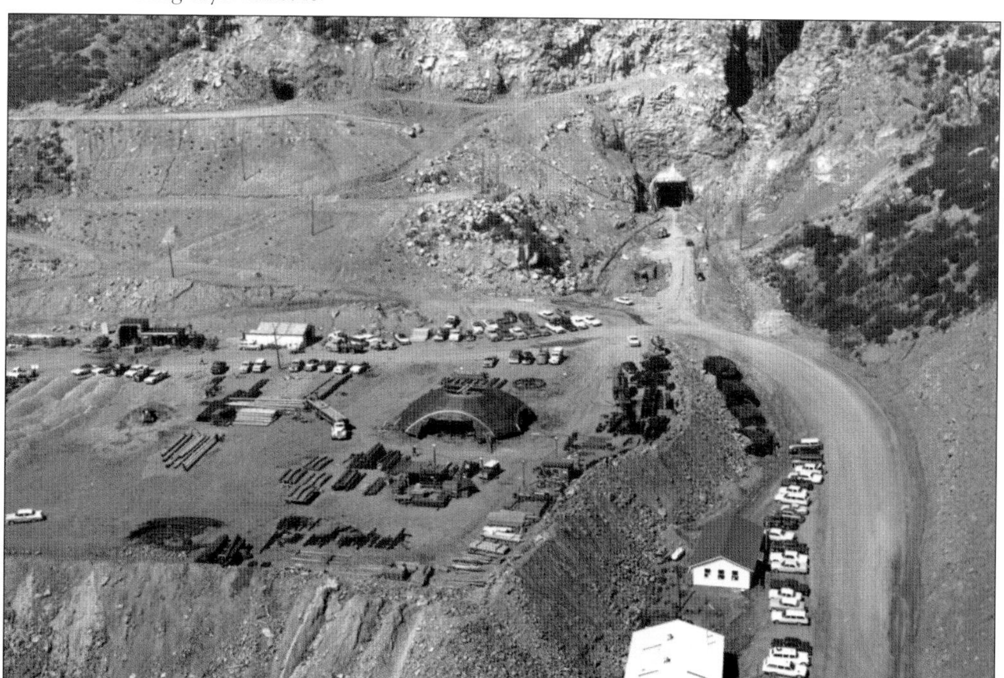

The area right outside the main entrance, the north portal, is where the construction crews had their equipment and offices. The area where all the equipment is now is sitting on top of the granite excavated from the mountain.

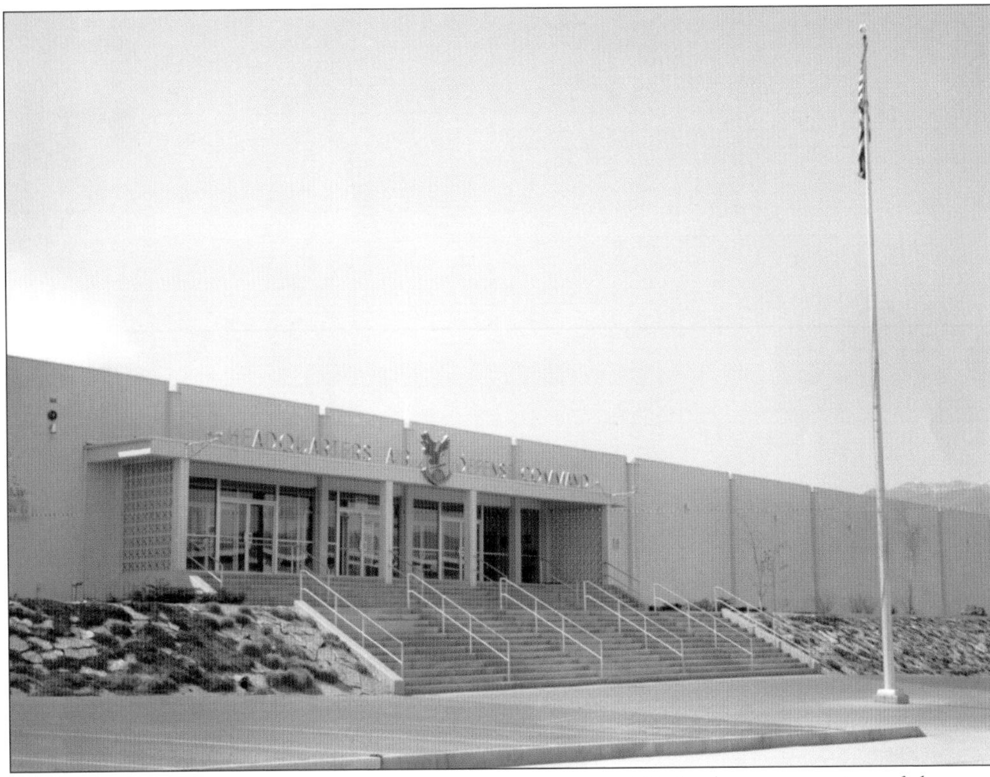

While the construction of the combat operations center inside Cheyenne Mountain was being finished, Air Defense Command moved into its new headquarters building, the Chidlaw Building. This building also housed the combat operations center until the new facility was finished. NORAD headquarters moved to the Chidlaw Building on February 15, 1963, from Ent AFB.

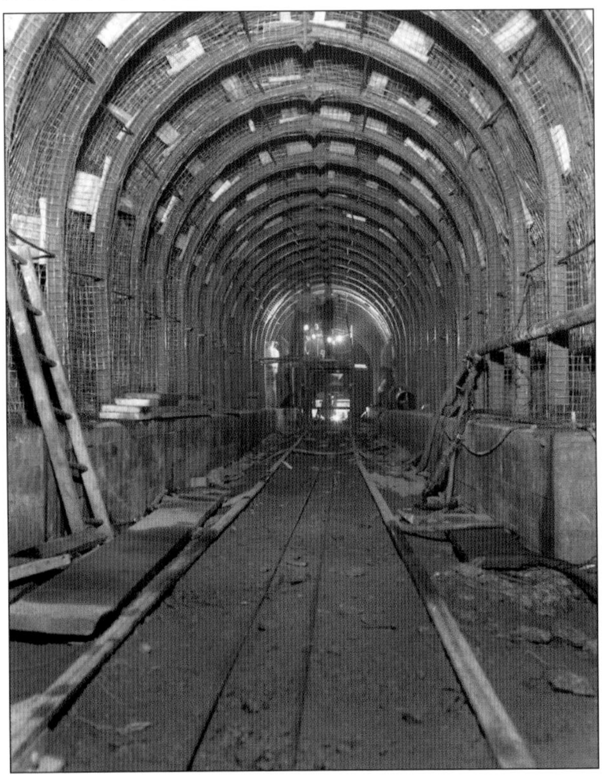

Structural strengthening of the tunnels was needed to ensure that cave-ins did not occur. Wood bracing, netting, and rock bolts were used to strengthen the integrity of the tunnels.

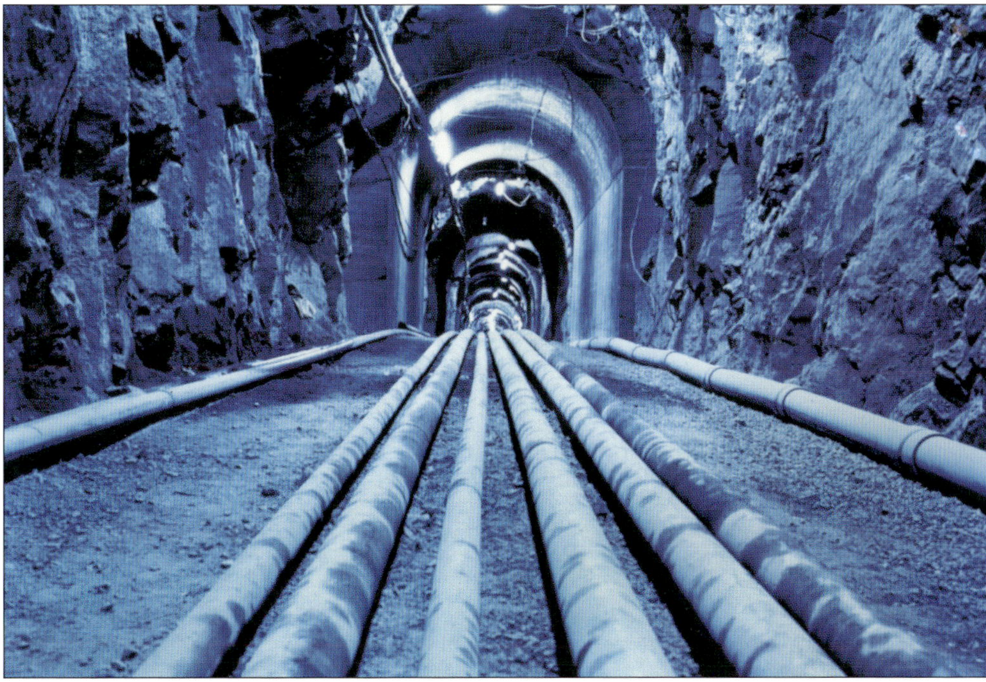

During construction, water, sewage, electricity, and air was brought in using piping. Once construction was completed, these pipes were either removed or relocated from the floor of the tunnels and caverns.

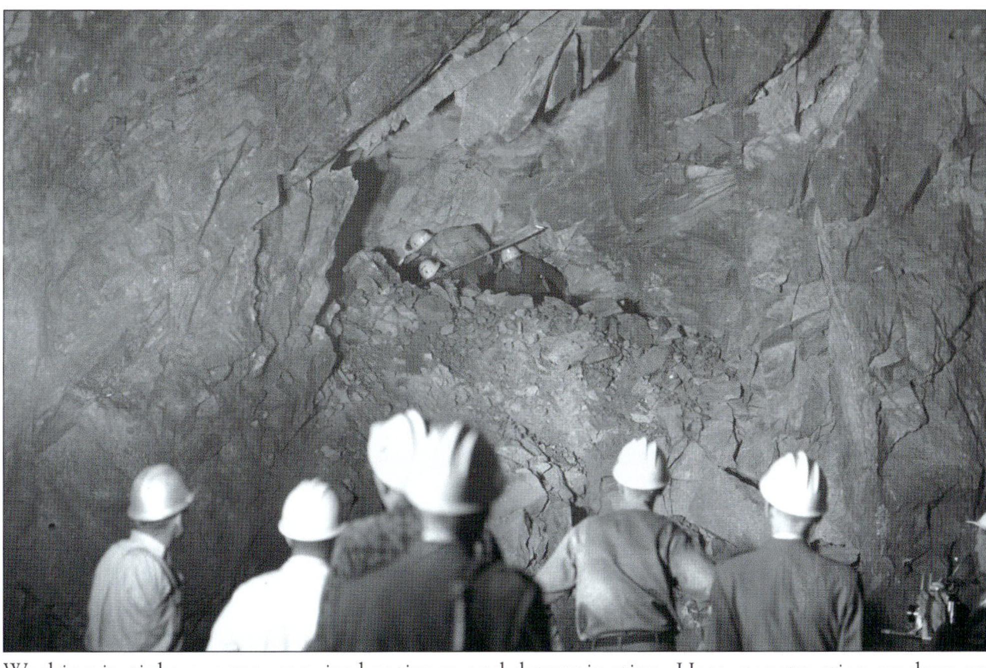

Working in tight quarters required patience and determination. Here, construction workers are checking areas of the mountain to determine the best course of action for excavation. During the excavation, workers discovered a fault in the mountain that required additional strengthening and moved the completion date months later than planned.

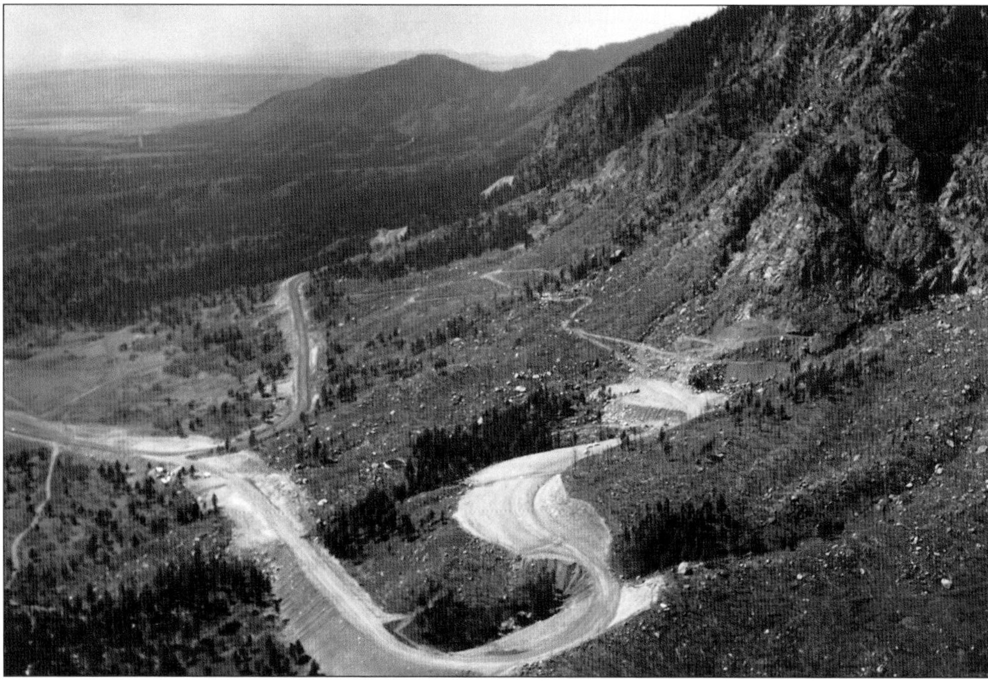

Looking to the south, this view shows the roadway and forks that lead to the main entrance (on the right) and the south portal (left fork). The flat area near the main entrance is leveled and will become the parking lot.

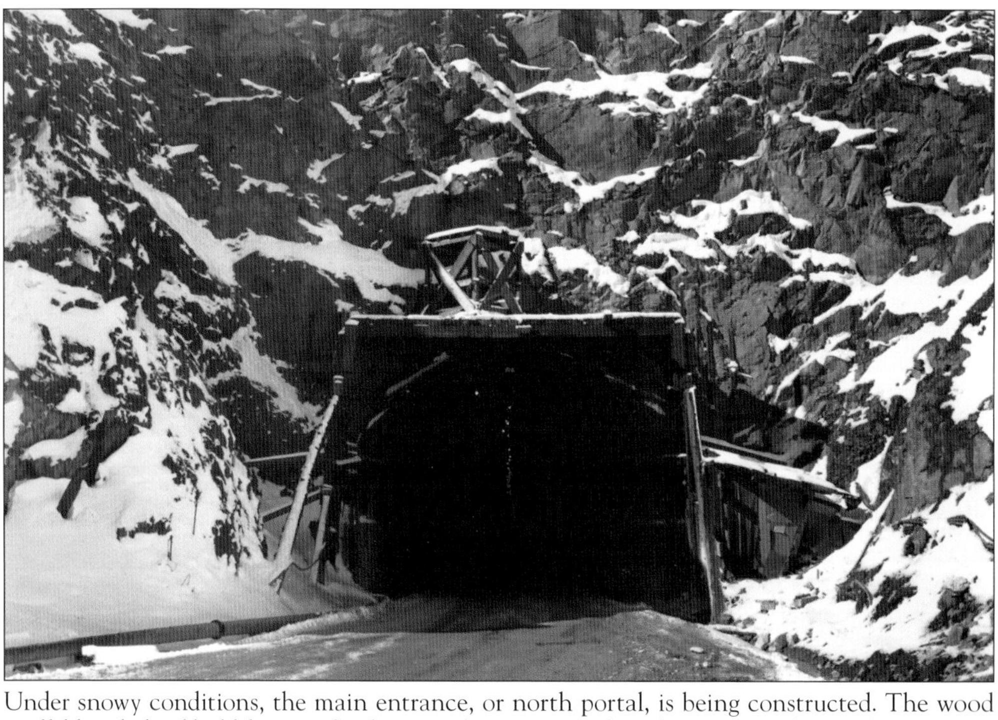

Under snowy conditions, the main entrance, or north portal, is being constructed. The wood scaffolding helped hold framing for the tunnel entrance and was later removed once the entryway was completed.

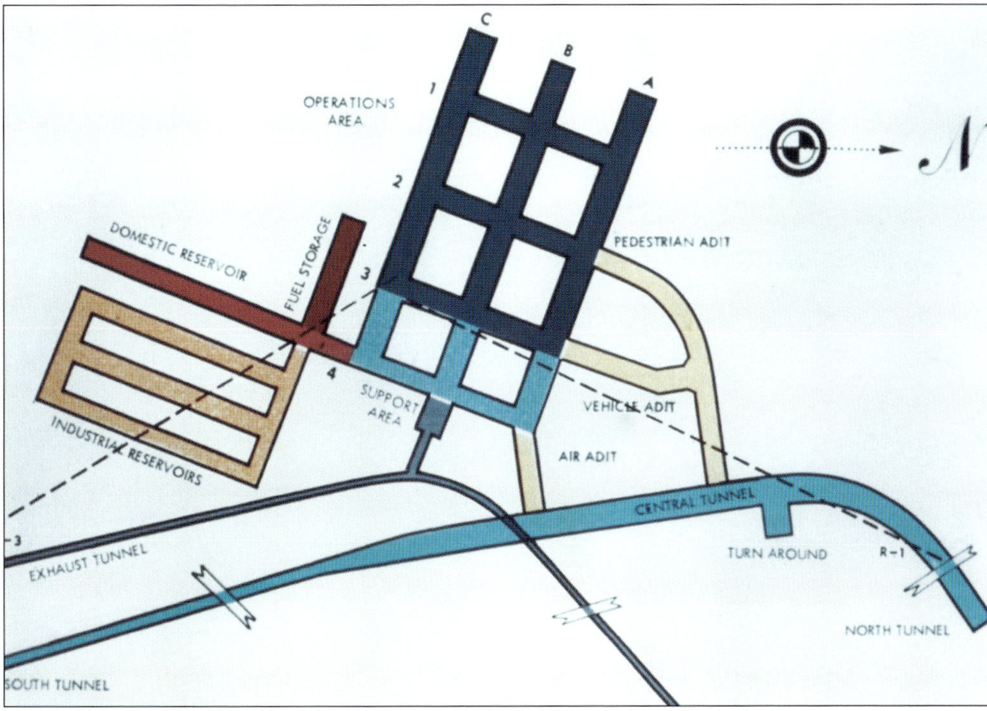

This architectural drawing shows the floor plan of the Cheyenne Mountain Operations Center. When one regards this plan and how all of it had to be excavated from the mountain, the complexity of the construction phase is evident.

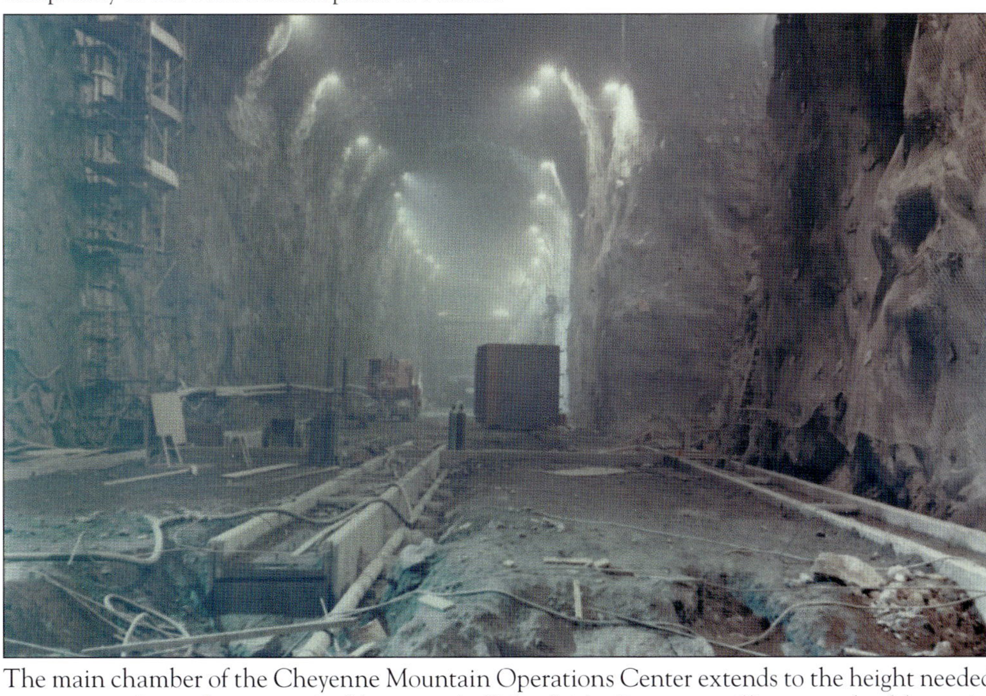

The main chamber of the Cheyenne Mountain Operations Center extends to the height needed to accommodate a three-story building, nearly 61 feet high. Over one million pounds of dynamite were used to clear the mountain.

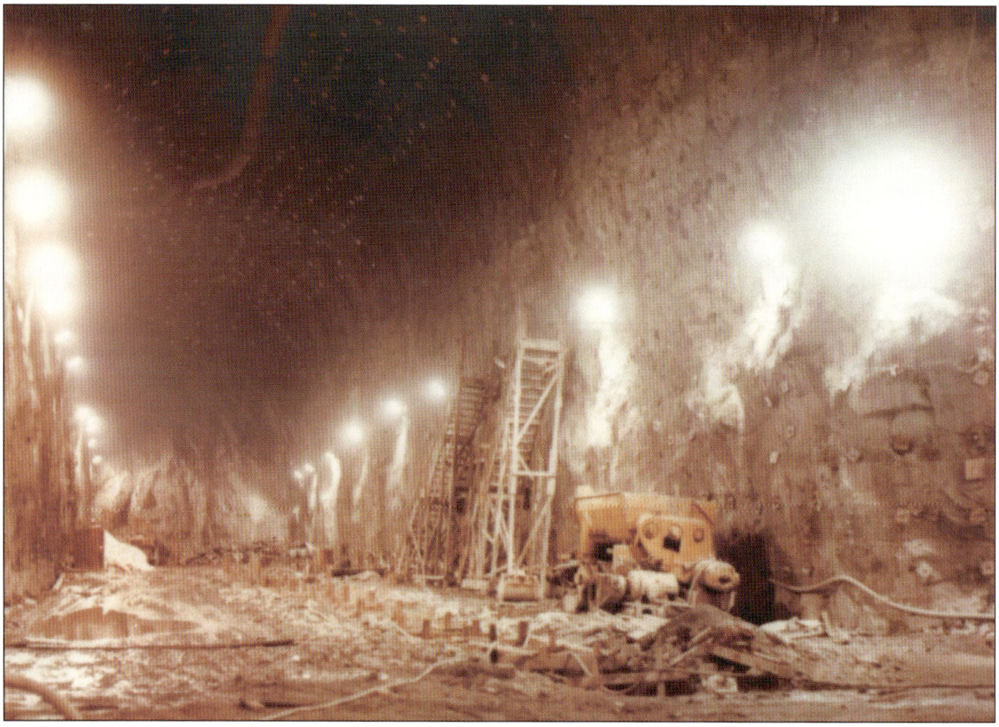

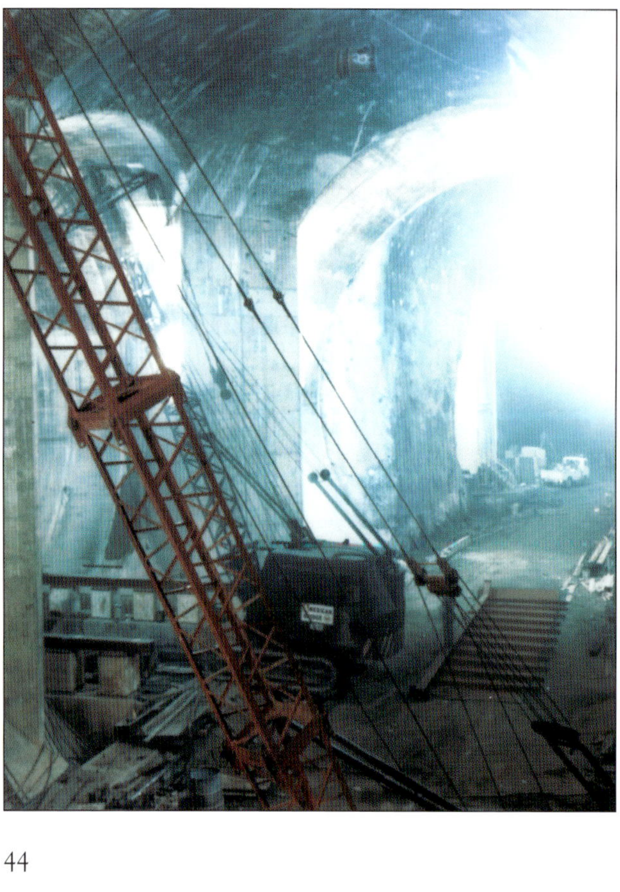

The depth and magnitude of the construction project is evident in this photograph, which shows some heavy machinery and other necessary equipment utilized to carve out the interior of the mountain.

During construction, a fault was discovered in the mountain. In order to assure the structural integrity of the interior, a dome had to be built over the main chamber. This caused a delay in the completion but ultimately made it safer.

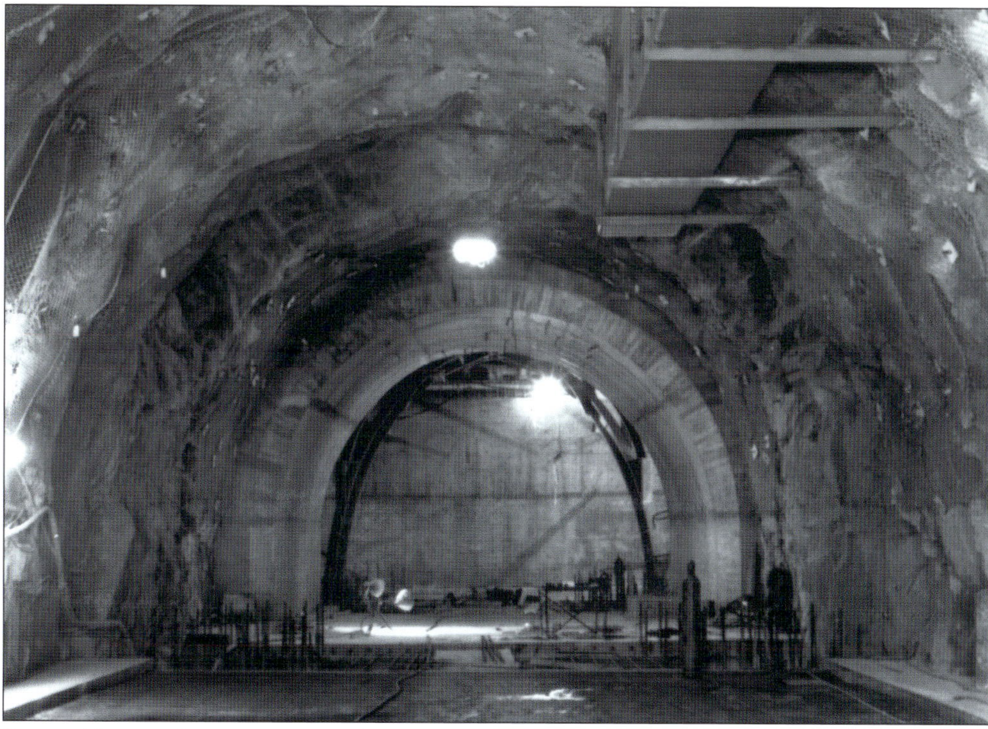

Pictured here is the interior tunnel arch during the construction phase. Also seen on the walls and ceiling are rock bolts and netting used to form a layer of compressed rocks that keeps the granite from crumbling back into the tunnels and chambers.

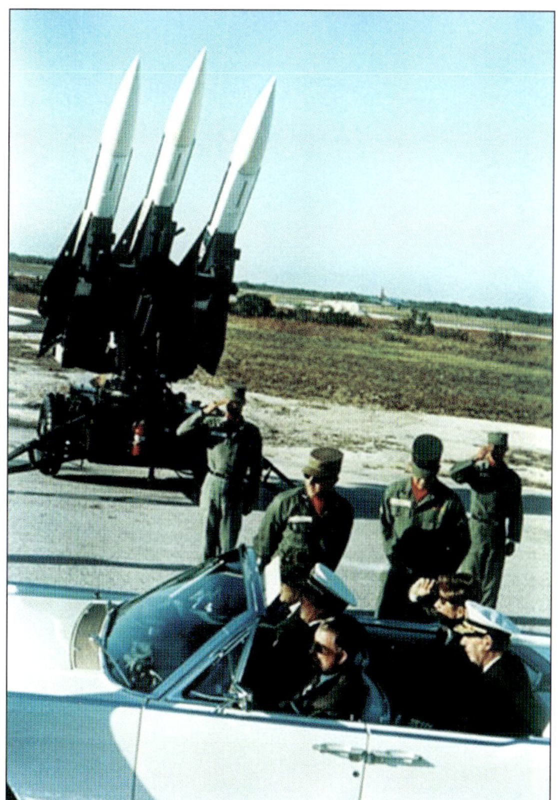

During the Cuban Missile Crisis, Pres. John F. Kennedy reviewed the air defense missiles on alert on the beaches of Key West, Florida. With Cuba only 90 miles away, Key West and southern Florida could have been the prime targets for Cuban missile launches and enemy aircraft. NORAD had a strong, alert fighter presence in south Florida.

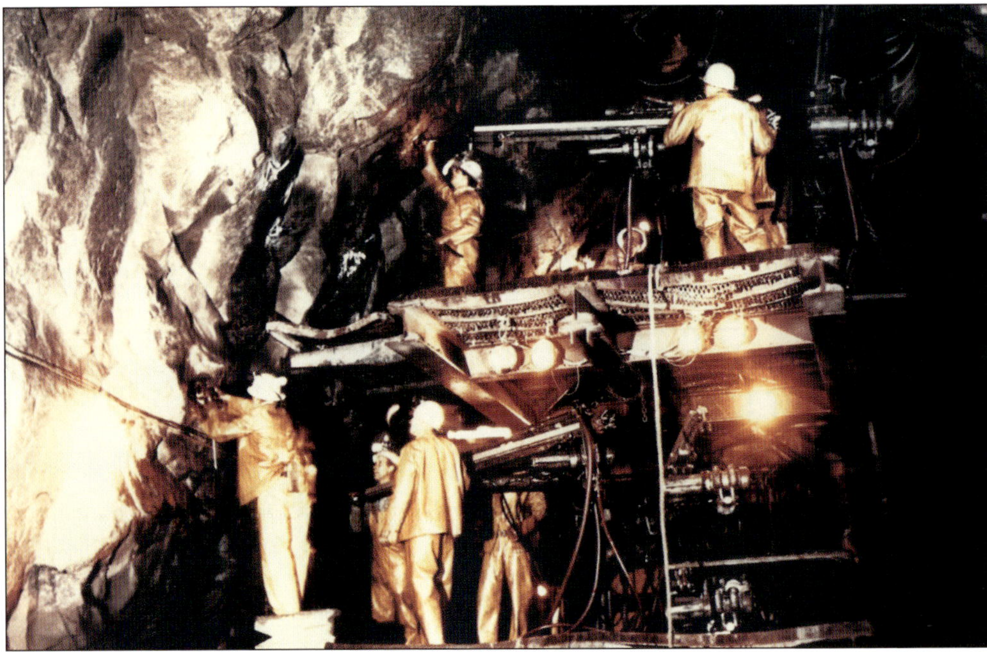

Crews are using large drilling equipment to drill holes in the granite for the rock bolts. Over 110,000 rock bolts were installed inside the mountain to help strengthen the walls. These bolts "fooled" the mountain into thinking it was solid so that debris would not fall into the tunnels and chambers.

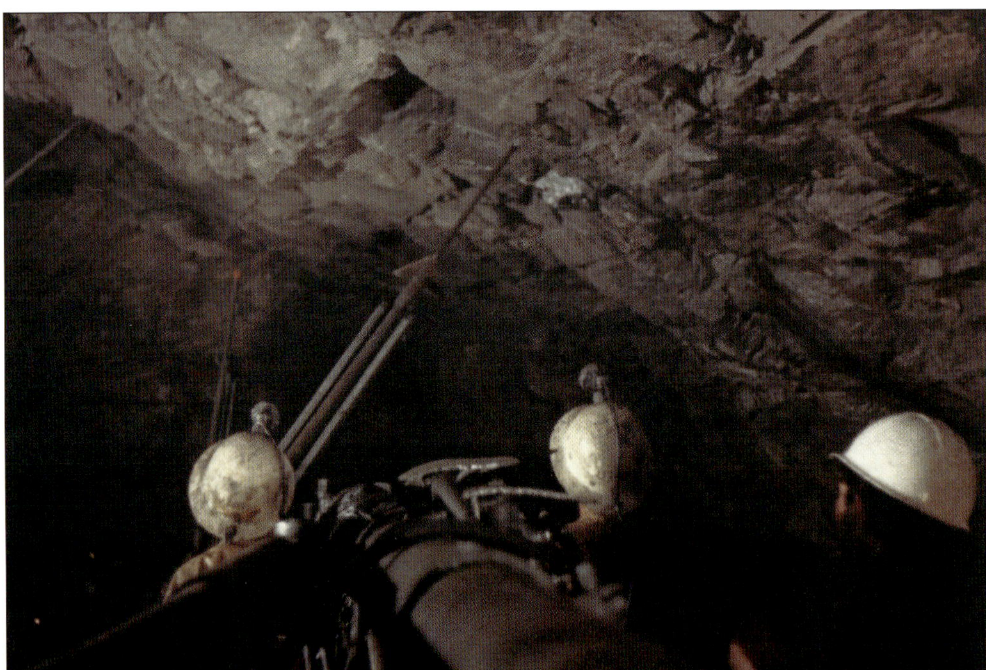

This is a closer view of the crews installing the rock bolts. These bolts ranged in length from six to 32 feet and were installed in the ceilings and the walls. These rock bolts are still in place today and are continuously checked for integrity and tightening if required.

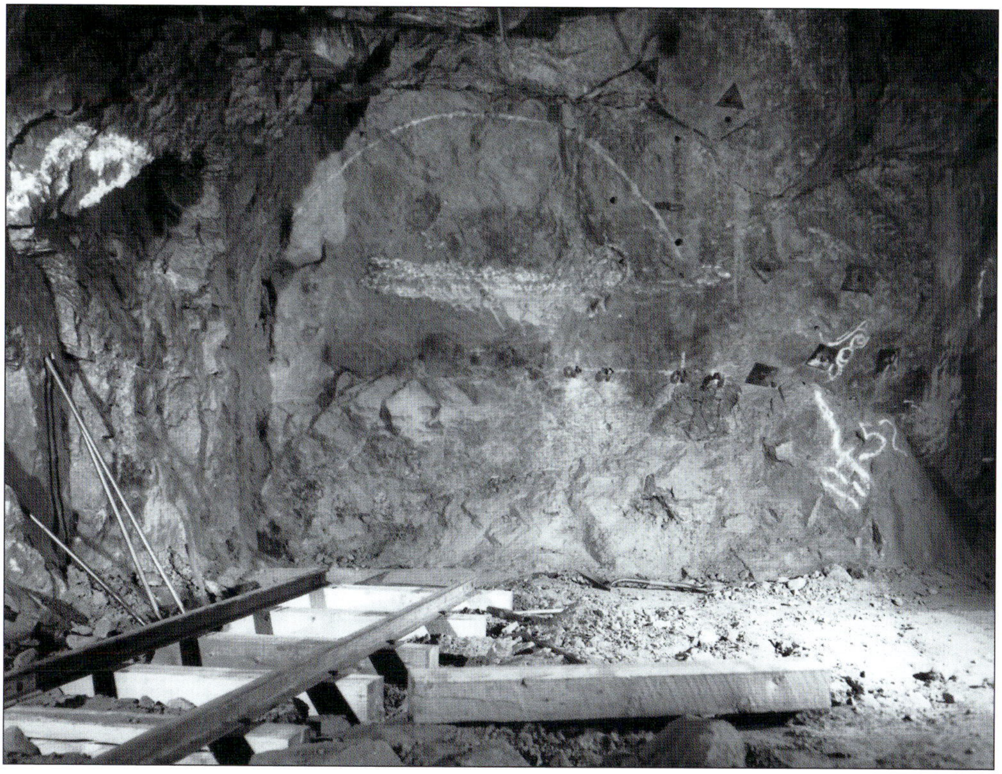

As engineers and construction crews excavated the mountain, they used numbers and drawings to show where excavating still needed to be done. After over 50 years, some of the writing and drawings are still visible on the walls of the mountain.

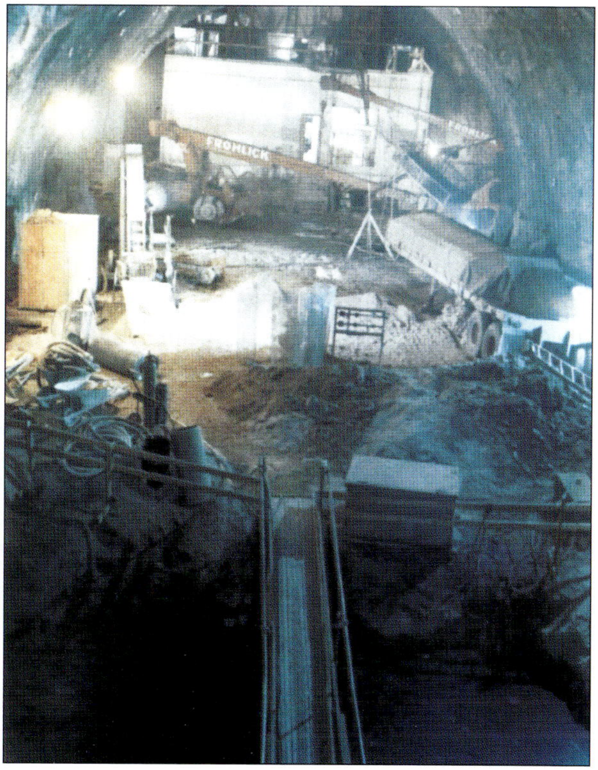

The water, air, and sewage was sent through these types of pipes during the construction phase. As the facility neared completion, these were either moved to other locations or removed.

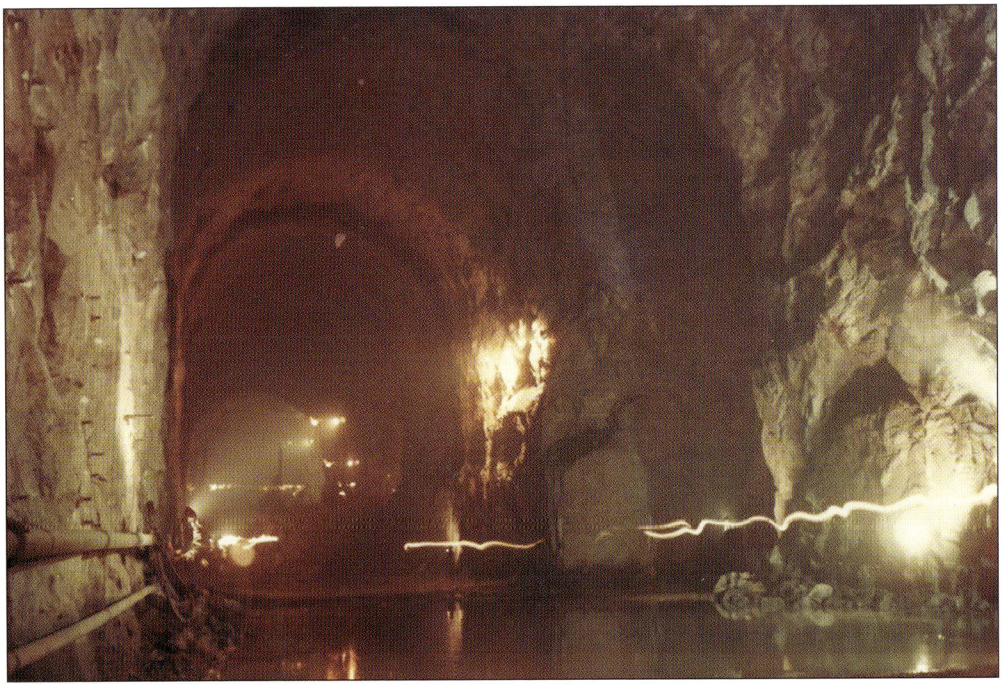

This is an interior view of the tunnel of the combat operations center, North American Air Defense Command (NORAD), being constructed inside Cheyenne Mountain south of Colorado Springs.

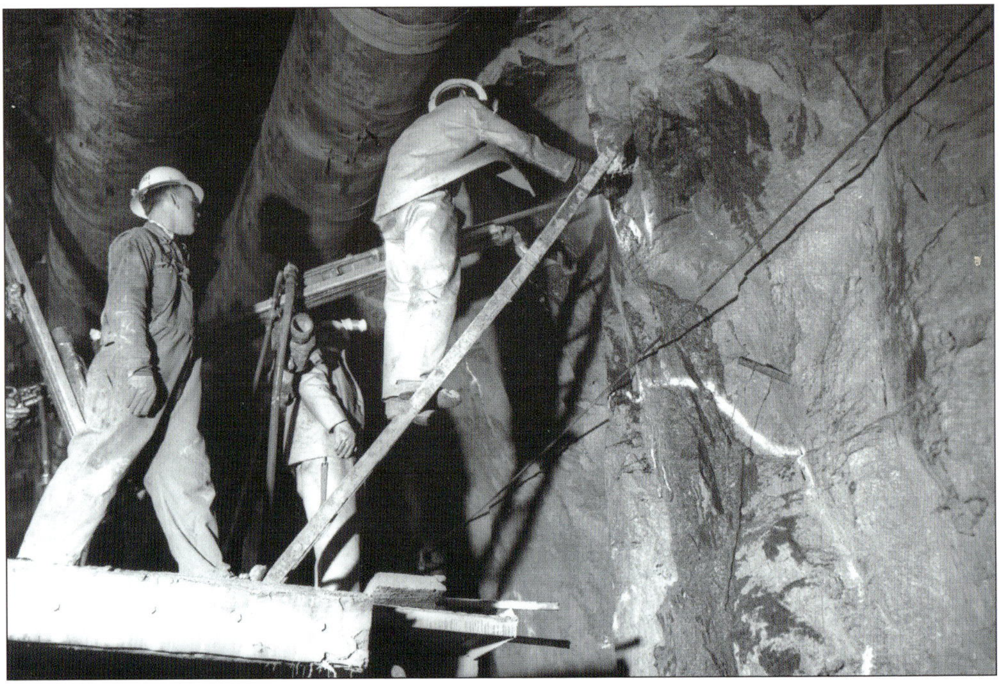

Construction crews work to install one of the thousands of rock bolts inside the mountain. Engineers had to determine the vulnerability of the location and then decide the length of the rock bolt needed.

One of the 15 buildings that were erected for the combat operations center is being assembled. The windowless city is set in a 4.5-acre grid of the excavated chambers. All buildings are freestanding and joined by flexible walkways.

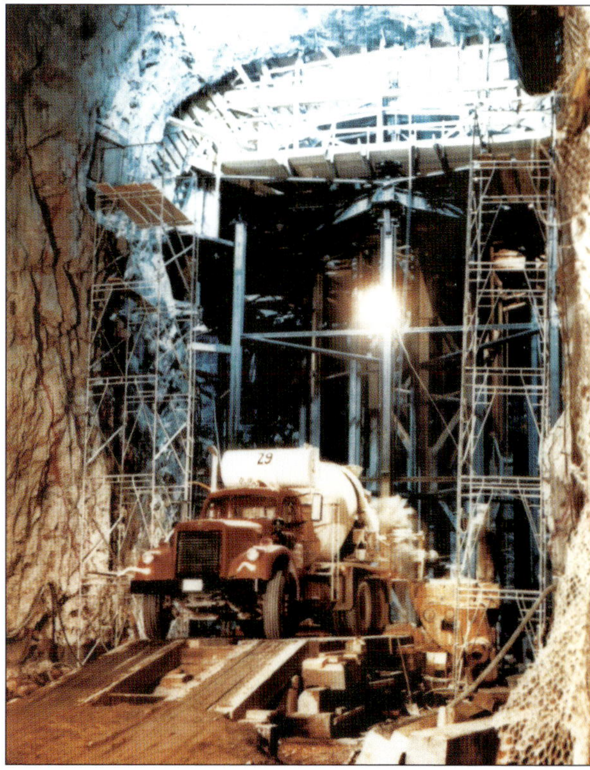

The main chamber of the facility houses the administrative offices and combat operations center. This shot shows the relative size of the chamber compared to the heavy machine installing wall supports.

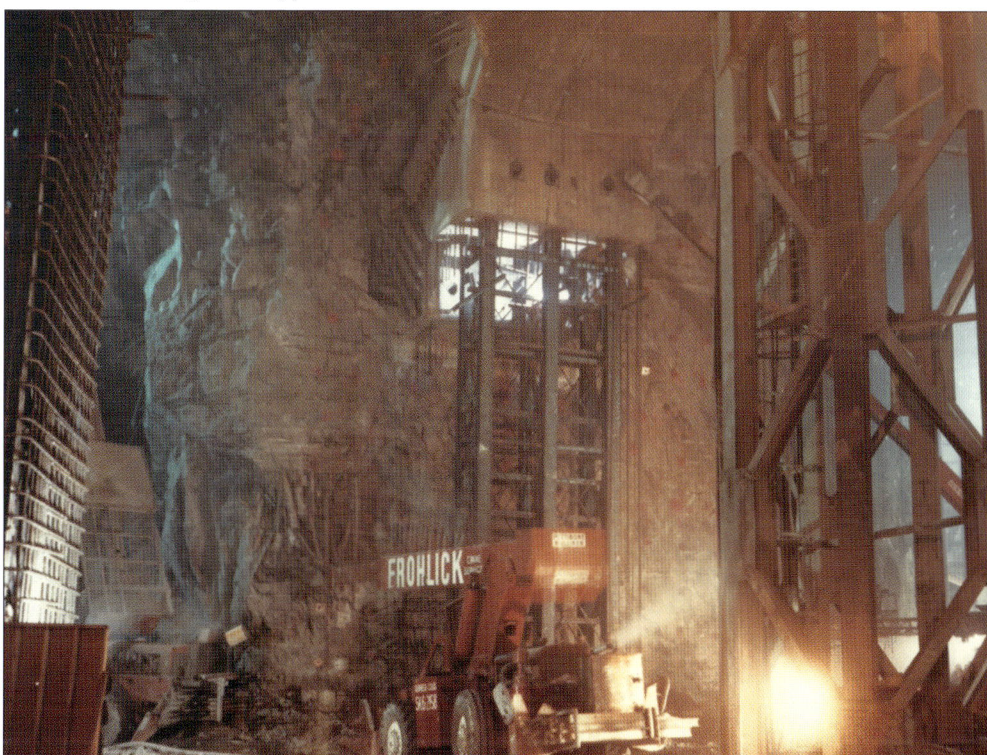

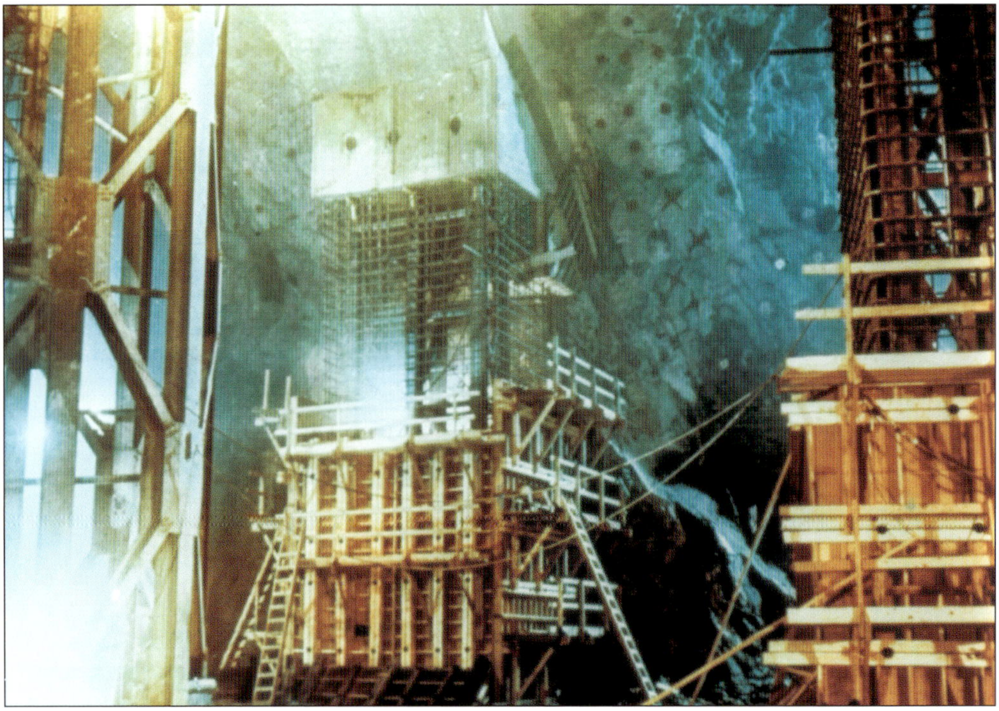

Pictured here is one of the main pillars that was cemented to provide an area of stability. This wood frame, a major project in and of itself, was where the cement was poured.

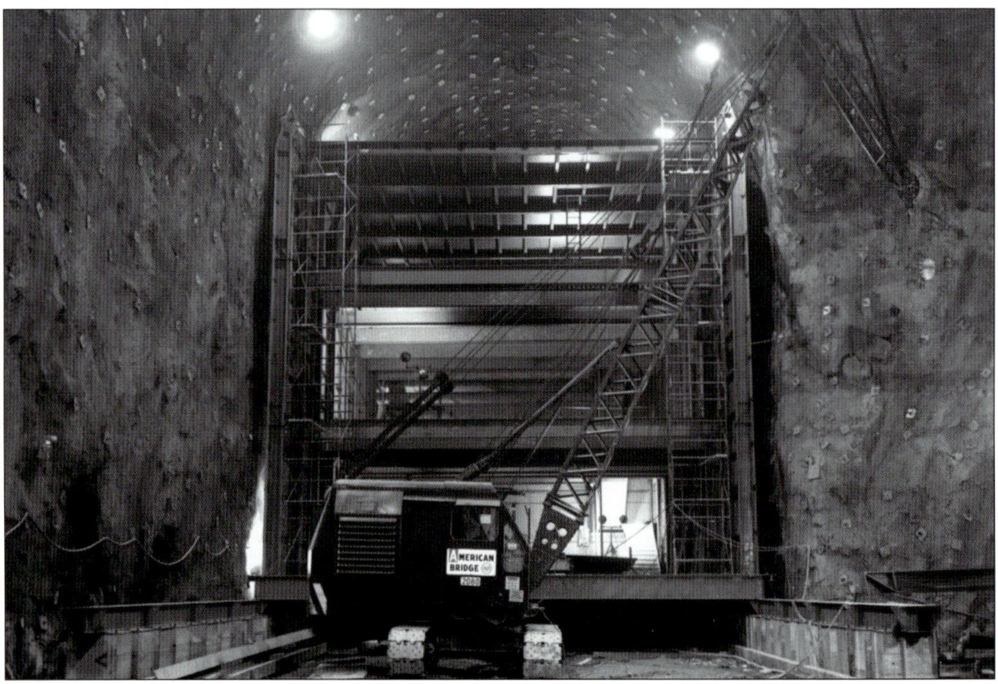

This is one of the three-story buildings inside the mountain. As evidenced here, the buildings do not touch the walls or ceilings of the mountain. There are 11 three-story buildings in the complex, made of steel plates three-eighths of an inch thick and resting on steel frames.

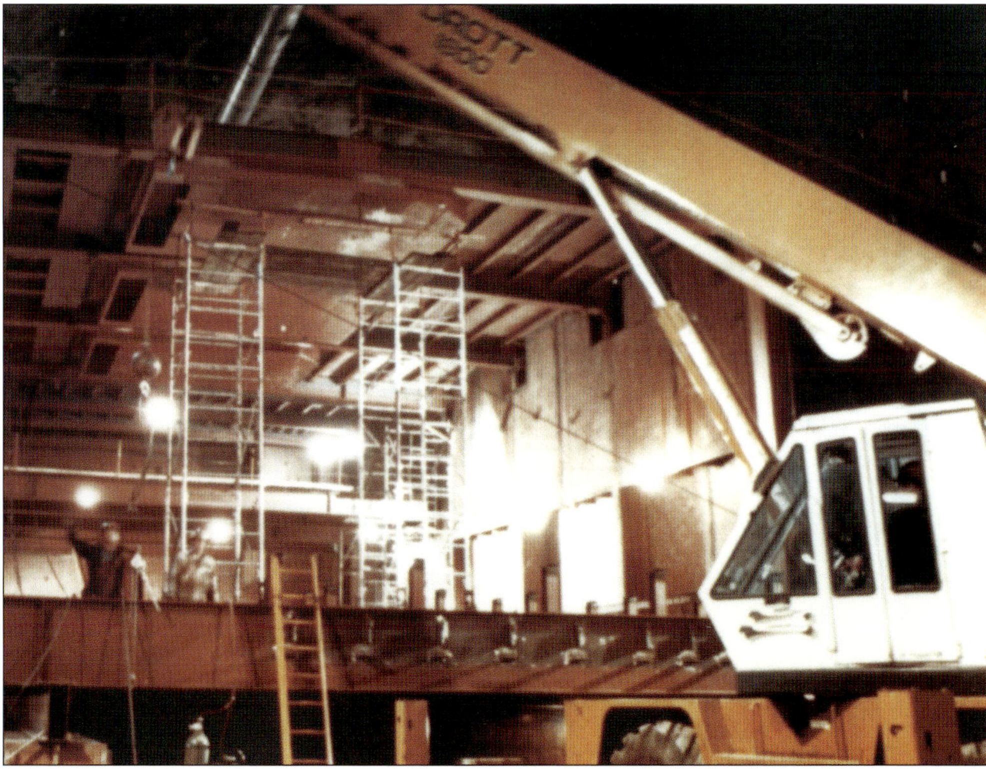

There are 15 buildings that make up the Cheyenne Mountain Complex, and most are three stories, with the rest reaching one or two stories. Combined, they provide over 200,000 square feet of floor space.

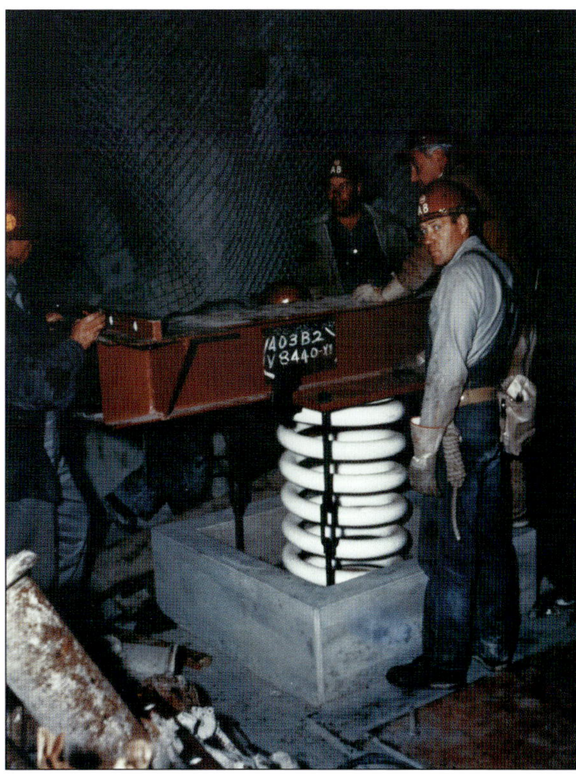

One of the shock-absorbing steel springs that all 15 buildings sit on is pictured here. Each spring is made of formed, three-inch steel rods and weighs 1,000 pounds. They are approximately four feet high.

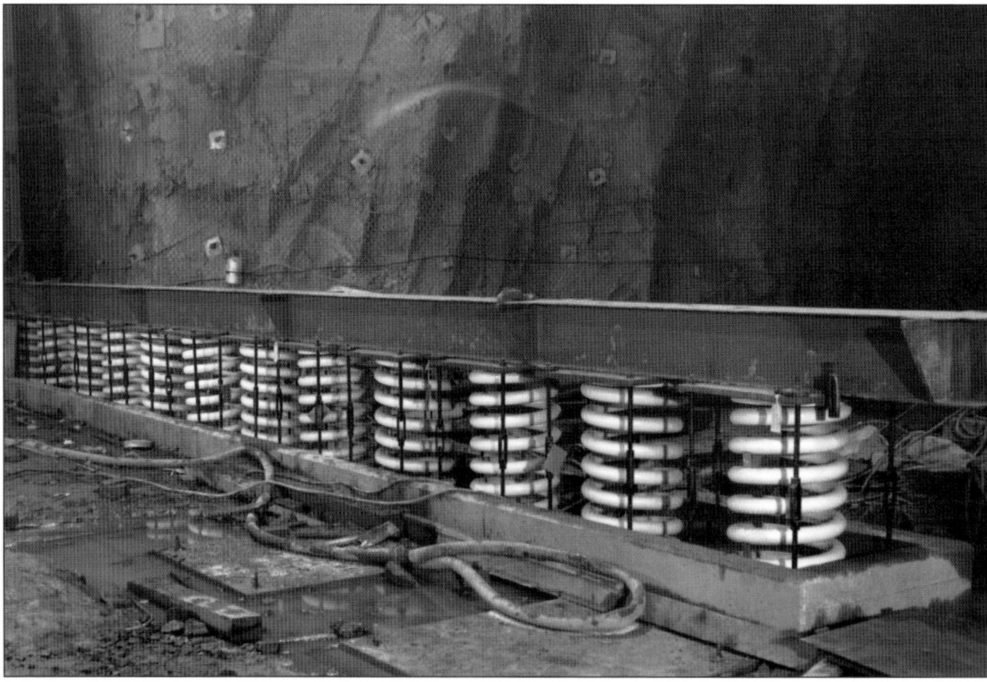

More than 1,300 springs were installed inside the mountain. These springs, placed in rows under the buildings, were designed to negate the potentially devastating earthquake effect of a nuclear blast.

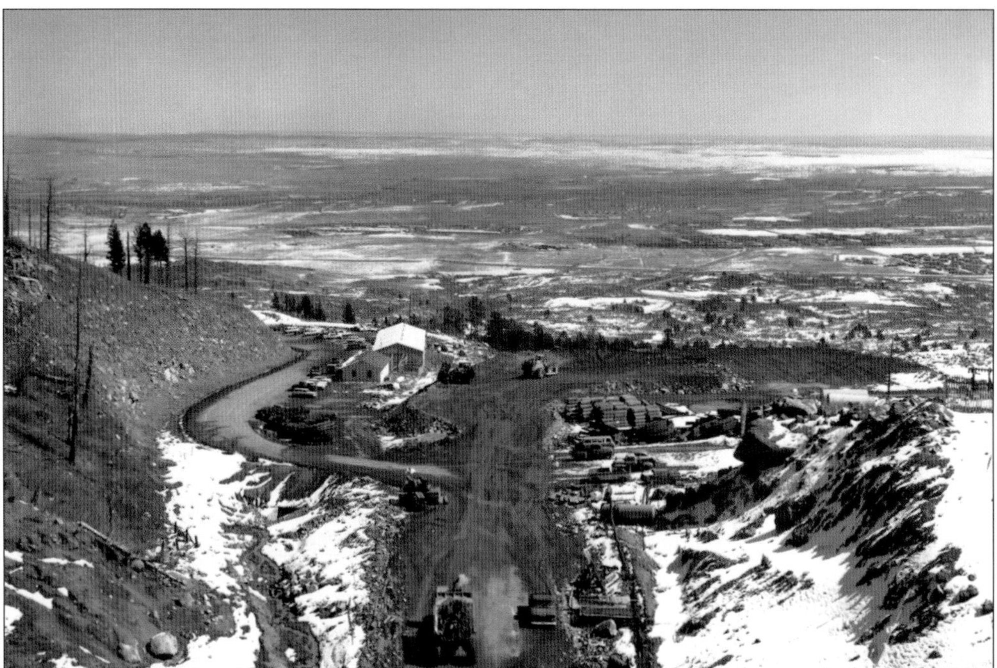

Looking east over Fort Carson, a heavy equipment hauler leaves the main tunnel. The construction team's equipment area is seen on the right. This area became the parking lot, which can accommodate over 600 vehicles.

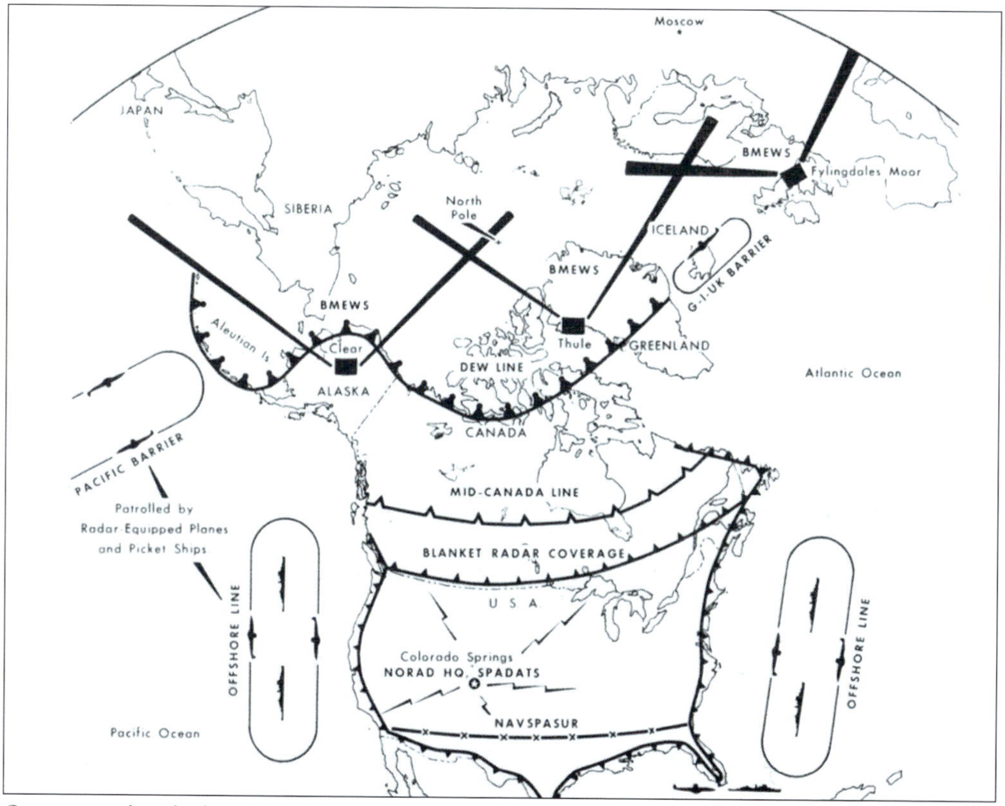

Once completed, the combat operations center will be the nerve center for the air defense of North America. This map shows the surveillance coverage in the early 1960s. The data was fed into Cheyenne Mountain's new center.

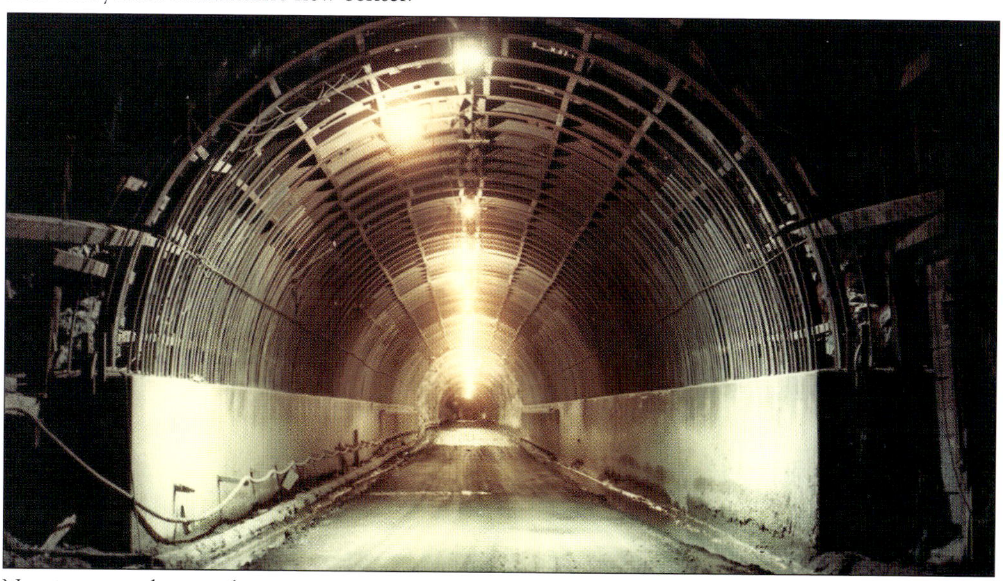

Nearing completion, the entrance to the Cheyenne Mountain Operations Center and the length of the main tunnel is pictured here. Nearly a third of a mile from the entrance to the first set of blast doors, this tunnel is the route used by vehicular and pedestrian traffic.

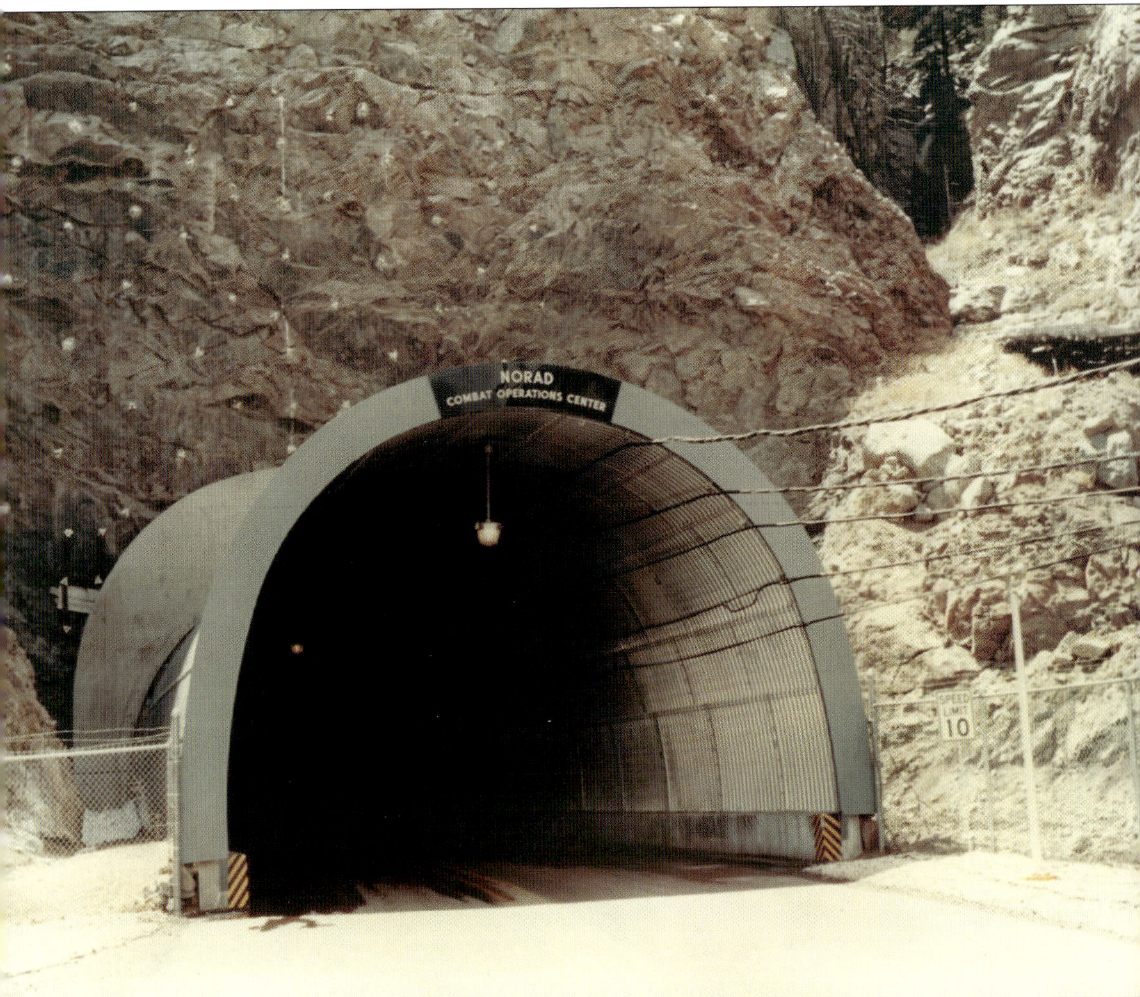

The north portal is completed in this photograph, and it is ready to become the entrance to the new NORAD Combat Operations Center. In operational use since 1966, the hardened facility is still an active part of the defense of North America.

Three

Cheyenne Mountain AFS

America's Fortress

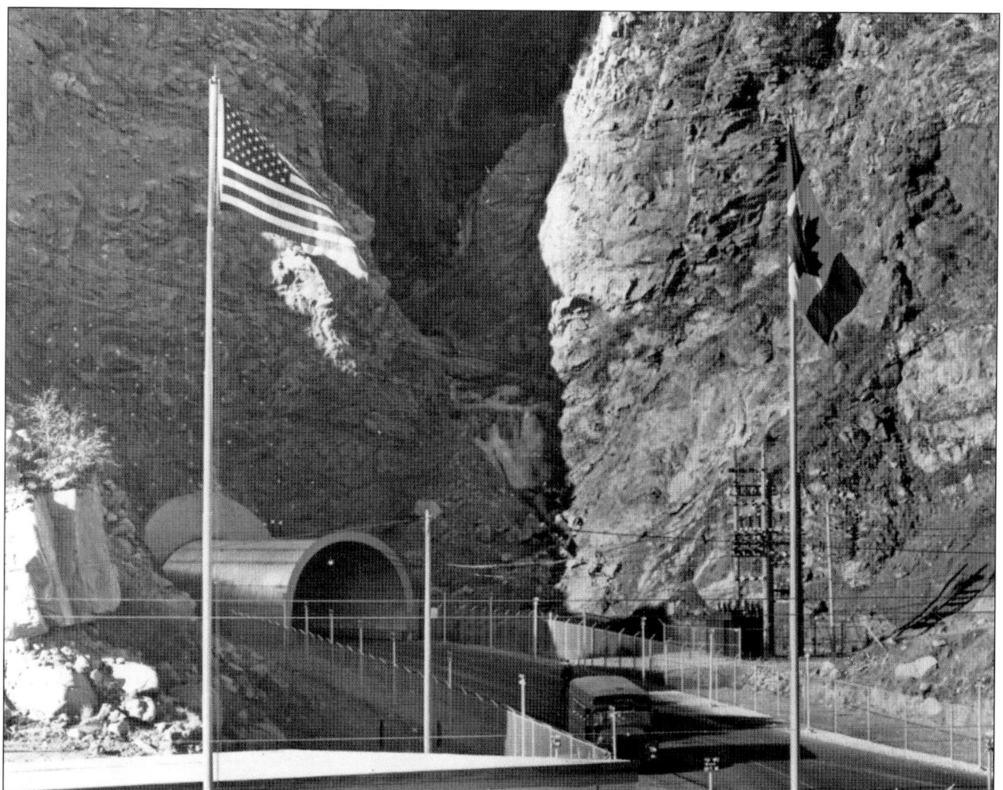

Pictured here is the main entrance to the Cheyenne Mountain Operations Center. This 1960s-era photograph shows a bus that is used to shuttle personnel into and out of the facility. Many choose to walk the third of a mile in the tunnel to the blast doors.

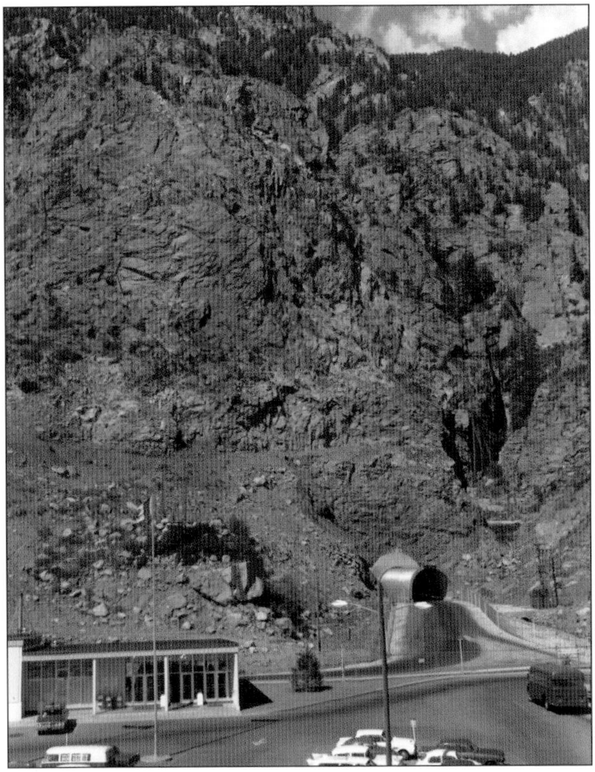

This photograph of the exterior of the north portal shows the security fencing around the facility. The building on the left houses the air police and secure entrance to the mountain.

The view in the command center shows the on-duty crew manning. The whiteboard displays the current air situation and unknown aircraft locations, alert force status, and radar site status.

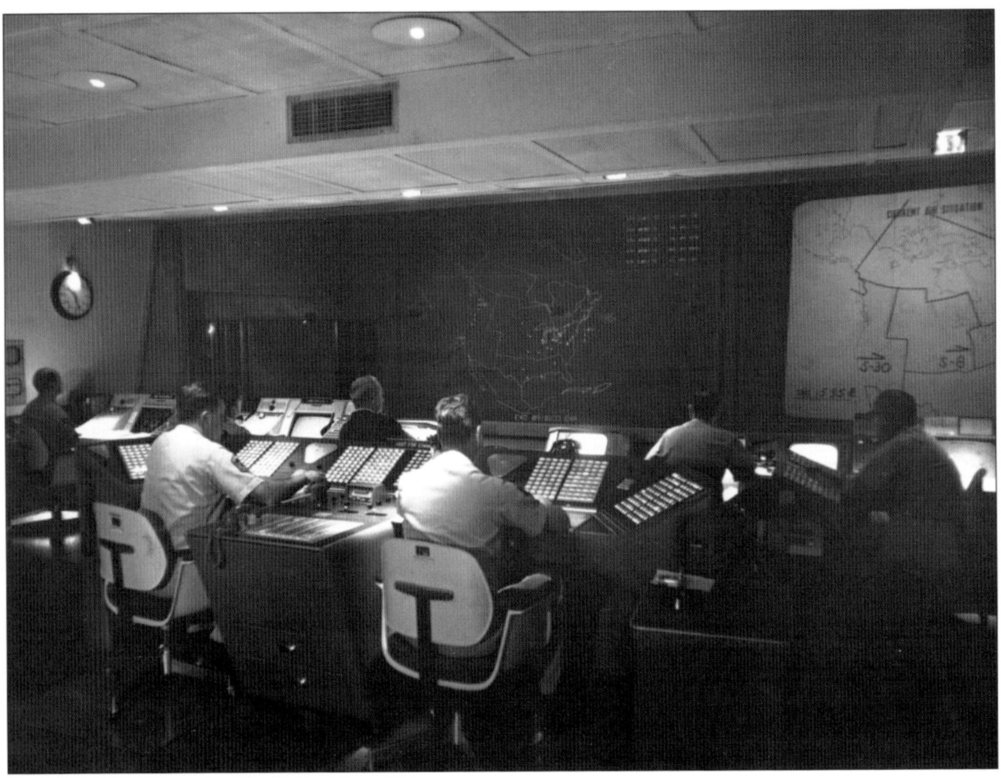

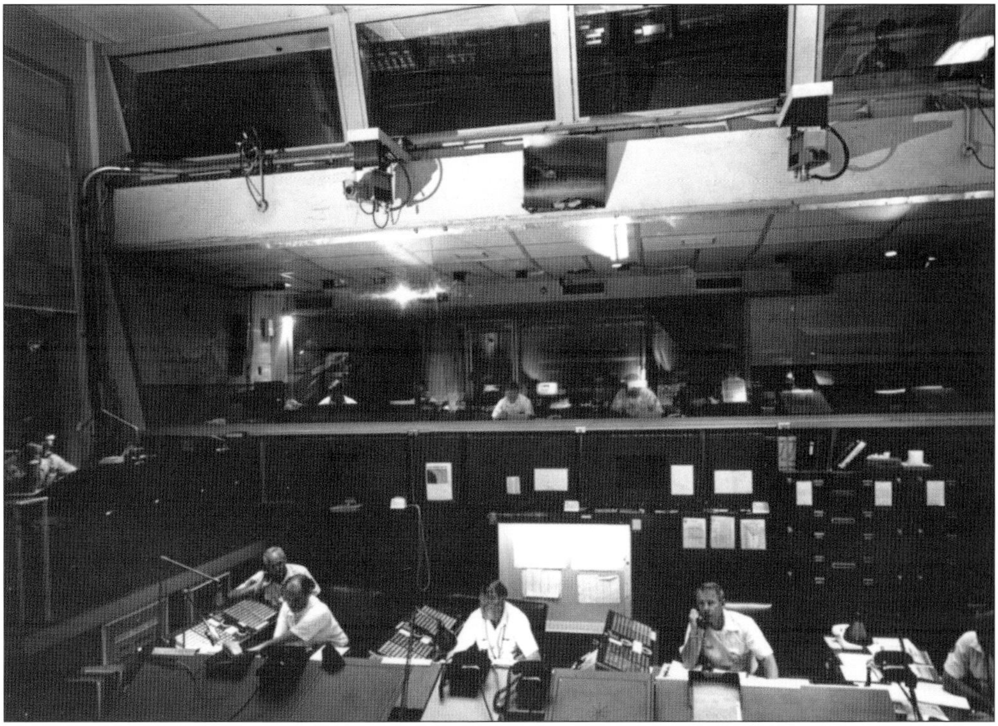

Pictured here is a view of the command center in the Chidlaw Building prior to the transition to Cheyenne Mountain. The on-duty crew monitors air, missile, and space domains for any threat to North America.

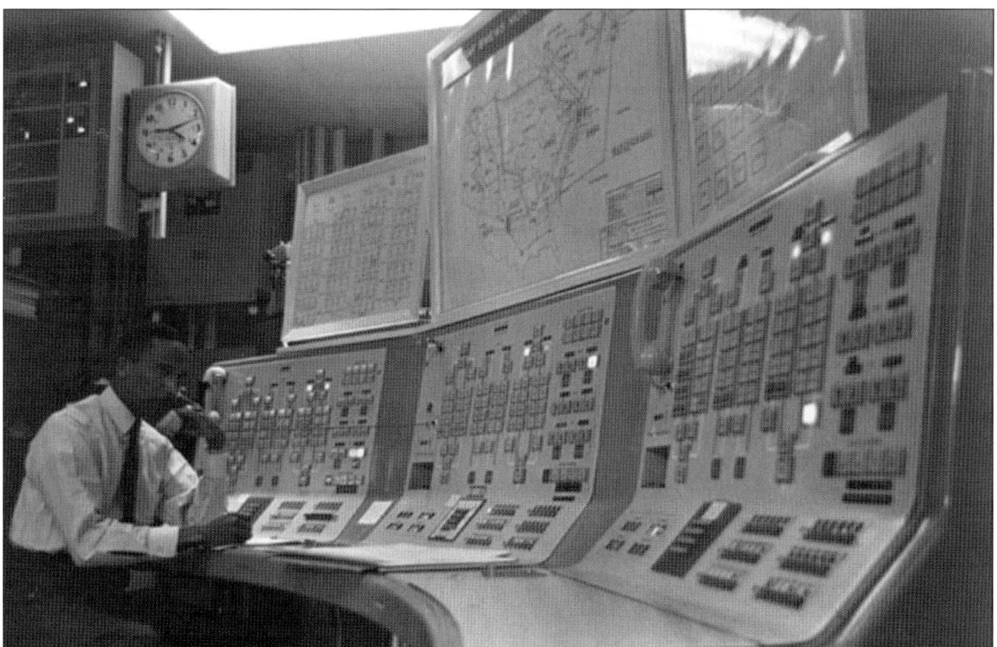

The missile defense center monitors the status of all air defense missiles, and the large whiteboard displays the status of the Ballistic Missile Early Warning System (BMEWS).

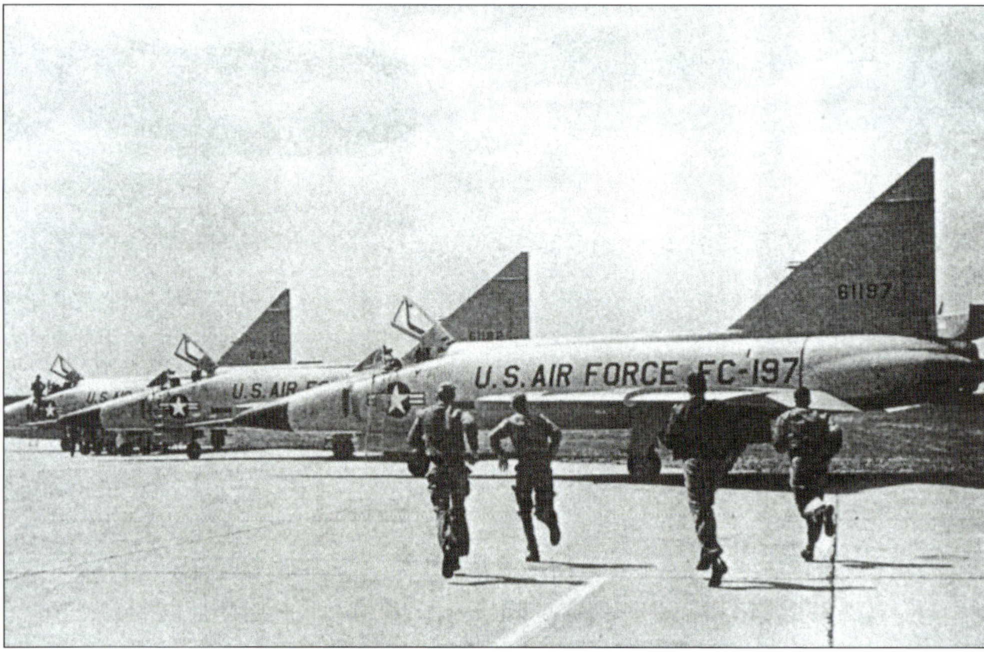

Pilots scramble to the alert fighters at an undisclosed base. The Cold War required pilots to be ready to respond to any air defense mission and their quickness provided every second needed.

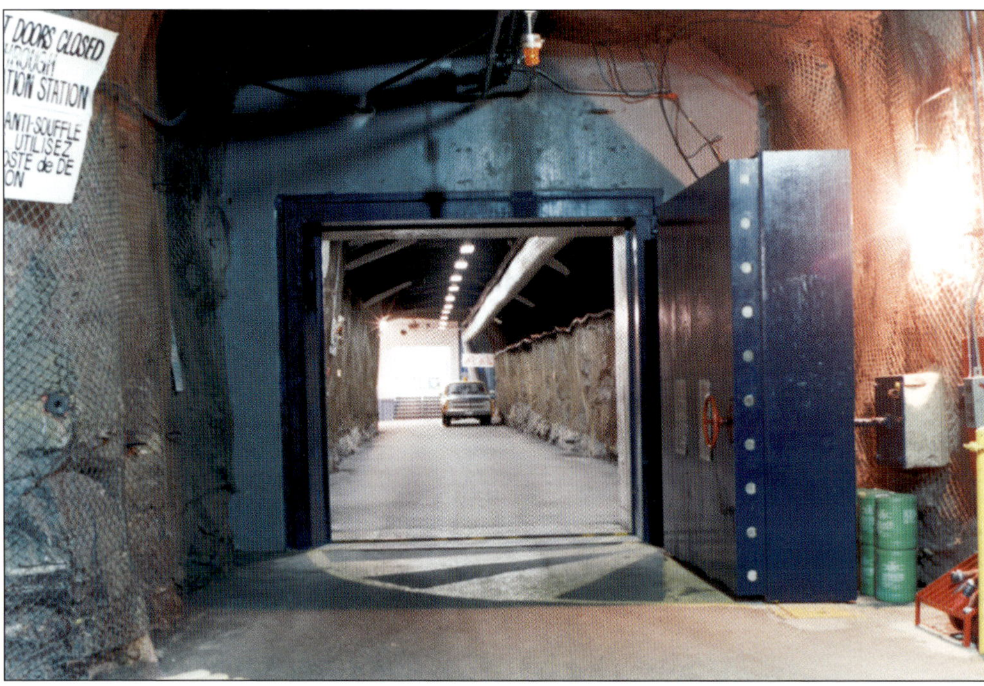

The Canadian NORAD Region in North Bay, Ontario, was an underground facility similar to Cheyenne Mountain AFS. The blast doors inside their facility provide the same type of protection as the ones located inside Cheyenne Mountain. Current operations have moved to a new facility.

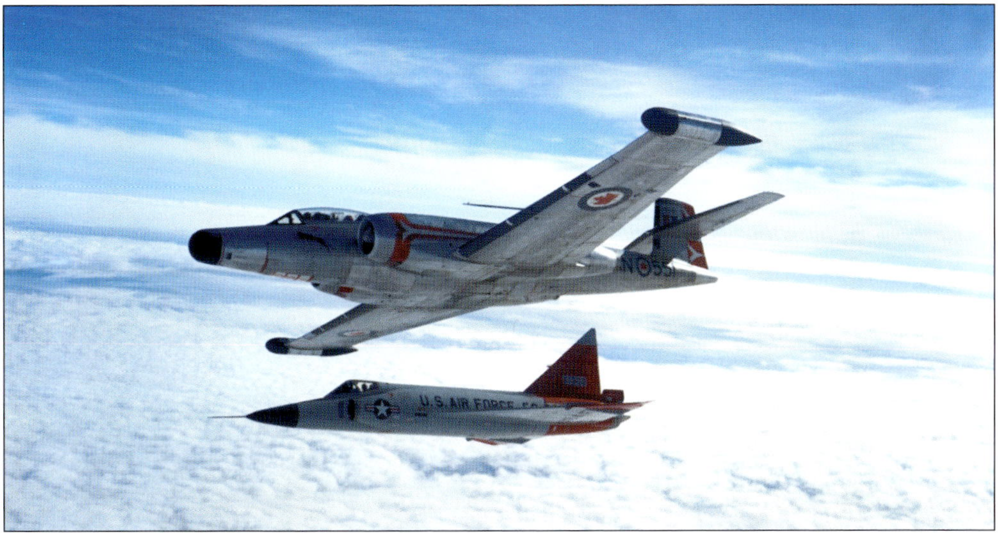

A US Air Force F-102 Delta Dagger and Canadian Air Force Avro CF-100 Mk 4B fighter-interceptor fly in formation. Both fighters were on alert for many years and intercepted numerous unknown aircraft. The CF-100's primary role was to attack enemy bombers detected by Distant Early Warning (DEW) Line radar stations in the Canadian Arctic.

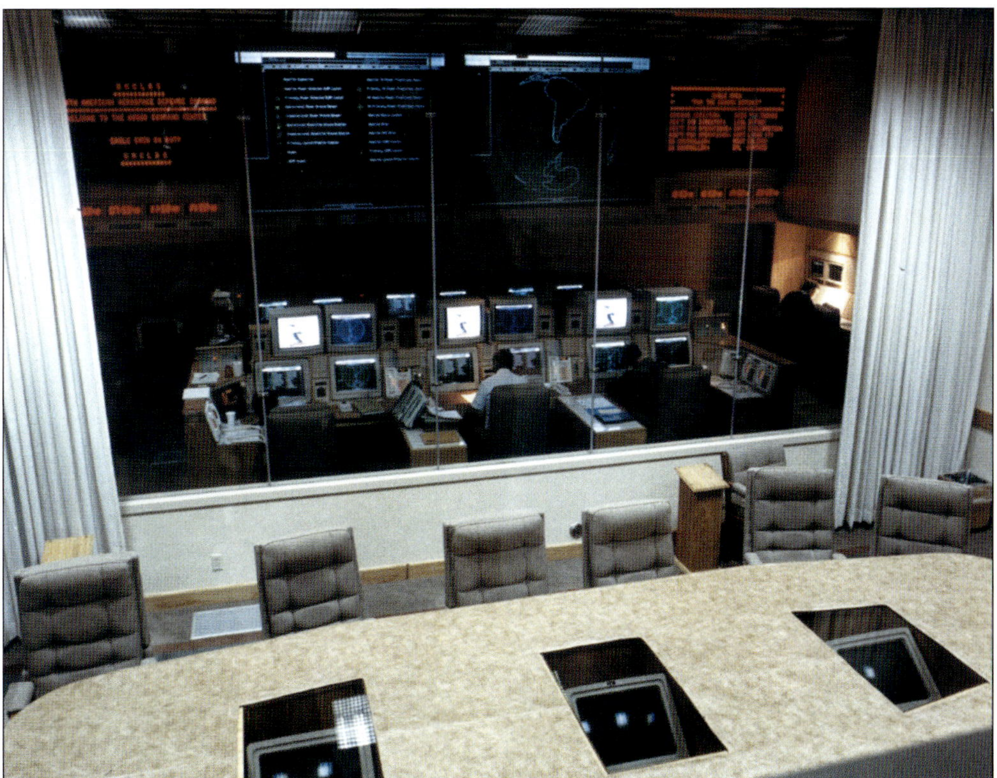

The NORAD Command Center inside Cheyenne Mountain is pictured here. Viewed from the battle staff area, the senior general officer sat in the center, surrounded by the crew, for ease of communications.

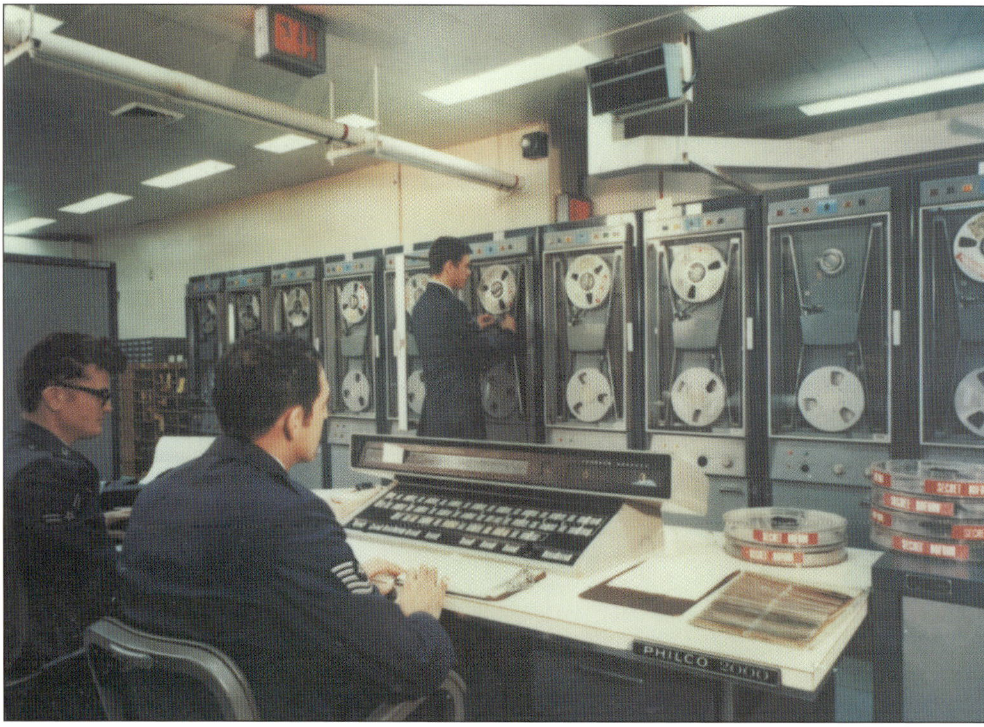

Inside the computer room at Cheyenne Mountain, US Air Force personnel monitor the status of the Philco 2000 Model 212 computer. Three of this computer model were installed in the mountain and operated until 1980.

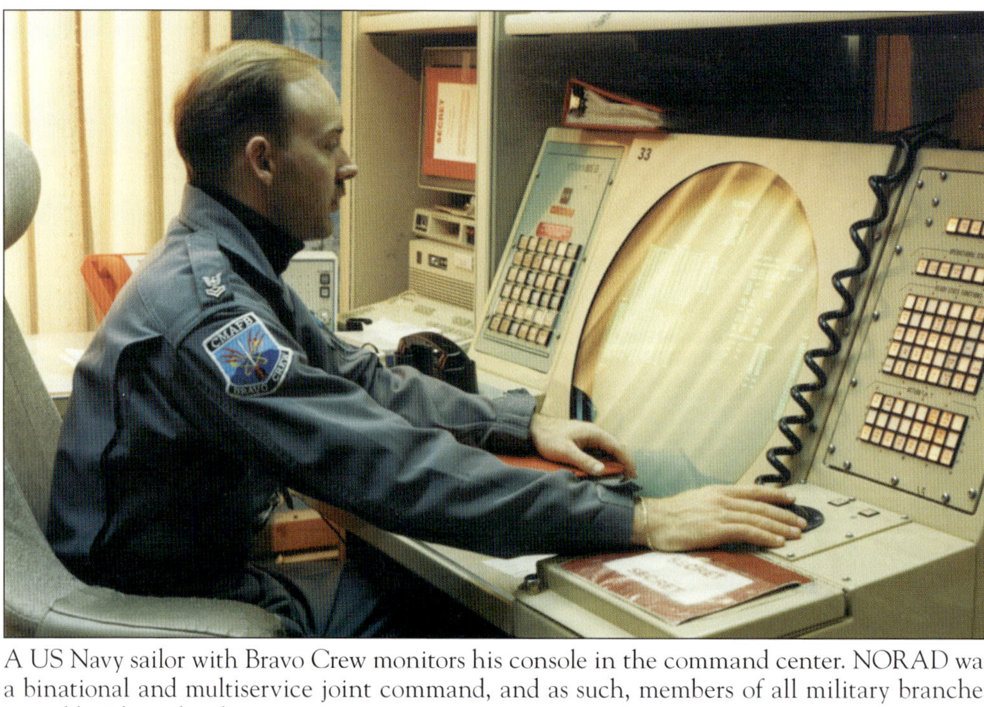

A US Navy sailor with Bravo Crew monitors his console in the command center. NORAD was a binational and multiservice joint command, and as such, members of all military branches served beside each other.

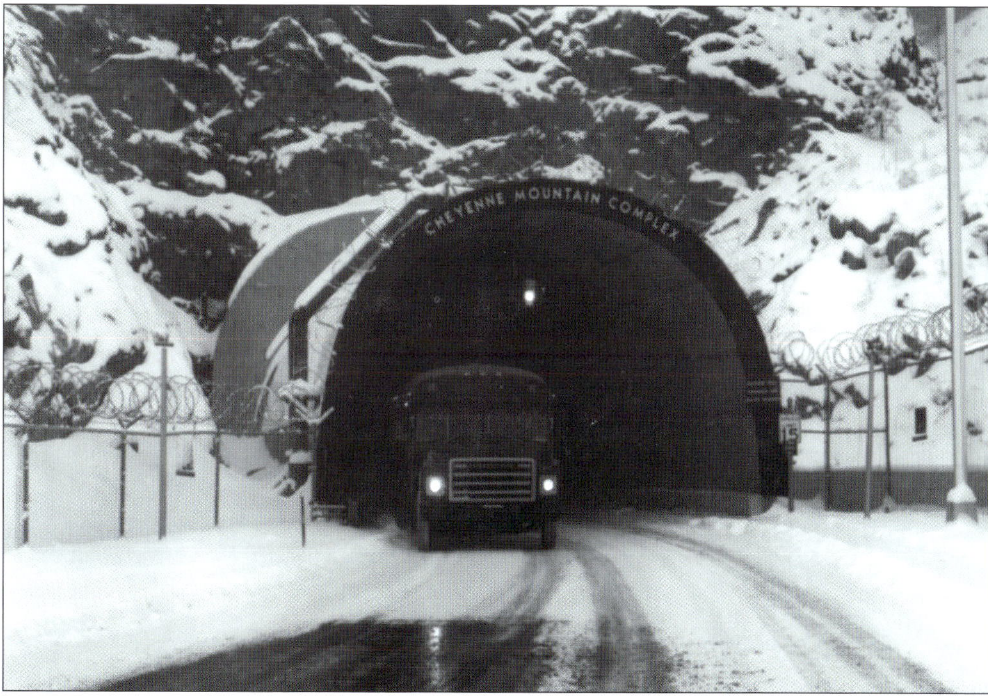

The tunnel bus shuttle emerges from the North Portal on a snowy day. Despite snow occasionally falling during the winter months, the crews of Cheyenne Mountain AFS operated 24 hours a day, 365 days a year.

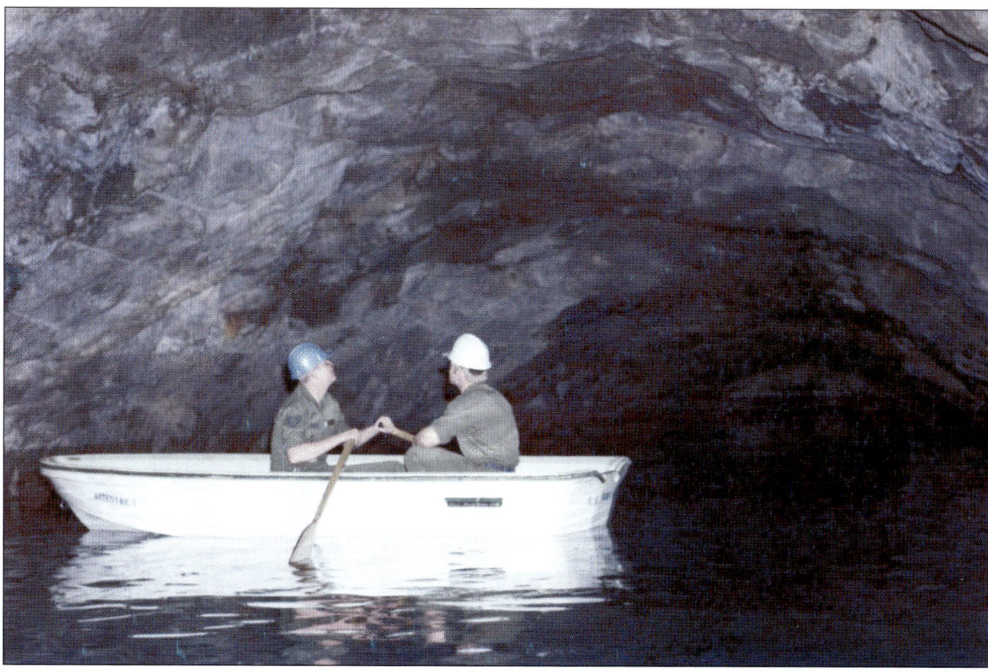

The US Air Force's navy is alive inside Cheyenne Mountain AFS. During the excavation of the mountain, crews discovered several natural springs. The artesian spring is used for drinking, cooking, and so forth. Crews monitor the reservoir and the rock bolts in the area.

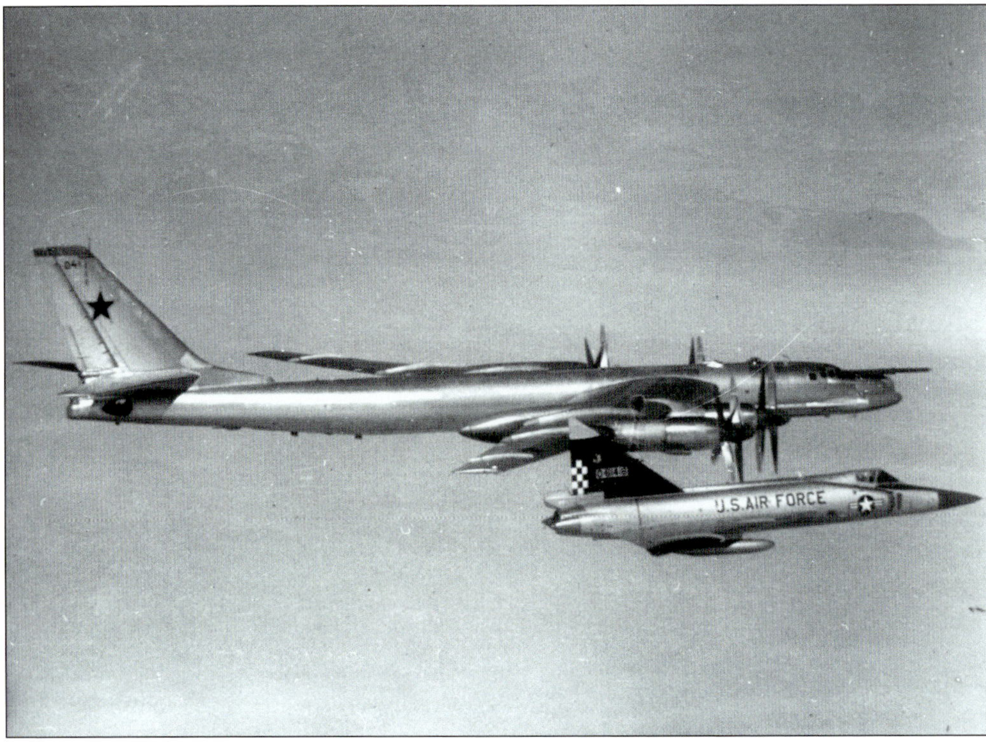

An F-102 Delta Dagger Fighter-Interceptor jet is escorting a Soviet Union Bear Bomber. These bombers were the prime threat to North America, and NORAD continuously monitored the skies for any incursions into sovereign airspace.

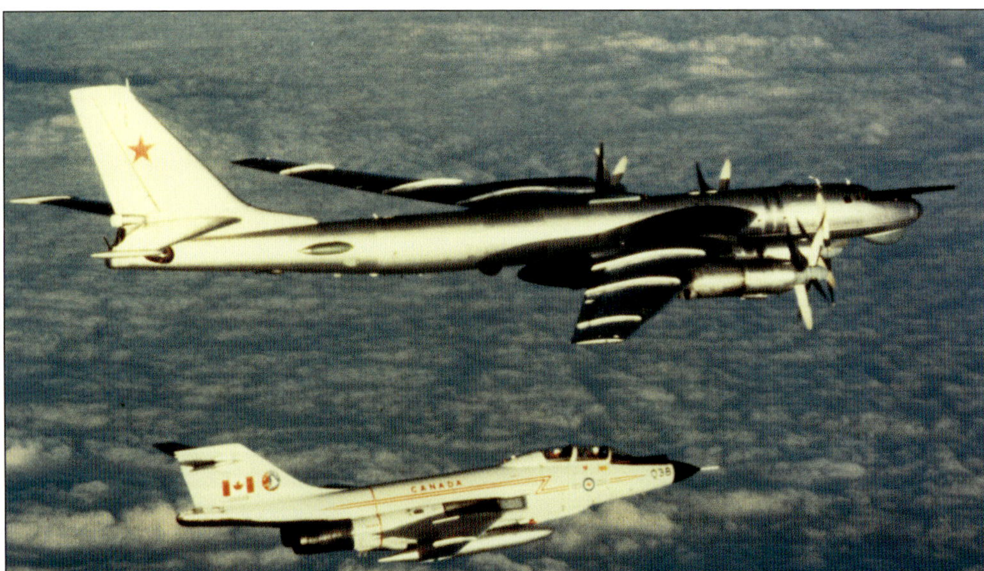

A Canadian CF-101 Voodoo Fighter-Interceptor escorts a Soviet Union TU-95 Bear Bomber during a mission near Canadian airspace. These bombers were the prime threat to North America, and NORAD continuously monitored the skies for any incursions into sovereign airspace.

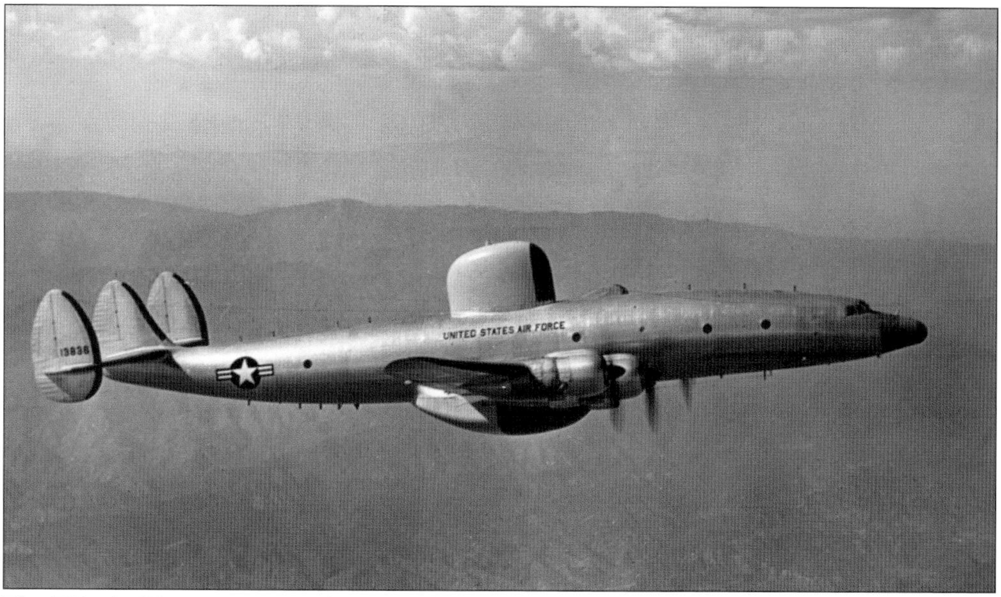

The EC-121 Warning Star Airborne Early Warning radar surveillance aircraft provided radar coverage where land-based radars could not reach. Operators on board the aircraft provided surveillance and fighter control when land-based systems could not.

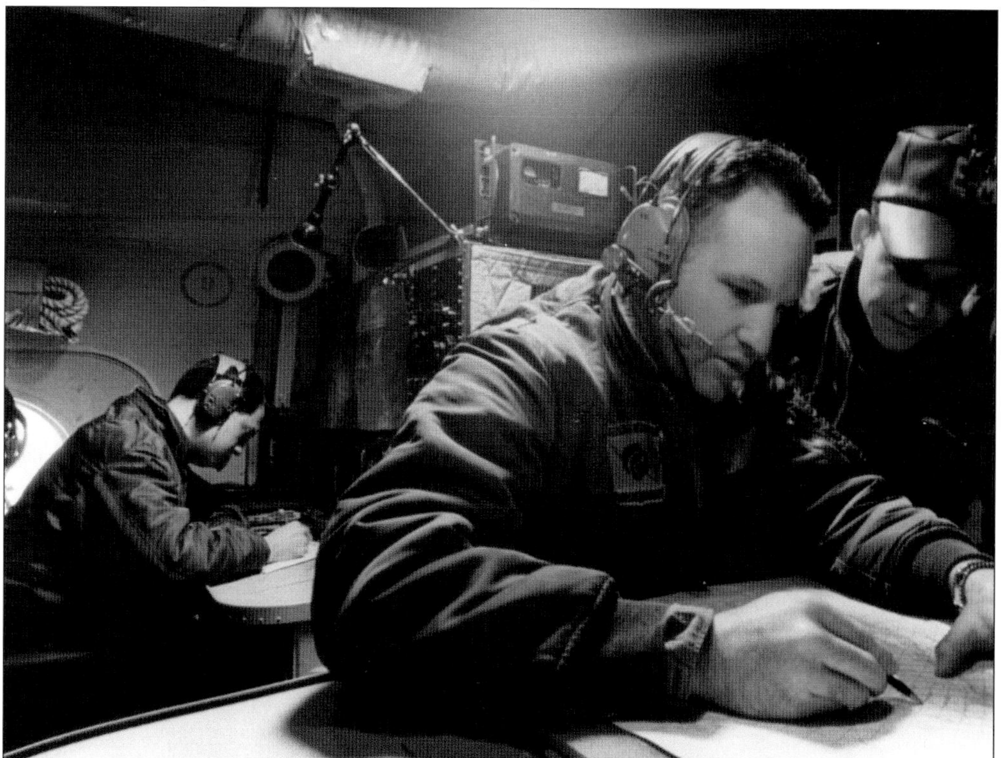

Crewmembers inside an EC-121 Warning Star aircraft plot strategy on a map. The EC-121, the forerunner to the current E-3 Airborne Warning and Control System (AWACS), was a major part of North America's air defense system until the late 1970s.

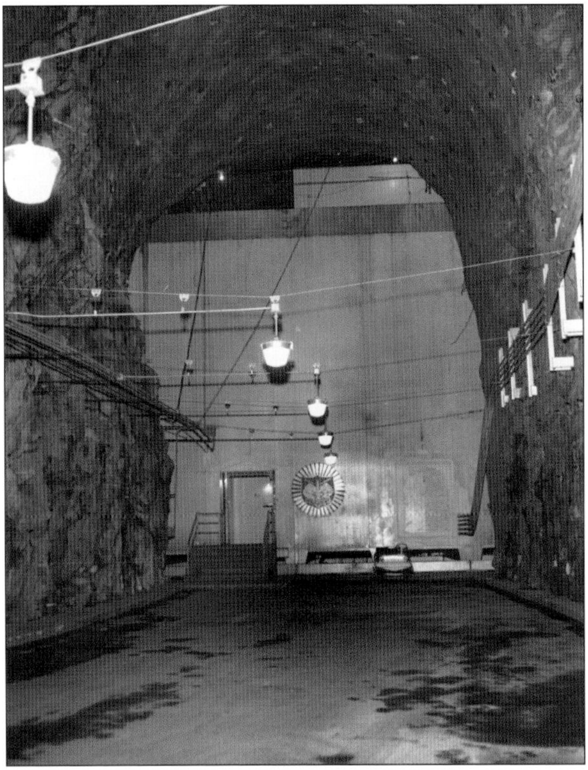

This is the entrance inside Cheyenne Mountain where dignitaries, visitors, and many workers enter. The NORAD commander's parking space is located to the left of this entrance.

This view of a three-story building demonstrates the amount of granite that had to be removed before an edifice of this size could be built. Each building was constructed inside the mountain using welding, rivets, and screws to bring them all together.

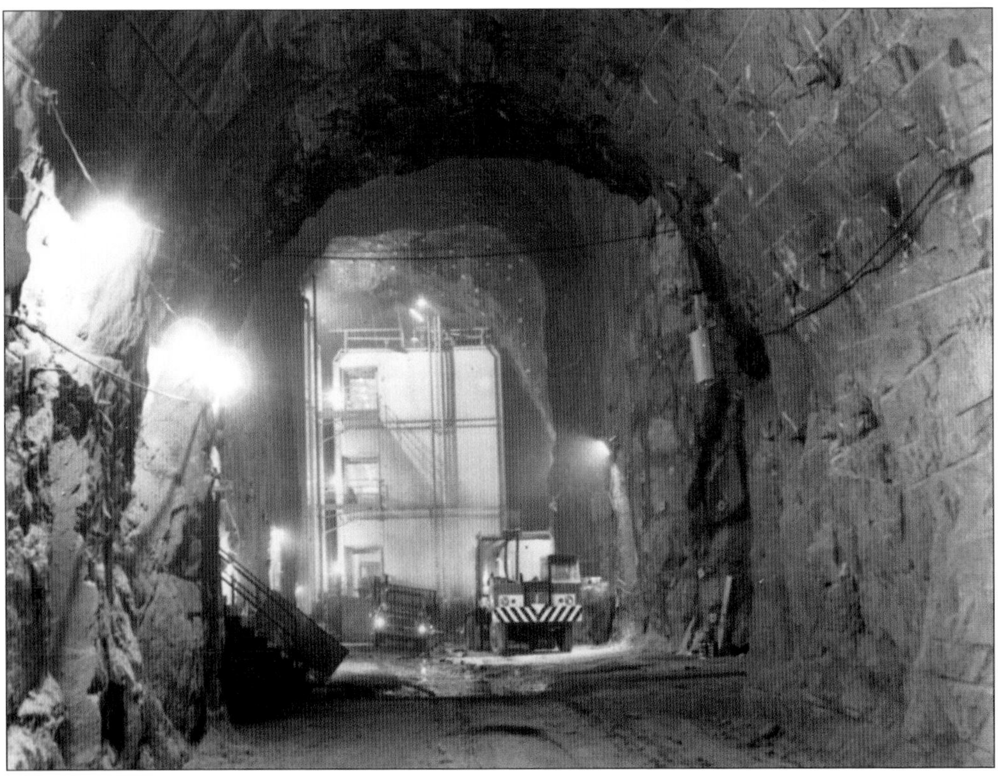

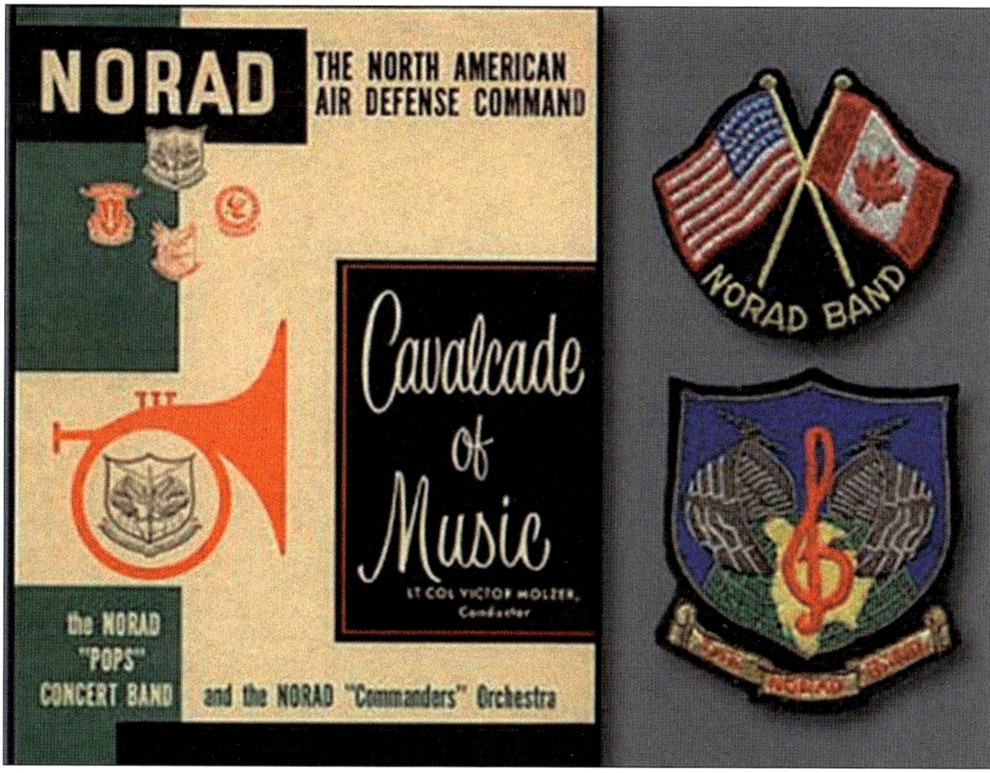

NORAD had its own band, which played at official functions and on television, performed concerts in local and national civilian areas, and even recorded several albums. Known as the NORAD Commanders, this orchestra became one of the elite musical groups of the armed forces during the Cold War and Vietnam era due to the plethora of talented young musicians being drafted into military service.

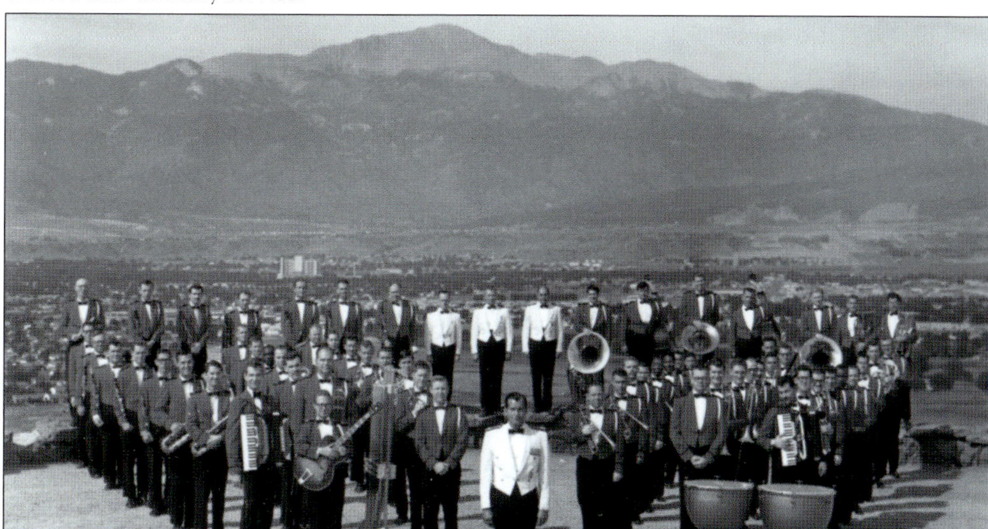

Established in 1959, the band was a American and Canadian joint armed services organization. It was a 90-member unit based out of Ent AFB, but members lived at nearby Peterson AFB.

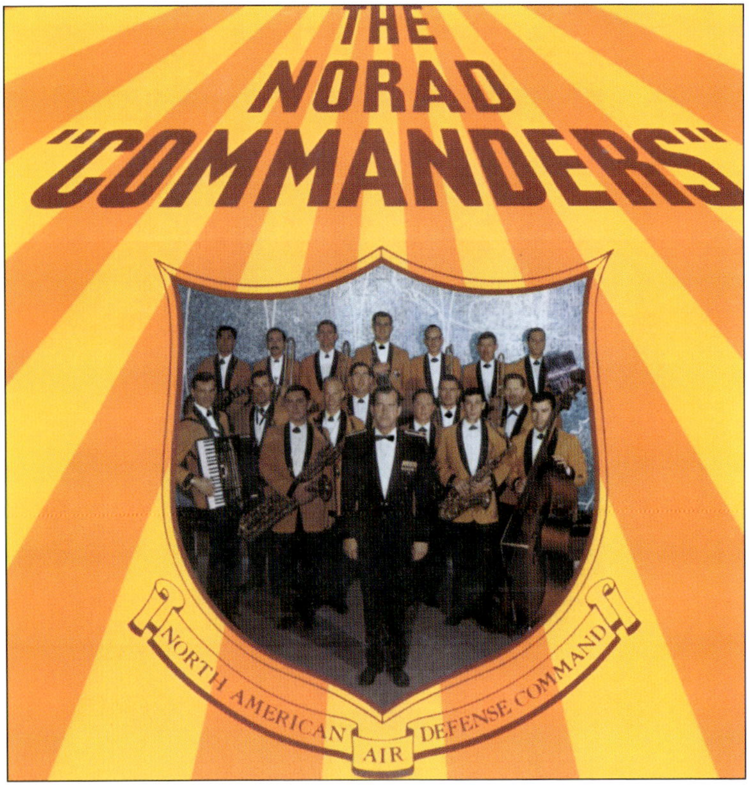

The band released several albums and performed on such popular television shows as the *Tonight Show*, *Steve Allen Show*, *Today Show*, and many others. The band also did high-profile performances at the famed Carnegie Hall, the New York World's Fair, and Expo 67 in Montreal.

Two F-102 Delta Dagger fighter jets soar in formation over Alaska. The F-102 provided NORAD's front-line air defense for many years.

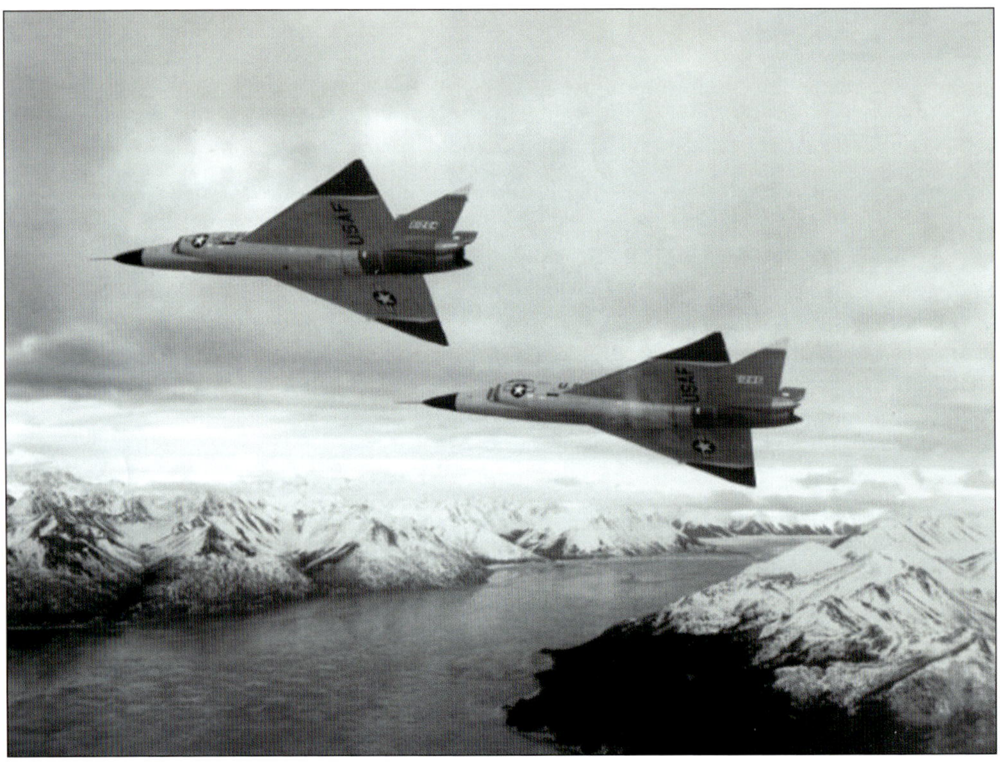

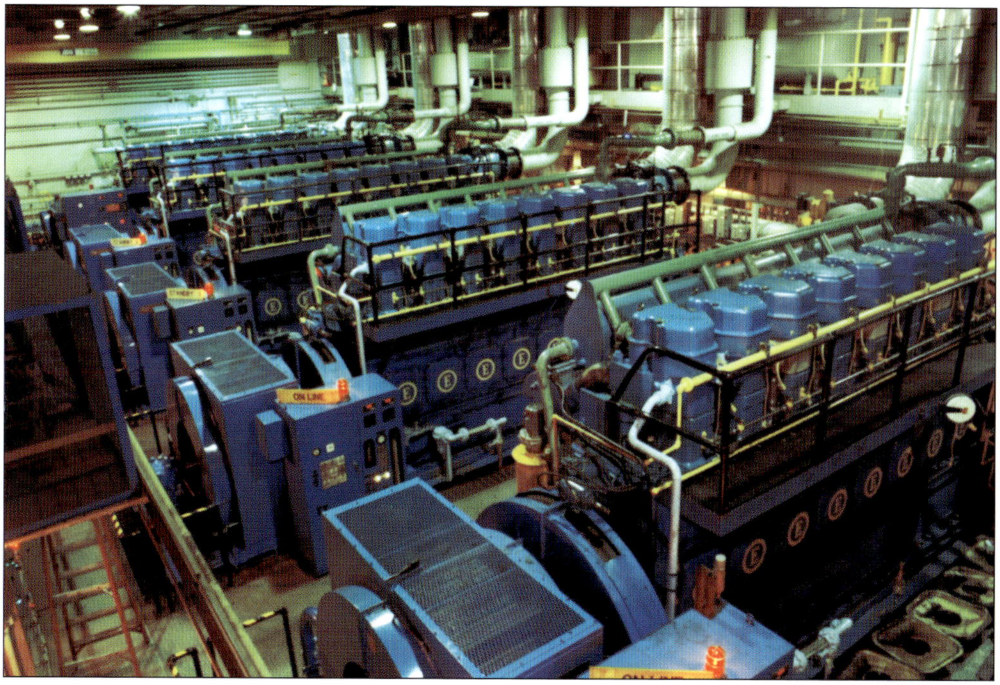

Six diesel generators (five pictured) are a back-up source for power to the Cheyenne Mountain Complex. The main power source is from commercial power purchased from Colorado Springs. These locomotive-sized diesels are operated as needed or as a standby during natural storms. Four generators can supply the power for the entire complex.

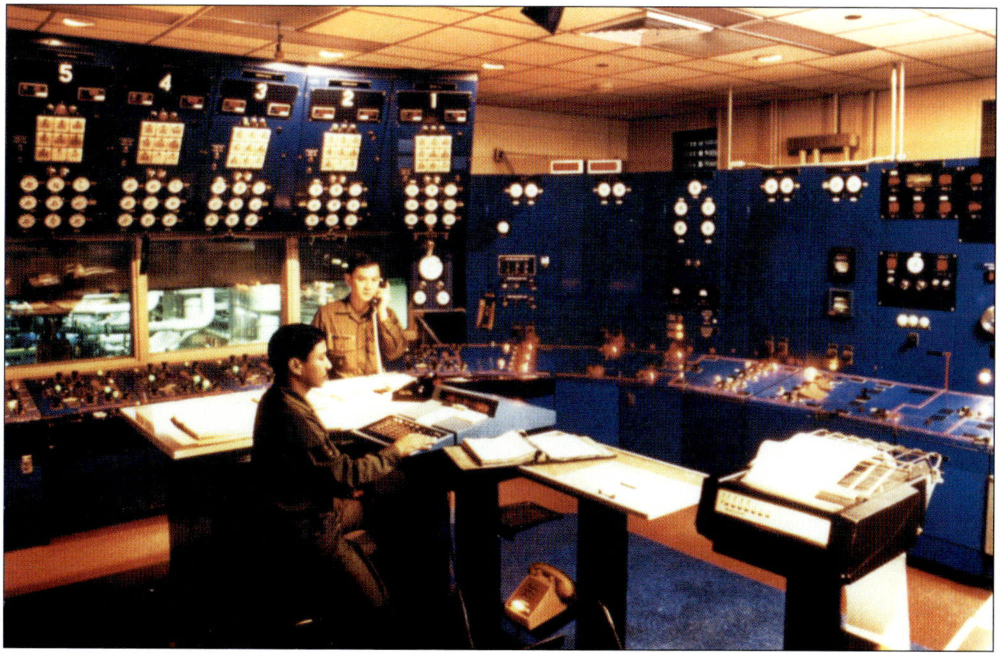

The generator-monitoring station is located a floor above the generators, with the windows looking out onto the six diesel engines. Each diesel generates approximately 2,800 horsepower and consumes about 110 gallons of diesel fuel per hour.

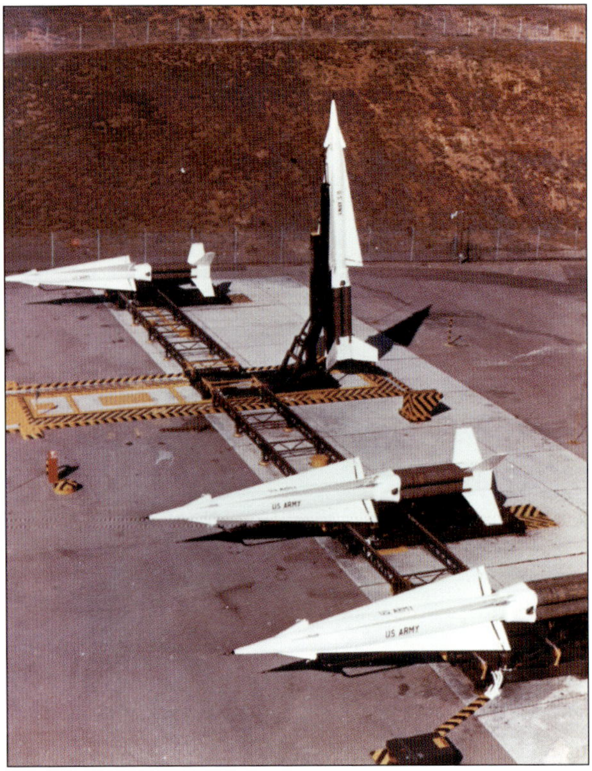

US Army Nike Hercules antiballistic missiles were on alert at strategic locations around the United States. The 27 Hercules batteries provided a shoot-down capability for incoming missiles until 1971, when they were released from air defense alert.

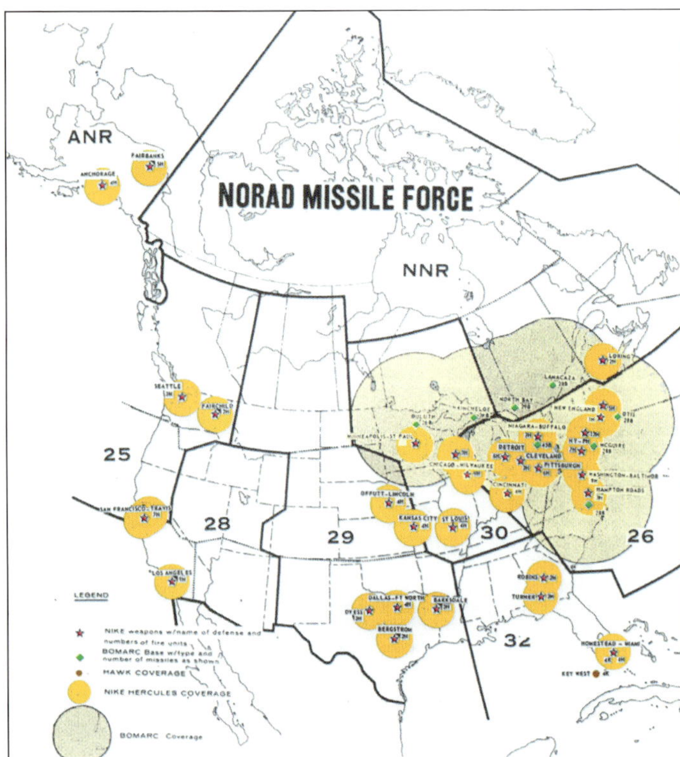

This map shows the location of the missile defense forces on alert throughout the United States. Under the operational guidance of NORAD and manned by US Army personnel, these missiles provided defense to any incoming ballistic missiles. Most were deactivated by the early 1970s.

One of NORAD's most enjoyable claims to fame is the yearly mission of tracking Santa Claus. Due to an accidental misprint of a telephone number (Continental Air Defense Command Operations Center phone) in a local newspaper advertisement that invited children to call Santa, Col. Harry Shoup, on-duty in the operations center, took the call. After several calls, Shoup directed his staff to find Santa on the radar screen and give children his location.

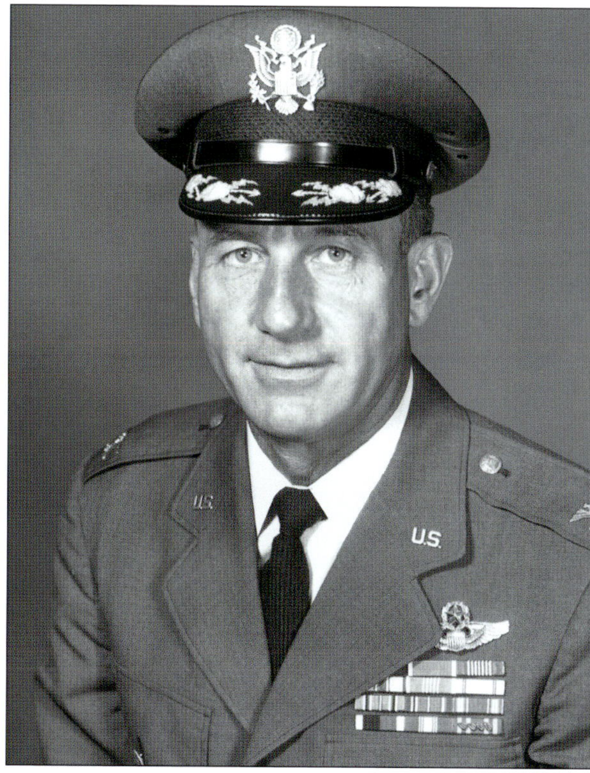

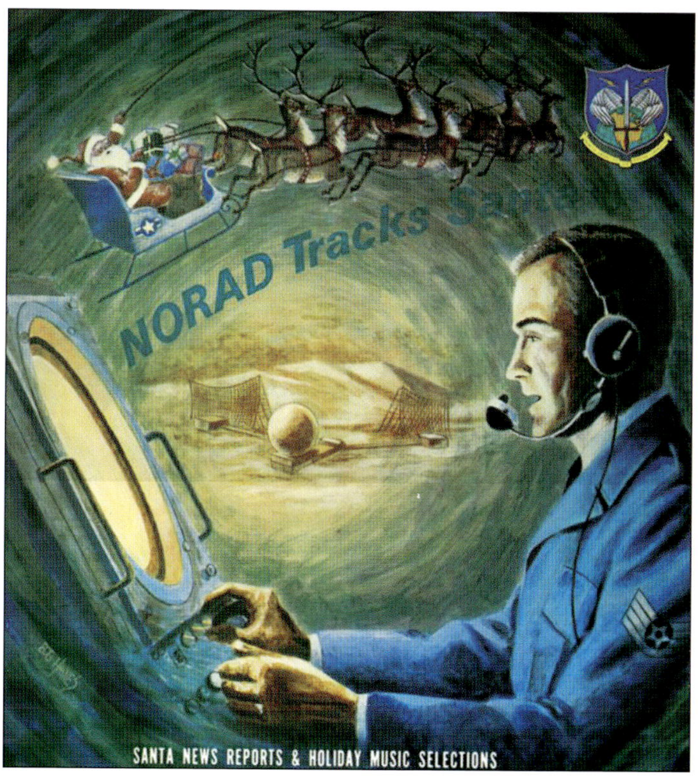

Since that Christmas Eve in 1955, the NORAD Tracks Santa Program has escalated to a worldwide phenomenon. Currently, on the Internet, nearly one billion hits occur each Christmas Eve, and millions more come through e-mails and telephone calls to the NORAD Tracks Santa operations center, manned by hundreds of volunteers.

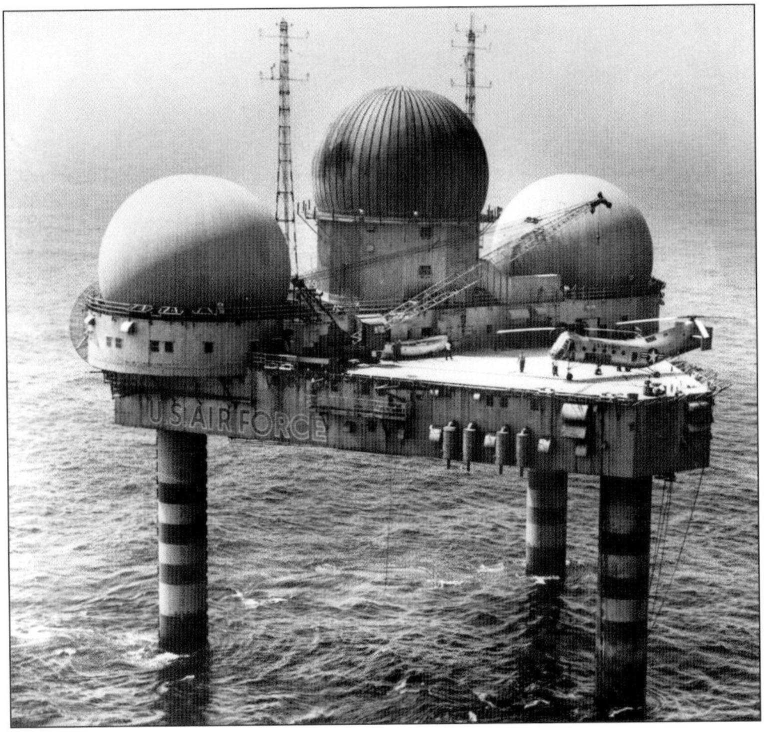

Among the most unique surveillance systems in the early years of NORAD were the Texas Towers. In the early 1950s, defending the northeastern United States was critical, and with the potential threat and capability of Soviet bombers striking that area, early warning was deemed a top priority. Located between 75 and 100 miles of the East Coast, these towers provided about 30 extra minutes of notification of pending threats.

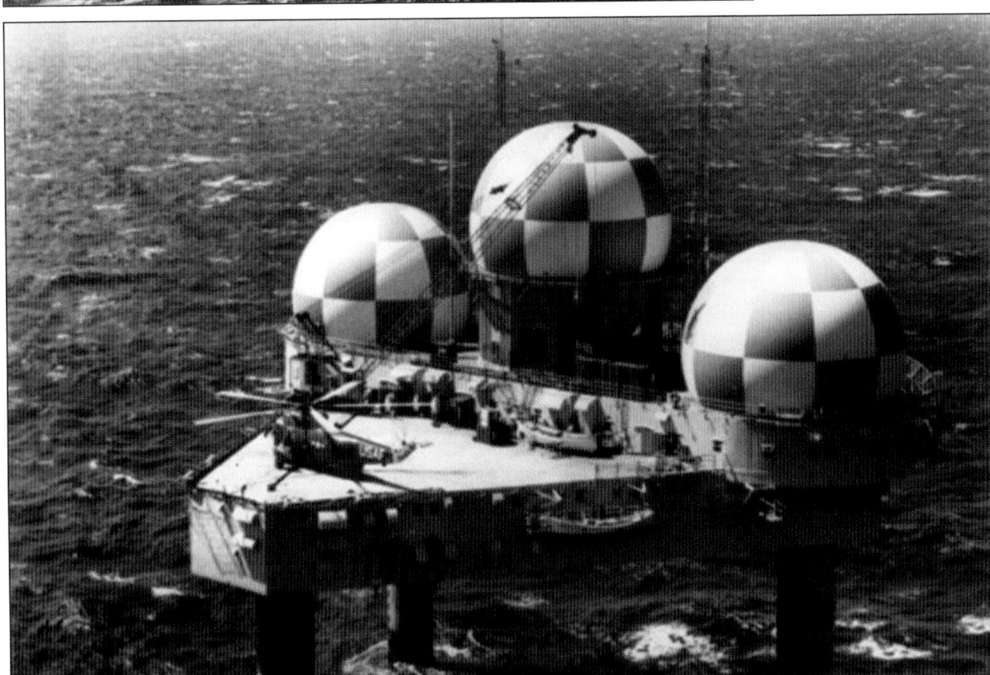

From 1955 to 1964 there were three Texas Towers erected. The stations looked much like the oil-drilling rigs in the Gulf of Mexico, and these radar sites were manned by US Air Force personnel who maintained the towers and monitored radar scopes. They all were semi-automated ground environment (SAGE) systems. SAGE was the modern air defense system for NORAD.

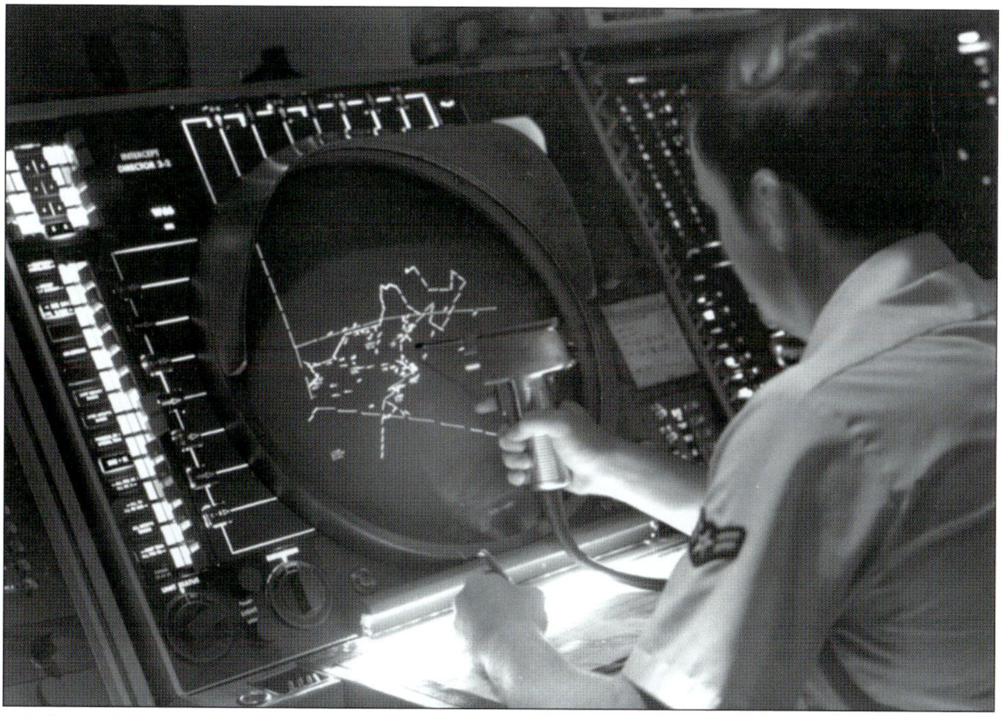

A US Air Force airman first class operates the console in a semi-automated ground environment control center in the 1960s. The airman is using a light gun, which acted like a modern day mouse, to pinpoint the location of needed computer actions.

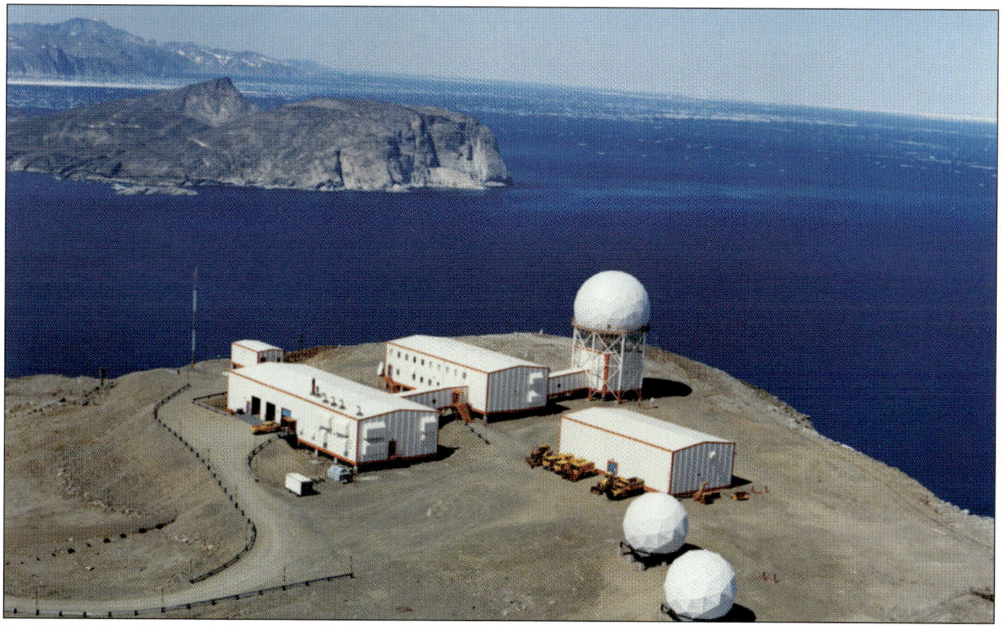

In 1987, the United States and Canada built the first segment of the North Warning System (NWS). The NWS is a series of radars stretching along the Arctic from Alaska to the eastern reaches of Canada. This system replaced the Distant Early Warning Line (DEW Line) with modern radars.

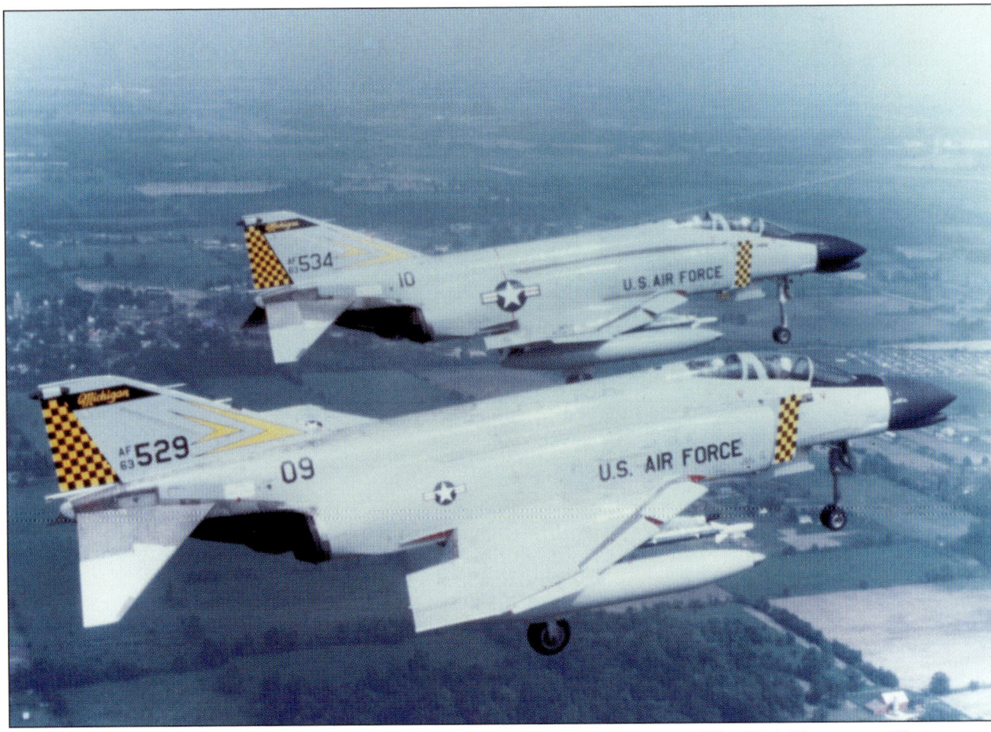

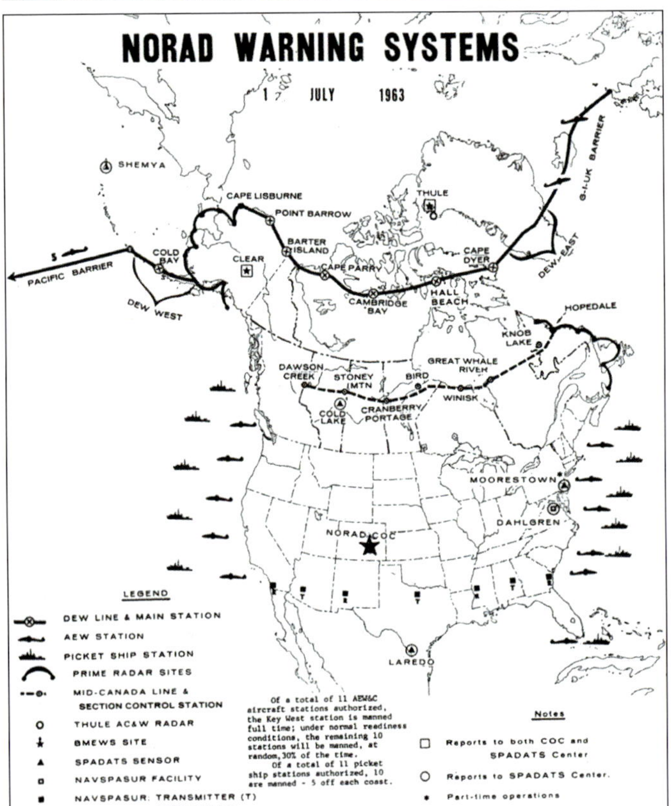

The F-4 Phantom II, a Vietnam-era workhorse, was the prime air defense fighter in the 1980s. Providing supersonic speed and proven combat capabilities, the F-4 intercepted numerous Soviet bombers before being replaced by F-15 and F-16 fighters for the air defense alert mission.

This map shows the NORAD warning systems in the 1960s and beyond. From the Distant Early Warning (DEW Line) system along the Arctic to the picket ships off the coasts, surveillance was a critical mission for the sovereignty of the United States and Canada.

Four

THE COLD WAR

DETERRING SOVIET AGGRESSION

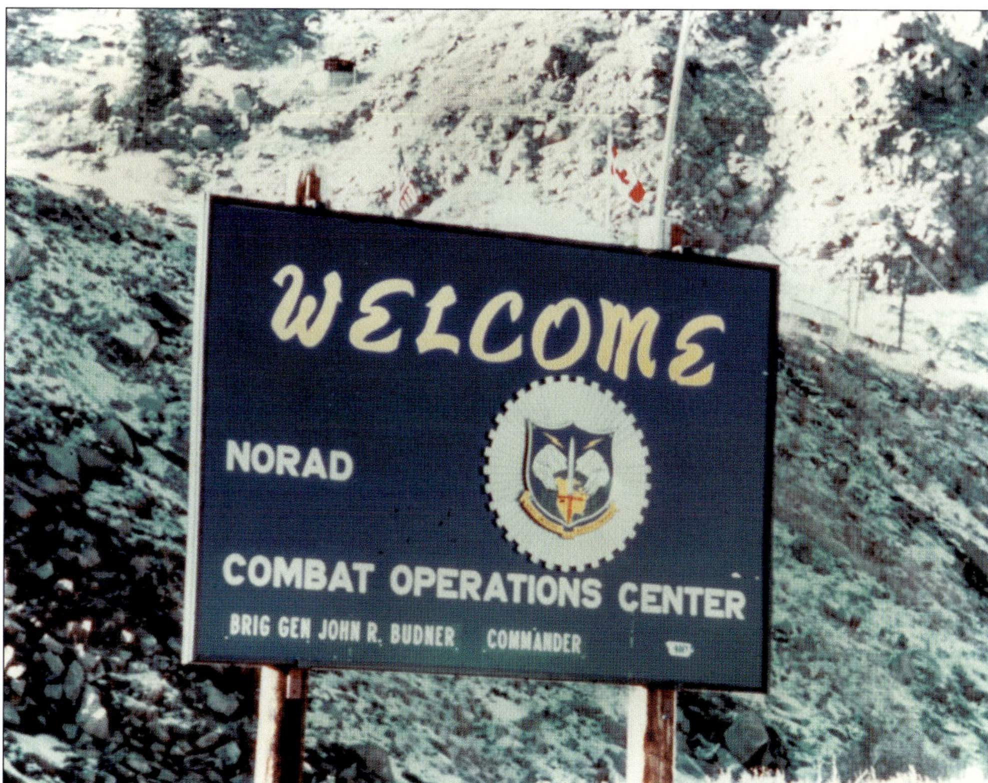

Pictured in the late 1970s, this sign was located near the top of the access road near the parking lot. General Budner was the commander of the operations center during this time.

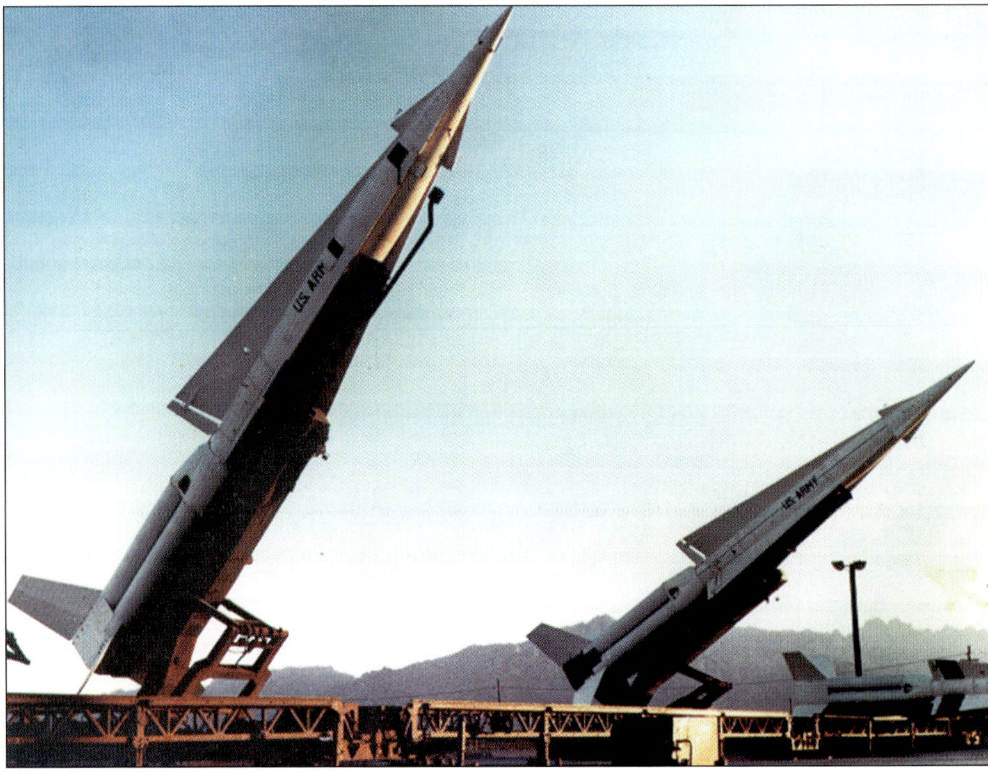

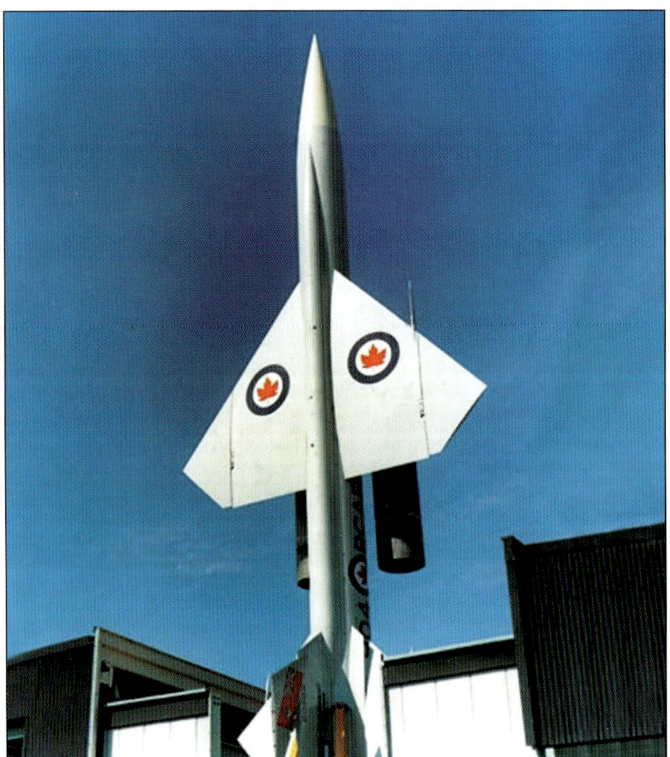

US Army Nike Hercules missiles are on alert at an undisclosed location. These missiles were on air defense alert around the United States for many years, and they were capable of shooting down a threat well before striking distance.

The Royal Canadian Air Force also had missiles on air defense alert. This Bomarc missile, in RCAF livery, is poised to launch at a moment's notice, protecting Canada's critical areas.

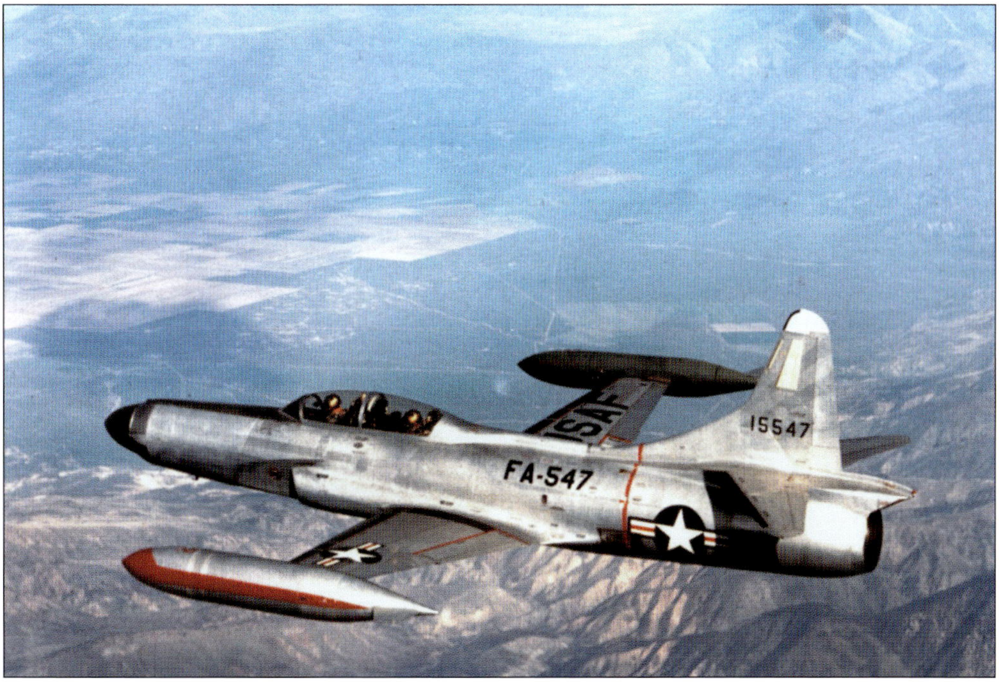

The F-94 Starfire fighter-interceptor jet was on air defense alert for many years. A subsonic jet, it was in service until 1959, when it was retired.

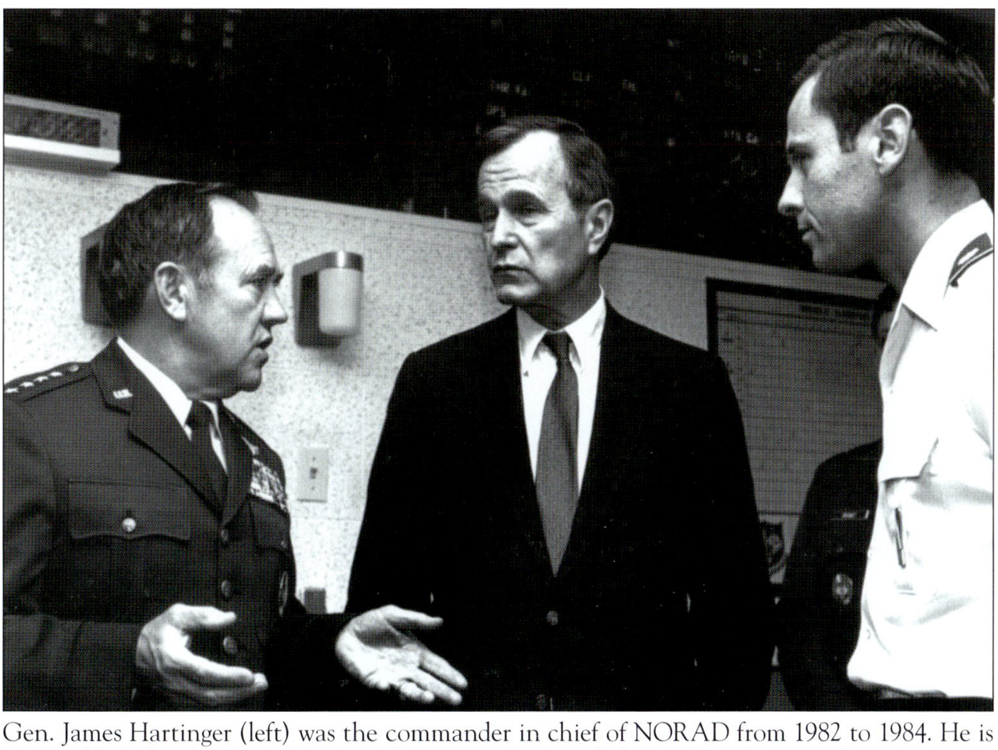
Gen. James Hartinger (left) was the commander in chief of NORAD from 1982 to 1984. He is pictured here briefing then-vice president George H. Bush (center) on the NORAD mission.

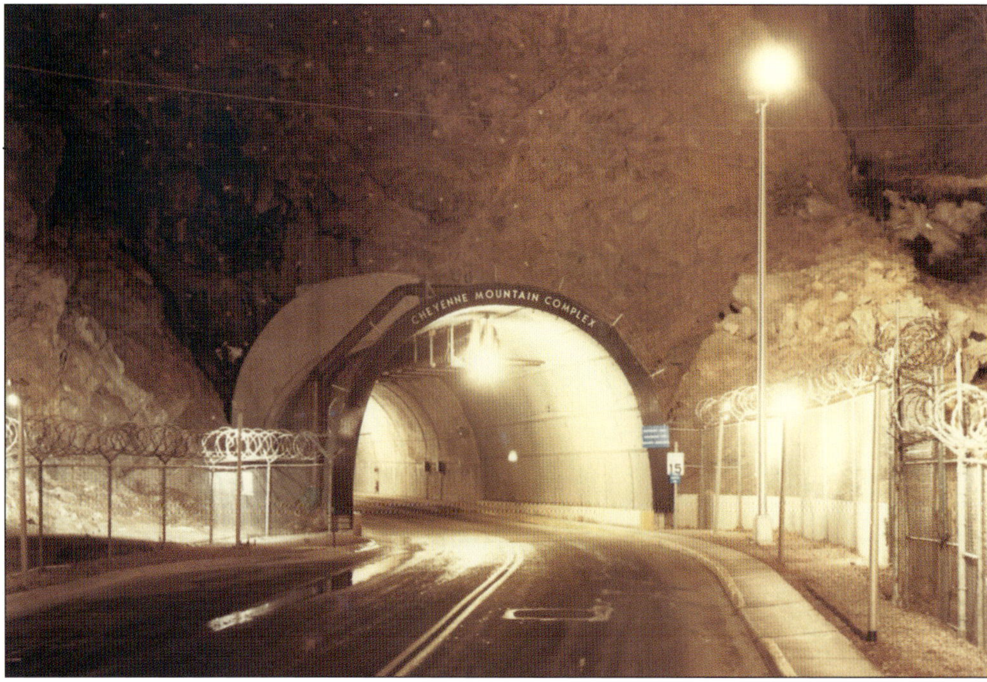

This iconic night shot of the main entrance captures how the tunnel into the Cheyenne Mountain Complex would have appeared in the Cold War era.

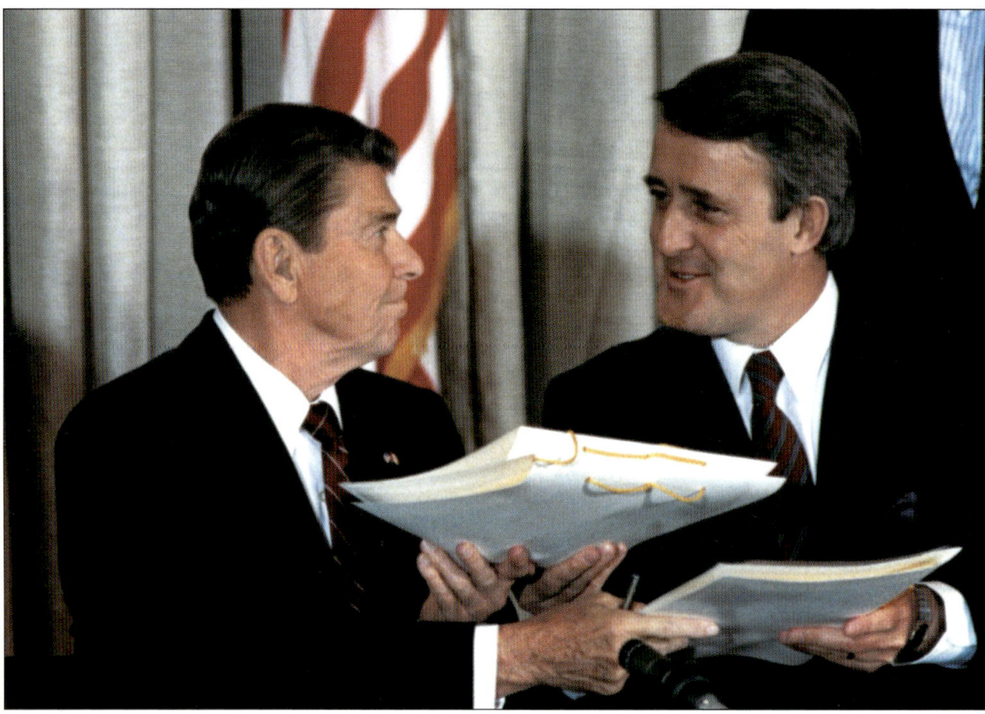

US president Ronald Reagan and Canadian prime minister Brian Mulroney exchanged signed copies of the NORAD Agreement in the mid-1980s. The close ties with Canada were strengthened with the signing of the agreement for another period.

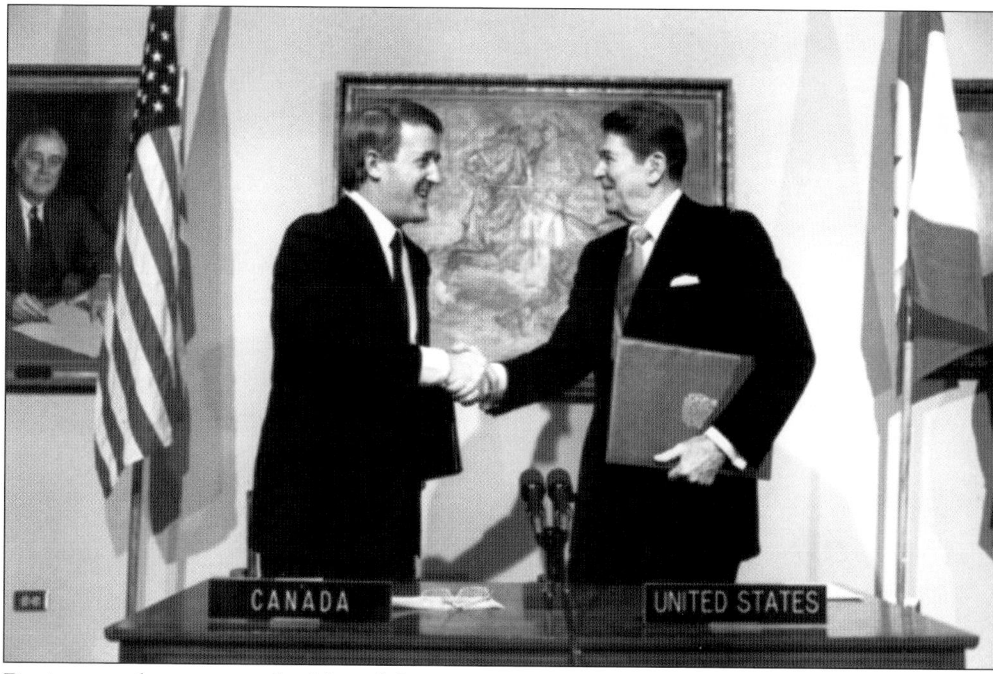

During another visit to the United States, Prime Minister Mulroney and President Reagan discussed defense issues between the two countries and renewed their commitment to protect North America from any threat.

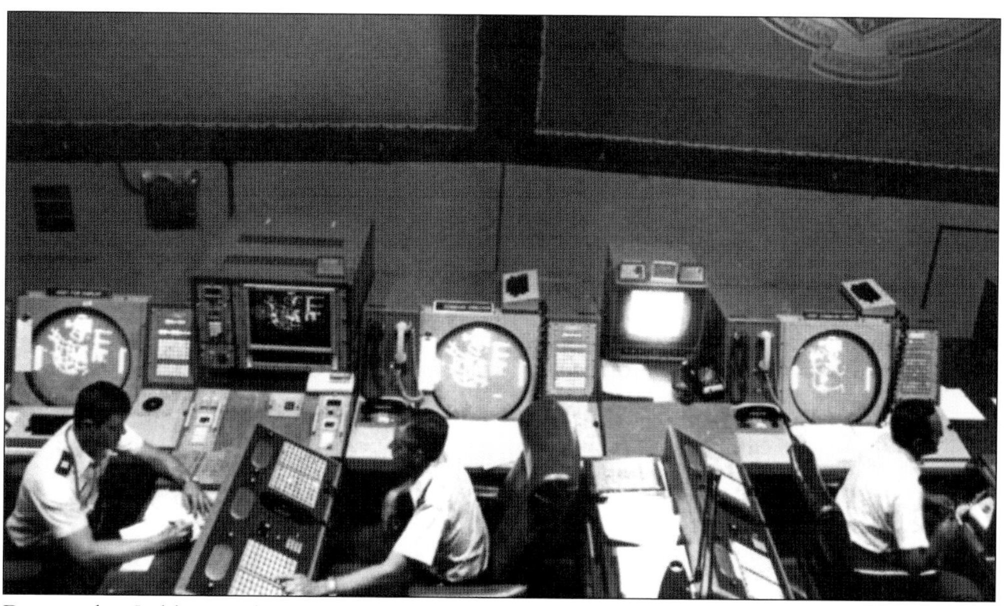
During the Cold War, the NORAD Command Center was a nerve center for watching North American sovereignty. The scopes in front of the leadership are Granite Sentry scopes, which displayed the air defense portrait of the United States and Canada.

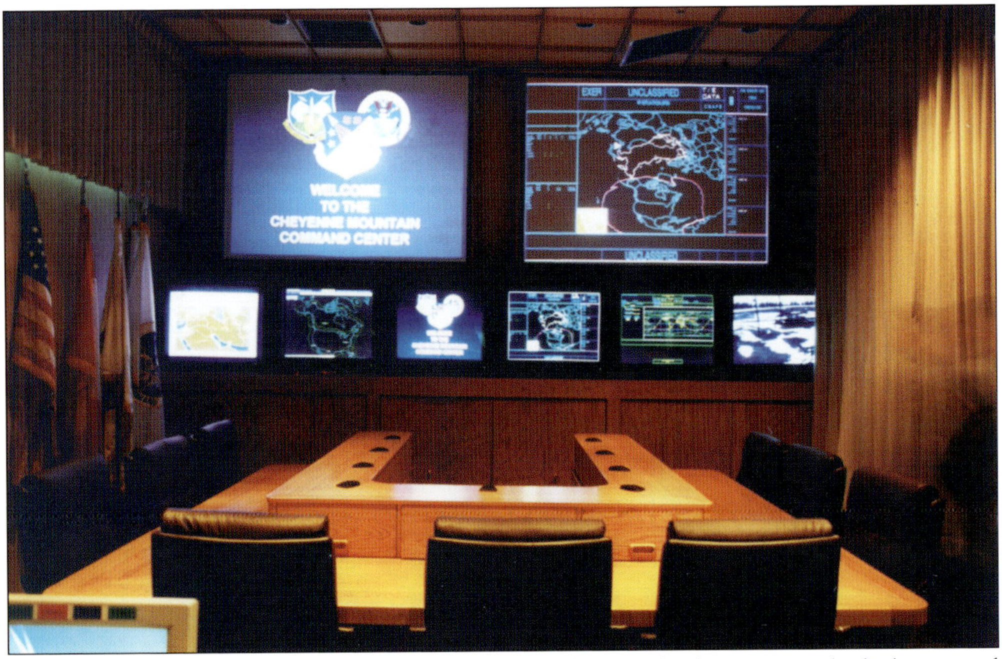

The command center senior battle staff area, pictured here, is the location in which the general and his senior staff assemble for exercise and real-world situations. CINCNORAD sits at the head of the table, with his deputies on either side. This is also the location in which VIPs are briefed on the Cheyenne Mountain Command Center operations.

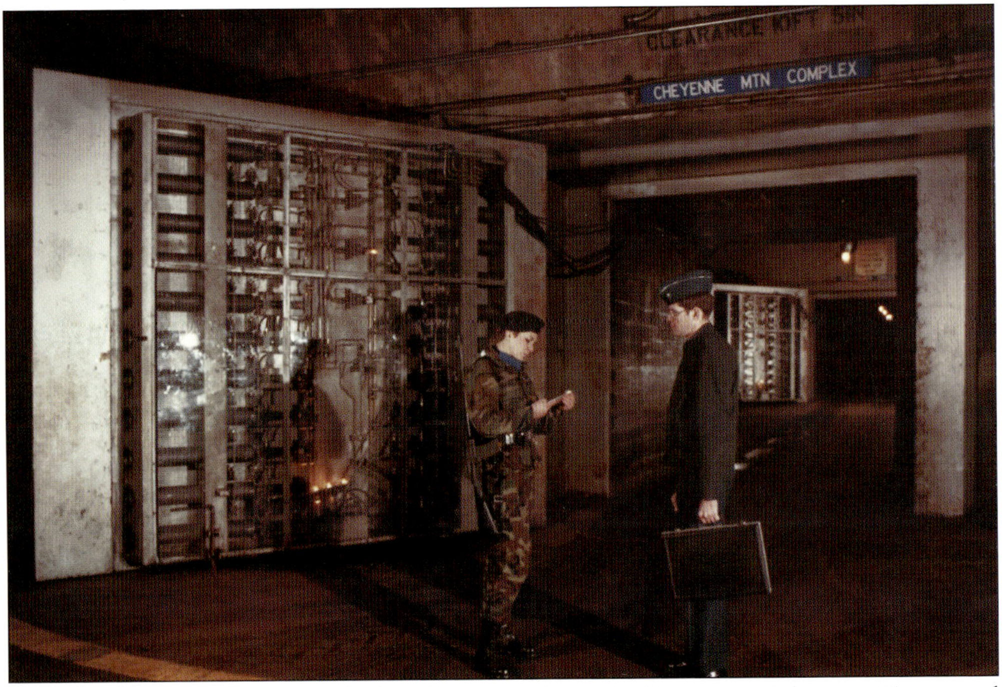

The first blast door located inside the Cheyenne Mountain Complex weighs over 25 tons and is made of concrete and steel. Security checks the access credentials of every person entering the complex.

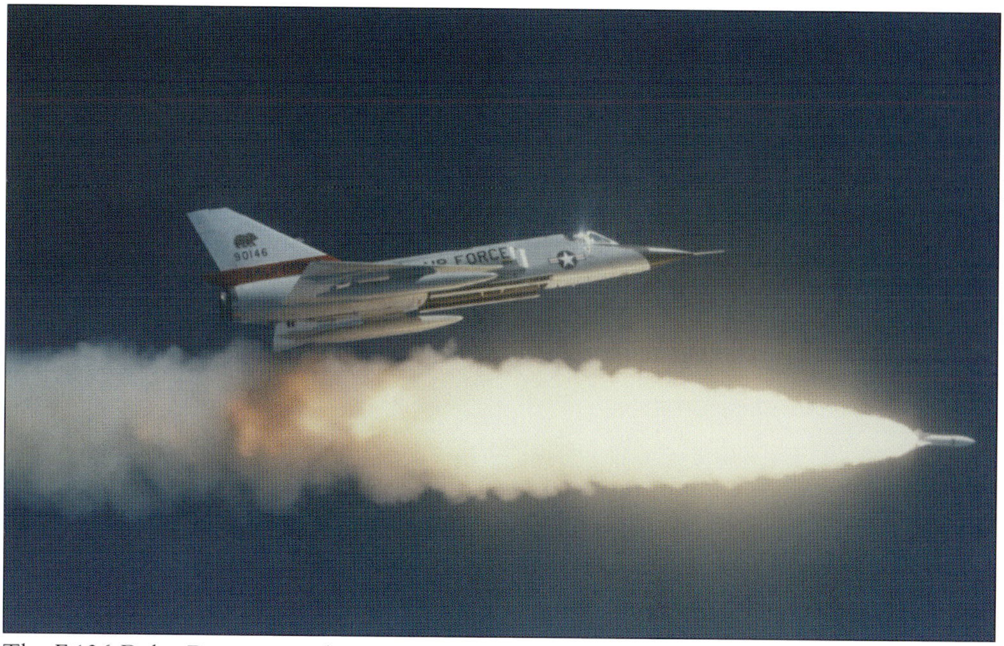

The F-106 Delta Dagger was the premier supersonic fighter-interceptor for air defense in the late 1970s and early 1980s. This aircraft, from the California Air National Guard 194th Fighter Interceptor Squadron (FIS), is launching an AIR-2A Genie test missile.

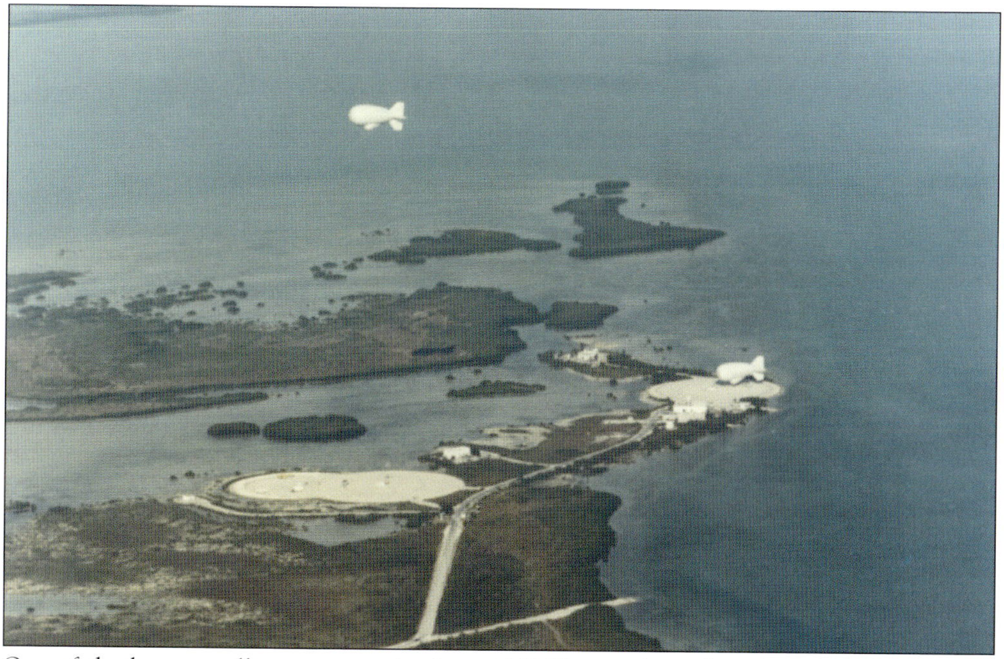

One of the key surveillance systems in the mid-1980s was the tethered aerostat radar system (TARS). Two US Air Force units located in Florida, one on Cape Canaveral AFS and the other near Key West (pictured), provided tracking of the Soviet bombers transiting between Russia and Cuba.

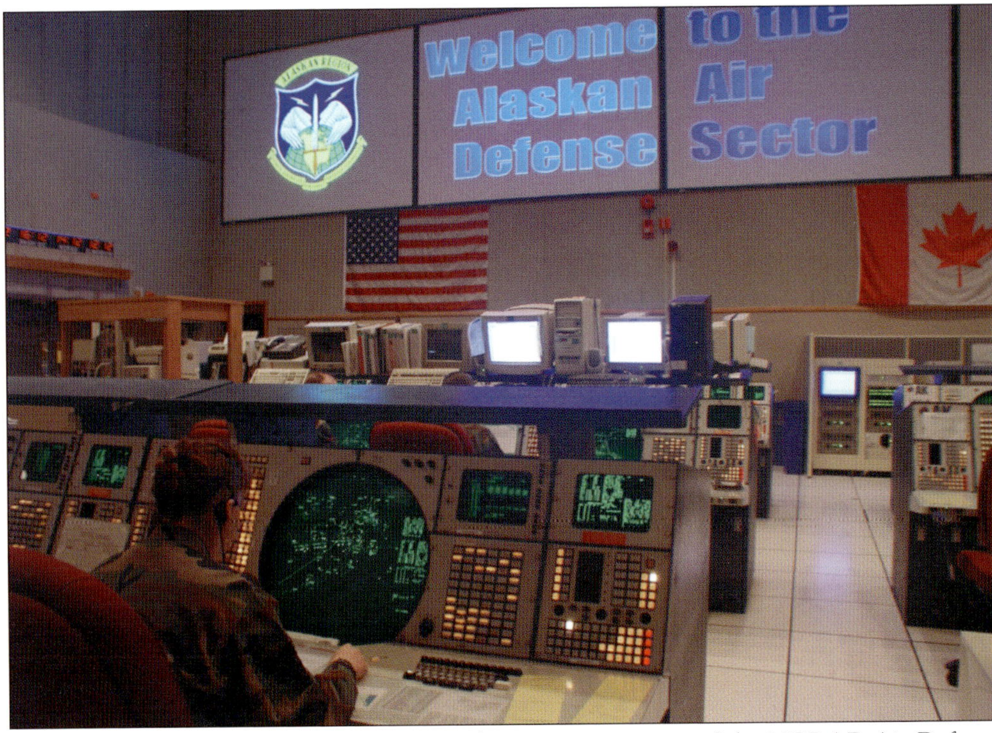

From the mid-1980s to 2009, the Q-93 was the operating system of the NORAD Air Defense sectors. Providing quick display of radar data, this system, located at the Alaskan NORAD Region at Elmendorf AFB, Alaska, was a huge improvement from the SAGE system it replaced.

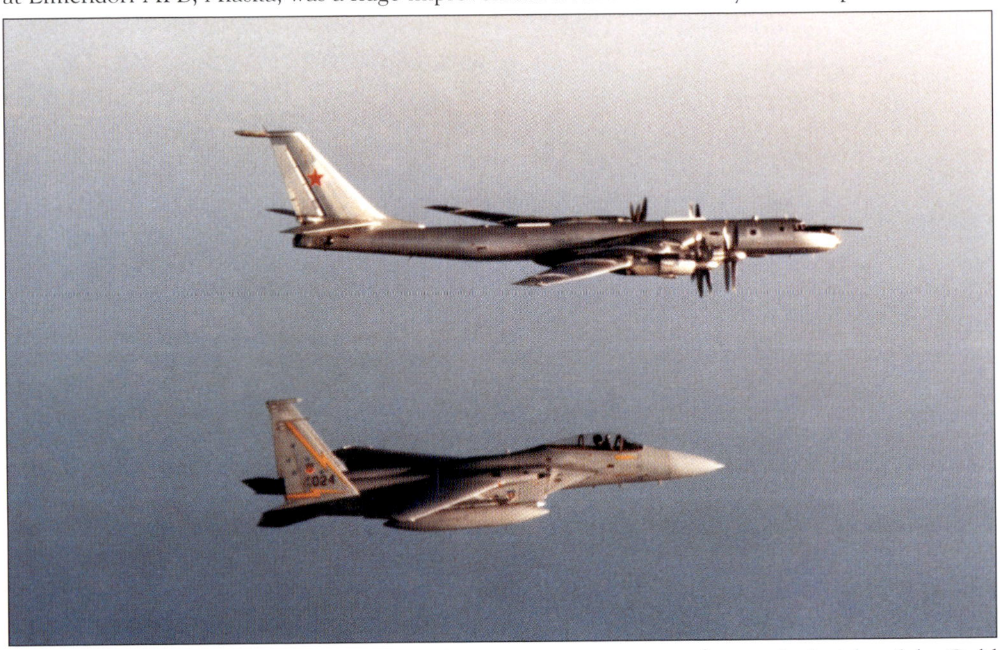

Soviet Bear Bombers were a threat to North American sovereignty during the height of the Cold War. Here, an F-15 is escorting the bomber as it transits near the US air defense identification zone. The Soviet bombers often tested air defense forces for response time.

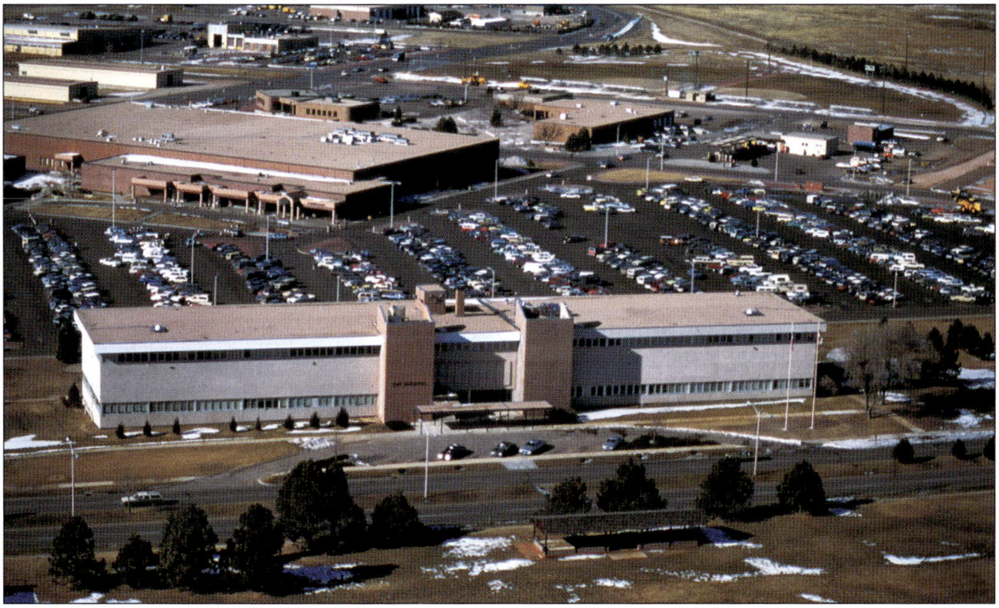

The Ent Building on Peterson AFB was NORAD headquarters for many decades. Named for the former location of NORAD headquarters, this facility was replaced by the new, modern Eberhart-Findley Building in 2003.

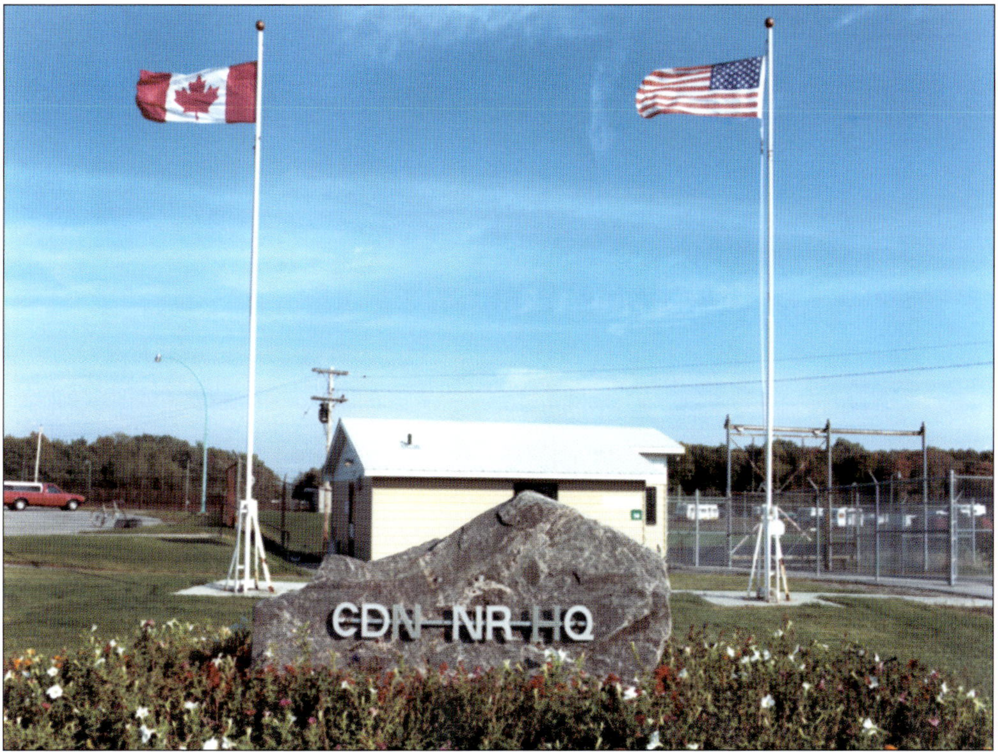

The Canadian NORAD Region, located at North Bay, Ontario, was also an underground facility until a new aboveground operations center was built. This photograph shows the entrance to the old underground facility, which is behind the gates on the right.

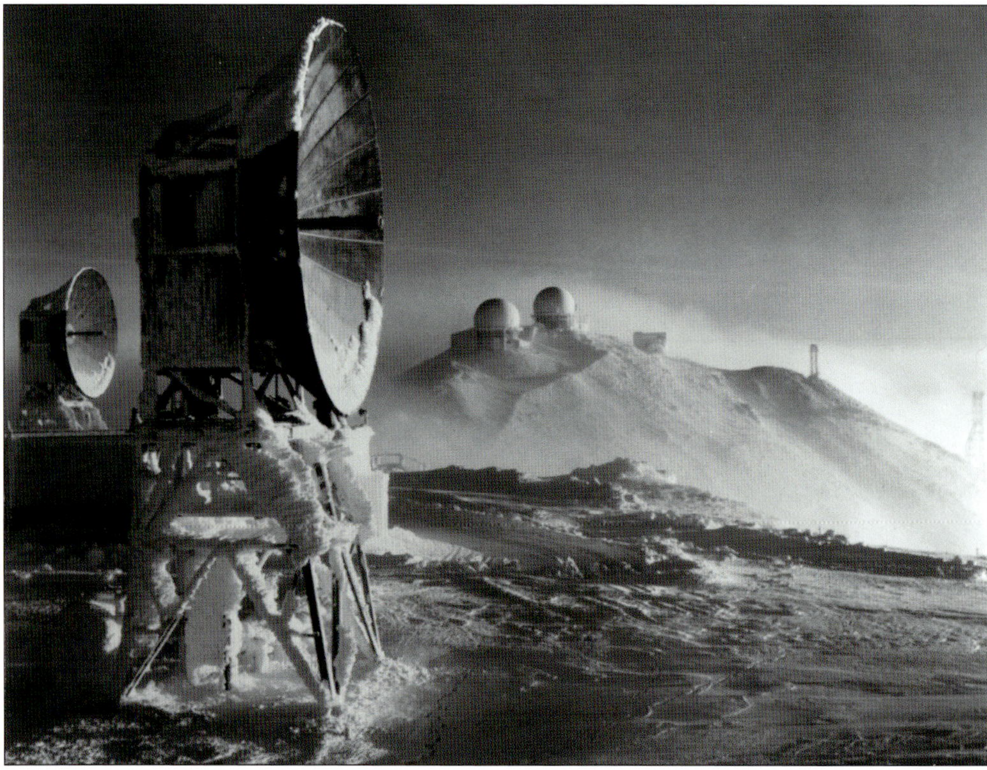

The radar sites located in the far north of Canada were built during the early years of the Cold War. Originally known as the DEW Line, for Distant Early Warning Line, the radar sites were manned until the upgraded North Warning System was built, and the sites were operated remotely. This photograph depicts the harsh winters that occur.

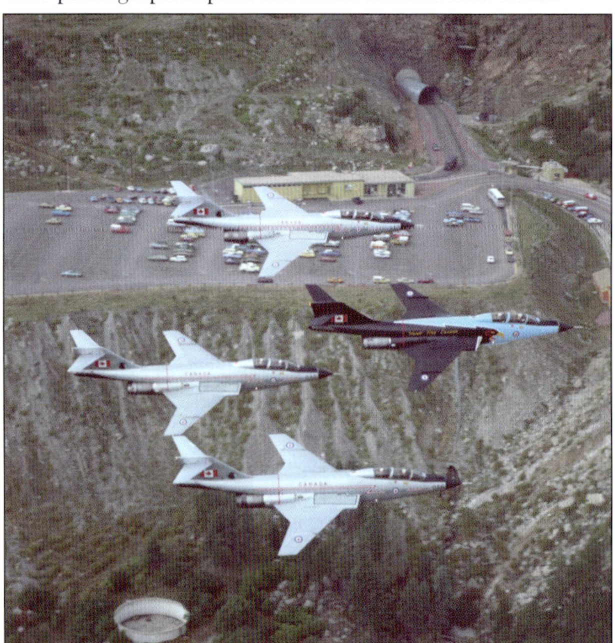

To honor NORAD's 20th anniversary, four CF-101 Voodoo fighters did a low-level pass over the Cheyenne Mountain AFS. The CF-101 was the primary Canadian air defense fighter until it was replaced by the technologically advanced CF-18 Hornet.

This mid-1980s map details the air defense sectors of the United States and Canada. The airspace of North America is continuously monitored for threat aircraft or aircraft in distress. Crews operate the consoles on a round-the-clock basis, ensuring all aircraft are identified.

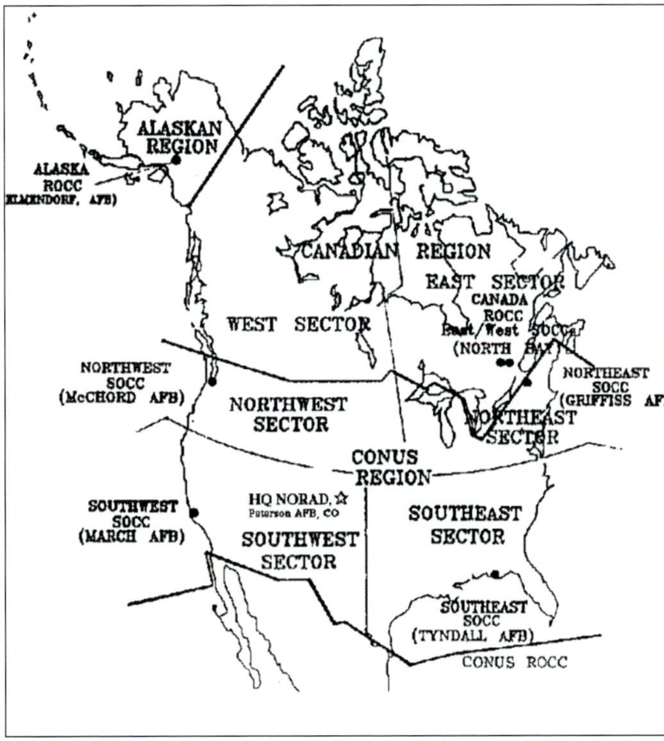

Pictured here is the tail gunner of a Soviet Bear bomber during a mission that came close to the North American air defense identification zone. This photograph, taken from an air defense fighter, shows a Soviet airman in the rear of the Bear bomber. The machine guns are in the up position, displaying nonaggression.

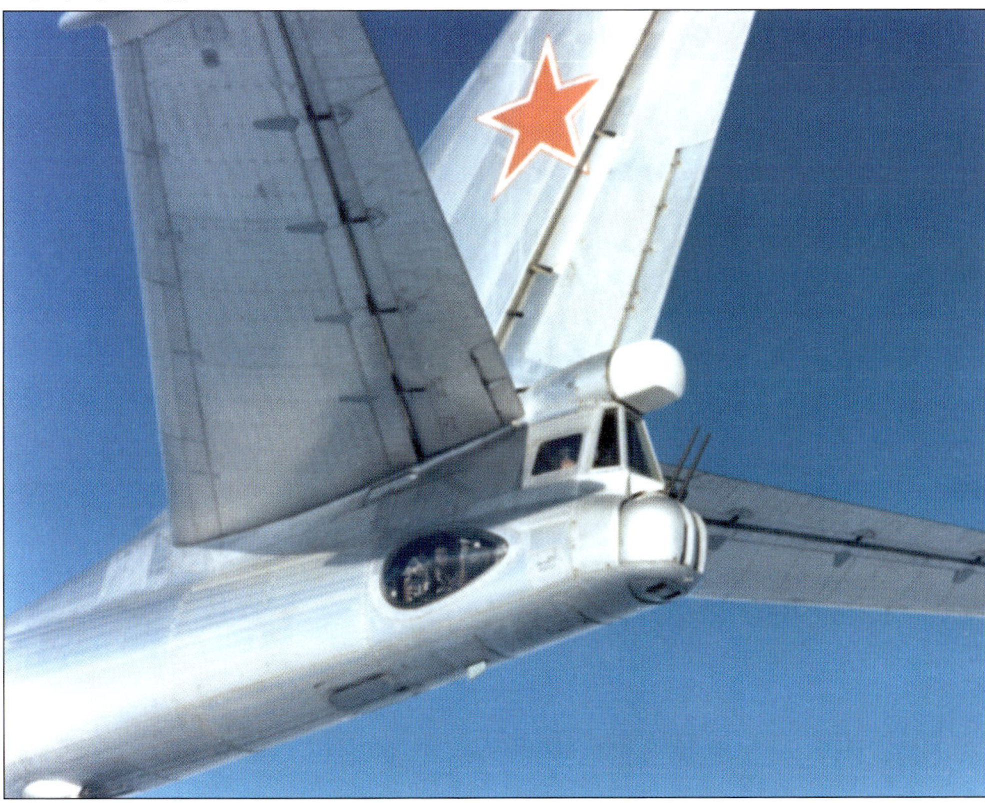

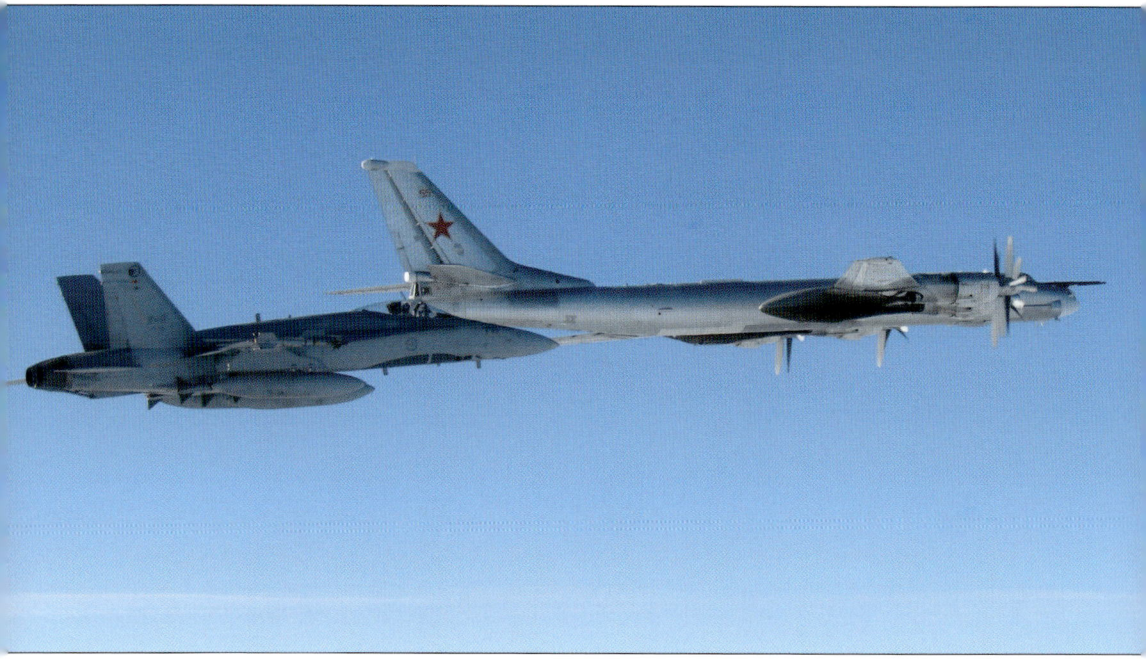

During the Cold War, the Royal Canadian Air Force (RCAF) flew the CF-18 Hornet as their air defense fighter. In this classic Cold War shot, a CF-18 has intercepted the Soviet Tu-95 Bear bomber off the Canadian coast. The RCAF has been on air defense alert since the NORAD agreement was signed in the late 1950s, ready to intercept unknown aircraft.

Five

9/11 AND THE WAR ON TERRORISM
NORAD'S NEW DIRECTION

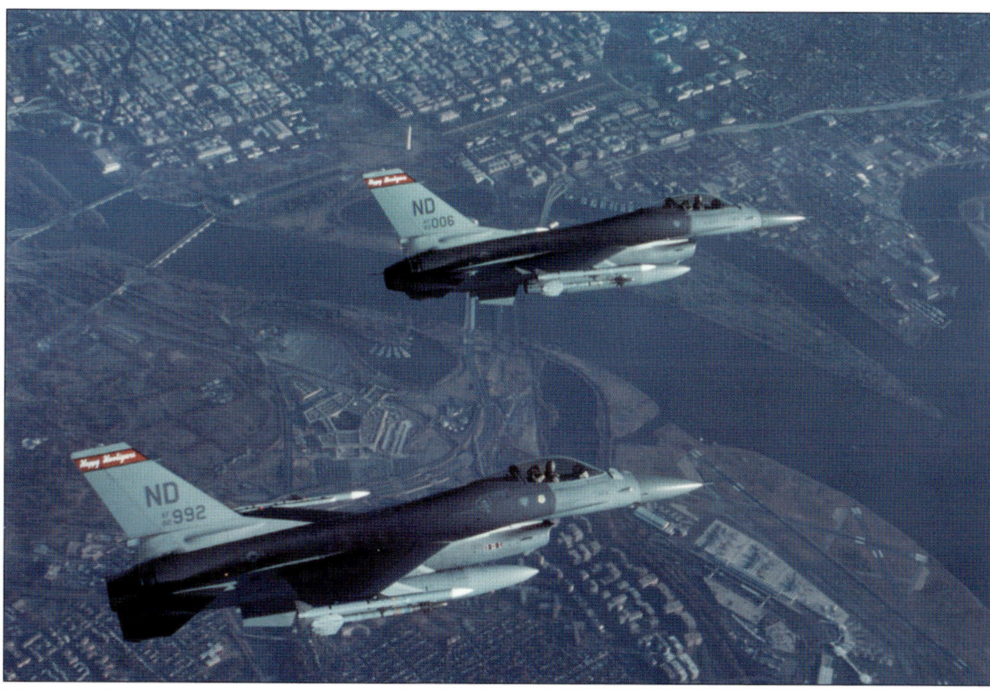

The attacks on September 11, 2001, forced NORAD to change its focus from watching aircraft approaching the borders to watching all aircraft in North America. After the attacks, alert fighters patrolled the skies 24 hours a day. Here, two F-16s from the 119th Fighter Group out of Fargo, North Dakota, fly a combat air patrol mission over the Pentagon.

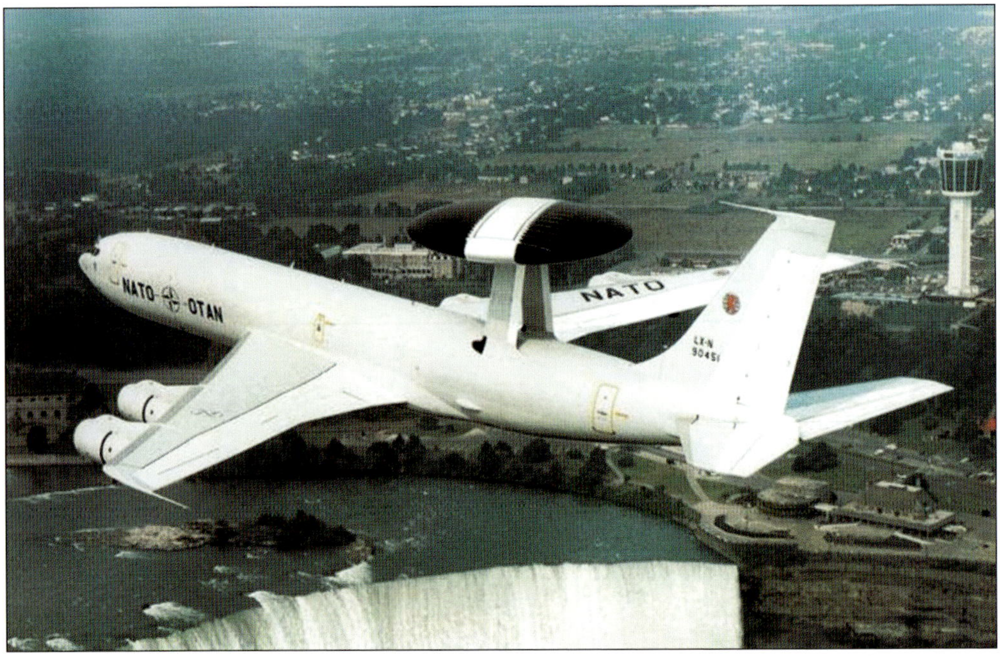

With US air defense forces tapped to the maximum after the 9/11 attacks, North Atlantic Treaty Organization (NATO) AWACS jets deployed to the United States to assist in the surveillance of airspace shortly afterward. This was the first time NATO forces had been deployed to the United States.

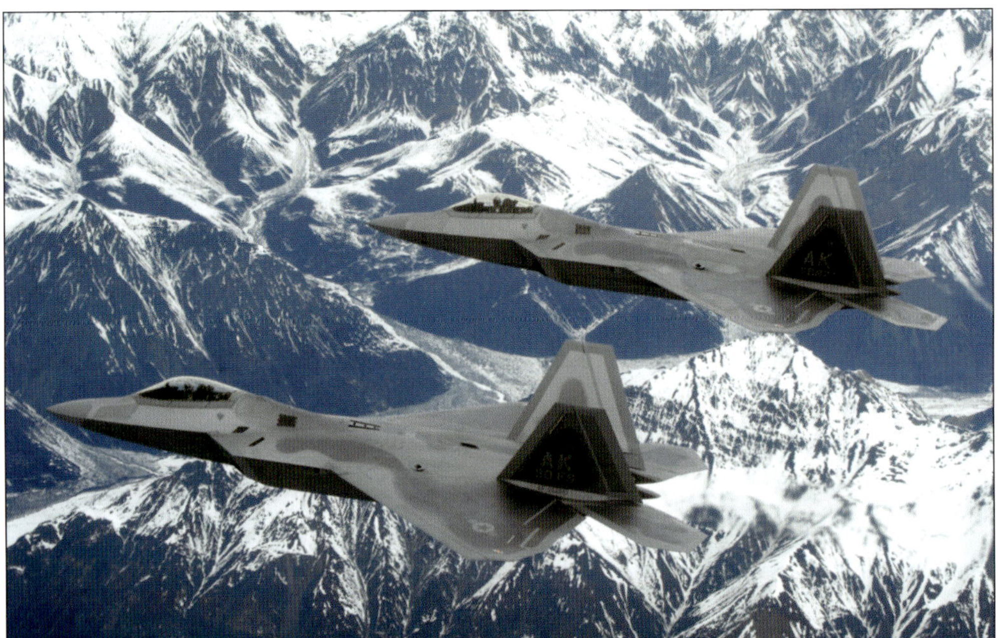

The US Air Force's newest air defense fighter is the stealthy F-22 Raptor. In this photograph, two F-22s are flying over Alaska on an air defense mission. Based at Joint Base Elmendorf-Richardson in Anchorage, the F-22s have intercepted Russian bombers outside the air defense identification zone on numerous occasions.

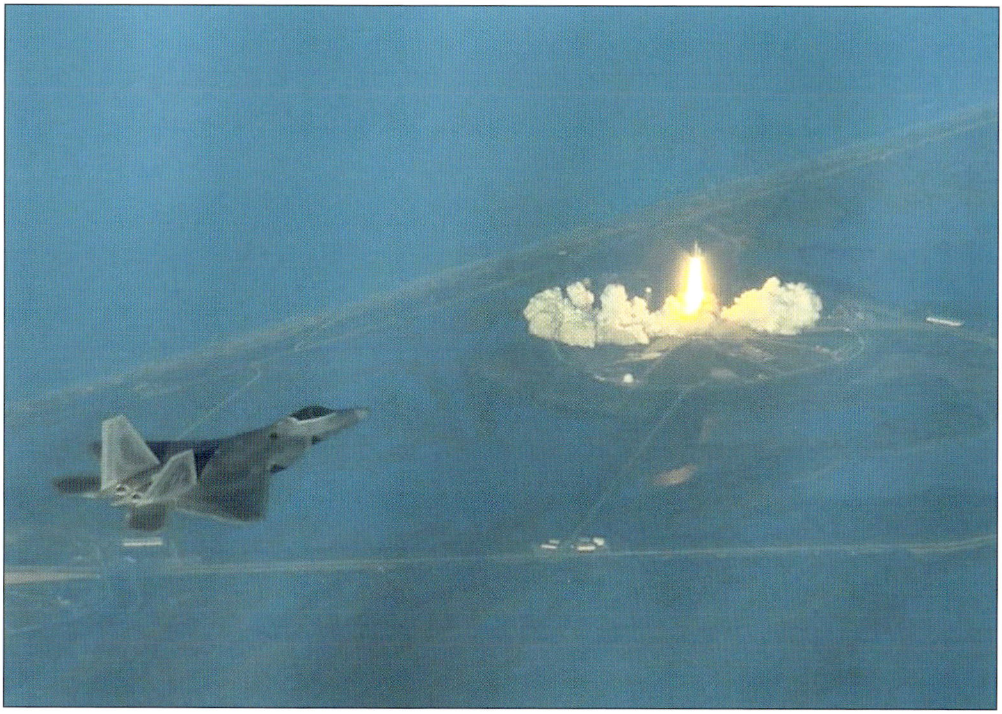

The F-22 Raptor has also guarded the skies over the Kennedy Space Center for the final space shuttle launches. Here, an F-22 monitors the skies for intruding aircraft that could pose a threat to the shuttle or other facilities at the launch complex.

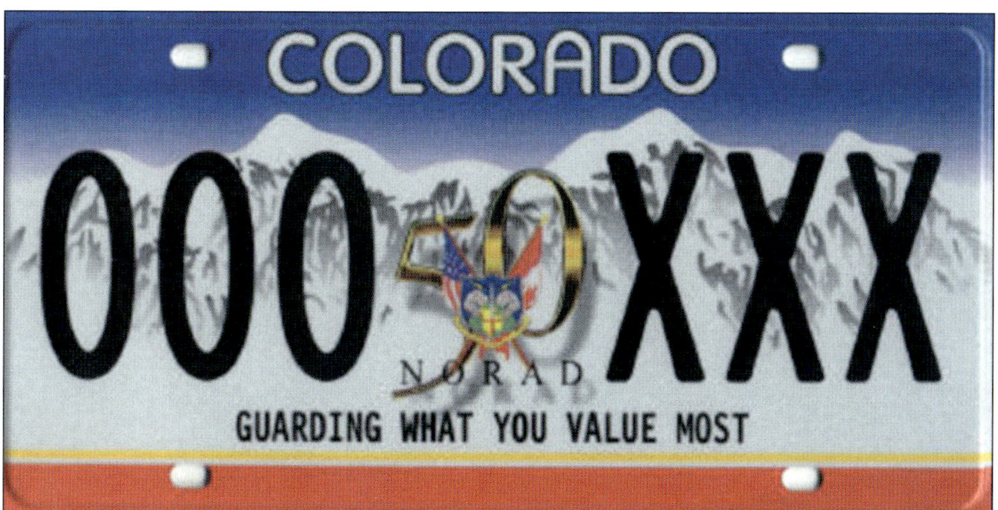

In 2008, NORAD celebrated its 50th anniversary. In honor of that milestone, approved by the governor, the State of Colorado issued this license plate. Hundreds of these plates were sold to anyone interested in honoring NORAD's 50 years of service.

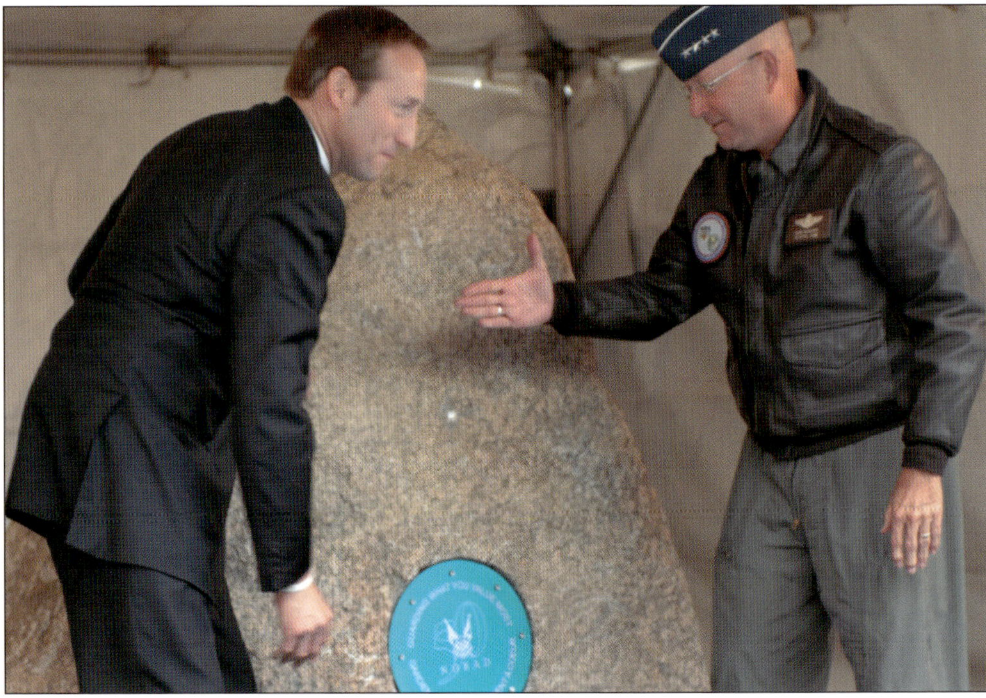

In honor of NORAD's 50th anniversary, a time capsule was buried inside a granite boulder excavated from Cheyenne Mountain. The capsule, to be opened on the service's 75th anniversary, contains artifacts from the local community as well as items celebrating NORAD's 50 years of exemplary service. Gen. Gene Renuart, commander of NORAD, and Canadian Minister of National Defence Peter MacKay sealed the time capsule.

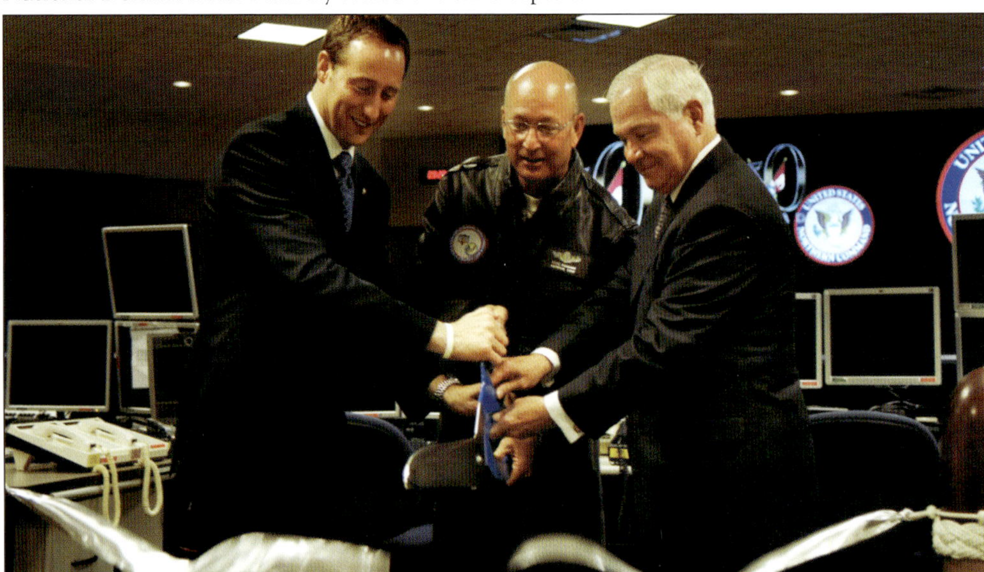

Minister of National Defence Peter MacKay (left), Gen. Gene Renuart, commander of NORAD, and Secretary of Defense Robert Gates cut the ceremonial ribbon officially opening the new NORAD-NORTHCOM Command Center on Peterson AFB. This new center takes over from the one inside Cheyenne Mountain AFS, which now will serve as the alternate command center.

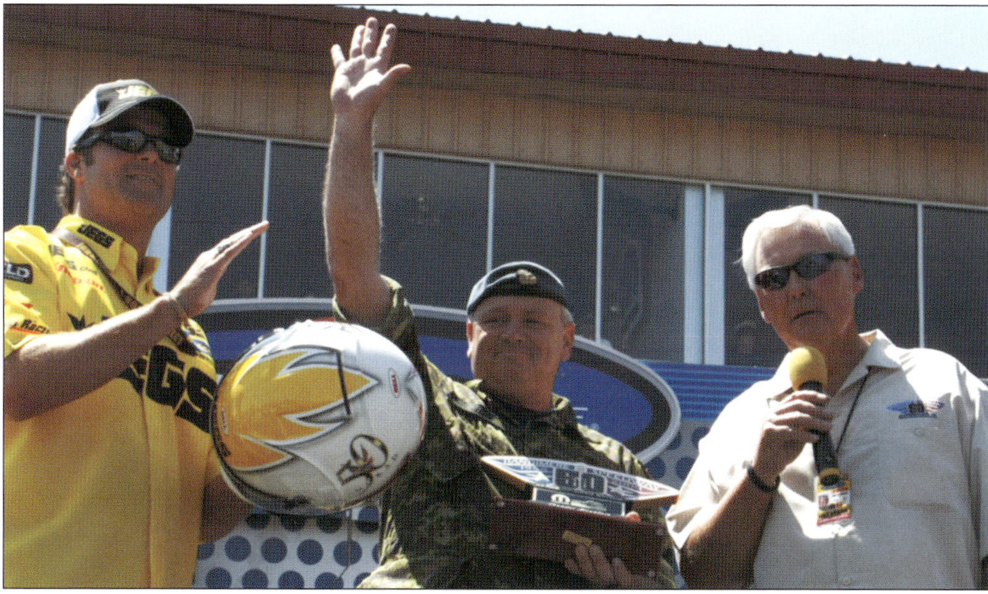

As part of NORAD's 50th anniversary celebration, six-time National Hot Rod Association World Champion Jeg Coughlin Jr. honored NORAD by displaying the NORAD 50th logo on his racecar and helmet. Additionally, Bandimere Speedway in Denver honored NORAD by having Canadian Lieutenant-General Bouchard as the honorary starter for the Mile-High Nationals. Here, Jeg Coughlin (left) is presenting the helmet to Lieutenant-General Bouchard while John Bandimere Jr., owner of Bandimere Speedway, presents the general with an honorary starter trophy.

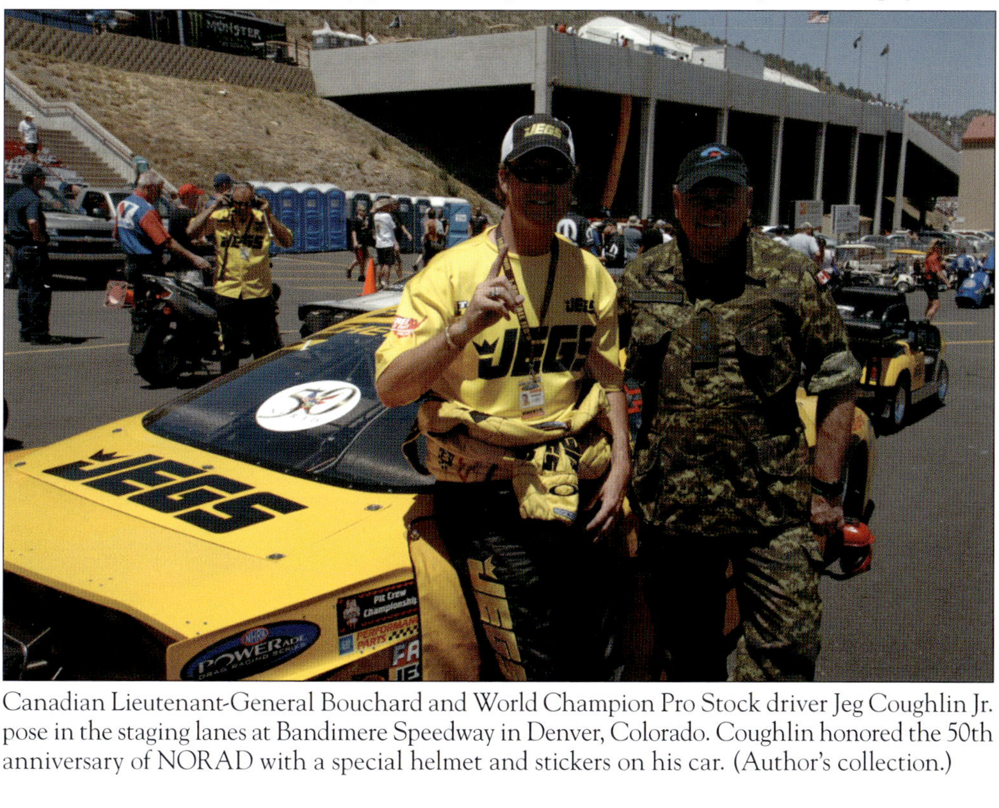

Canadian Lieutenant-General Bouchard and World Champion Pro Stock driver Jeg Coughlin Jr. pose in the staging lanes at Bandimere Speedway in Denver, Colorado. Coughlin honored the 50th anniversary of NORAD with a special helmet and stickers on his car. (Author's collection.)

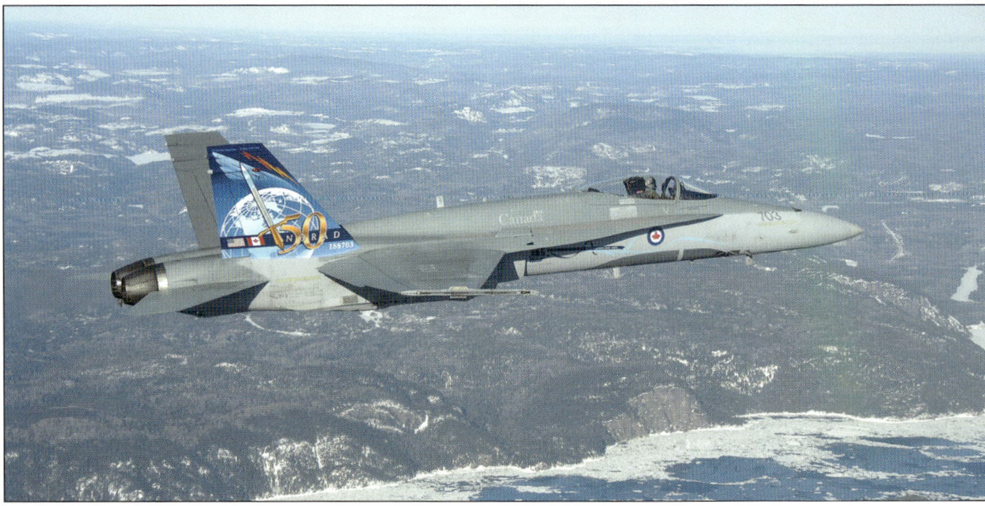

In 2008, to honor the NORAD's 50th anniversary, this RCAF CF-18 Hornet had a specially painted tail fin for the year. This CF-18 Hornet flew throughout Canada and the United States to various air shows and displays, showing off the special paint scheme and telling the NORAD history in the process.

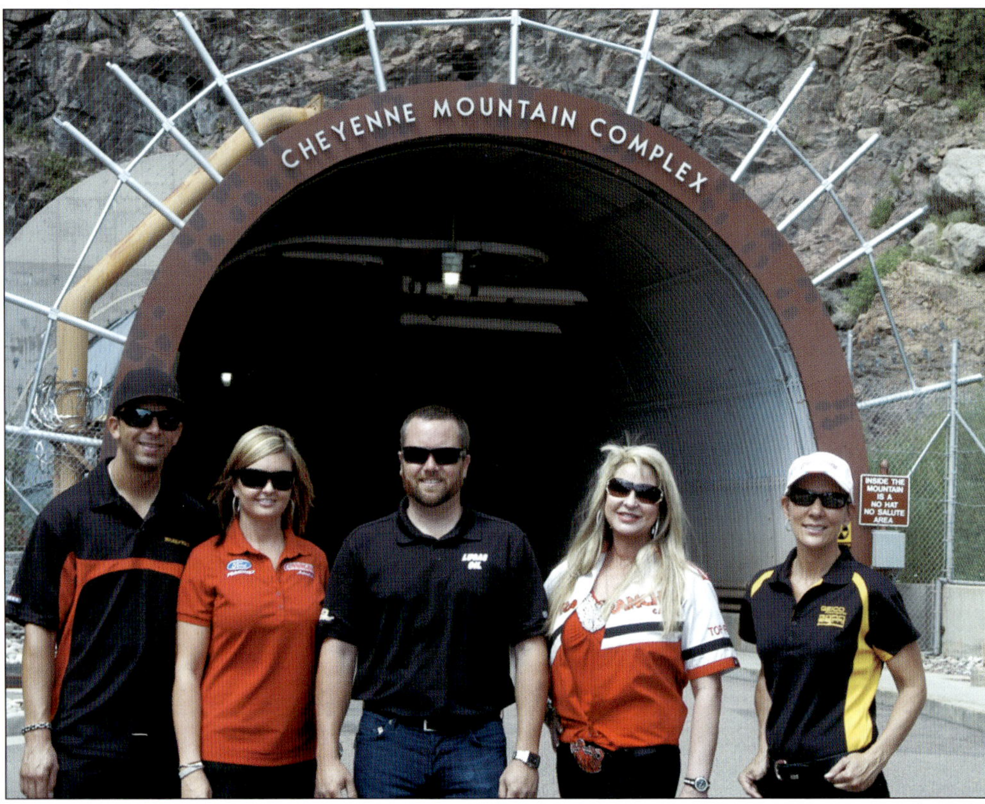

Professional athletes often come to Cheyenne Mountain, not only see the famous facility, but also to thank the troops for their service. Professional drag racing drivers, from left to right, Richie Stevens, Erica Enders-Stevens, Shawn Langdon, Lori Johns, and Karen Stouffer pose in front of the north portal.

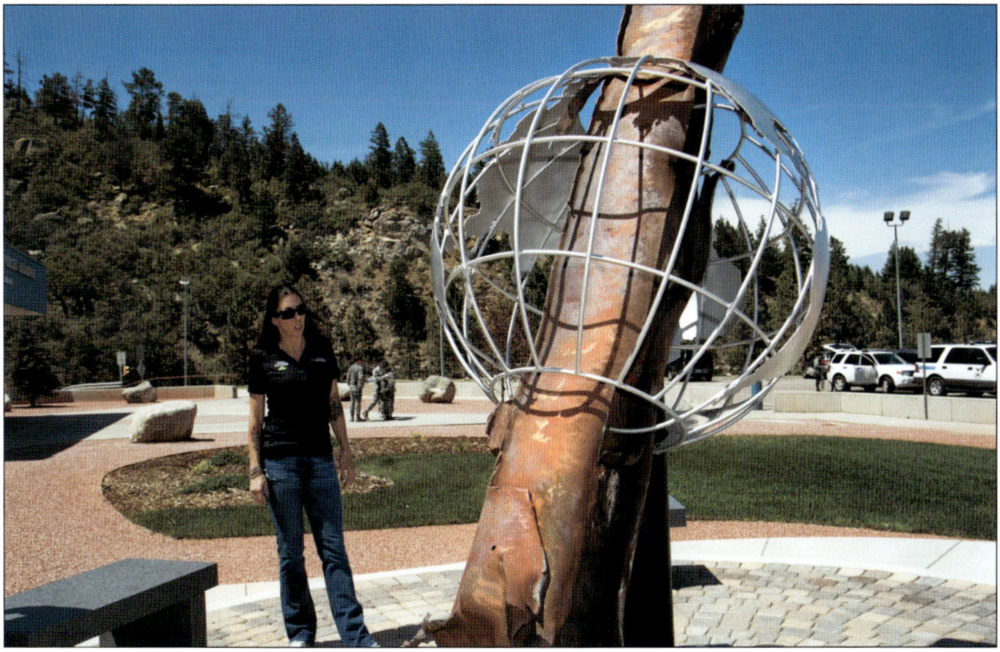

National Hot Rod Association Patrón Tequila Funny Car driver Alexis DeJoria, whose father is a Navy veteran, looks at the 9/11 Memorial at Cheyenne Mountain AFS in 2012. She and other drivers were VIP guests for a tour of Cheyenne Mountain and also met with the troops and their families.

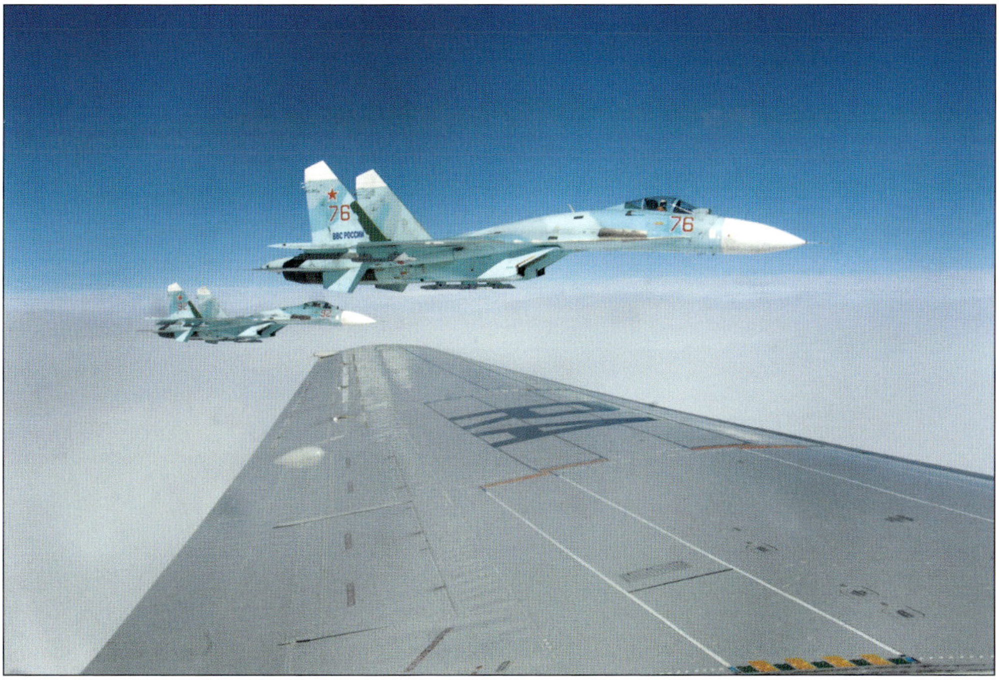

With terrorism as a worldwide issue, the continued military cooperation with Russia has opened combined exercises. Here, two Russian Su-27 Flankers shadow a simulated hijacked airliner prior to handing off the intercept to US fighters.

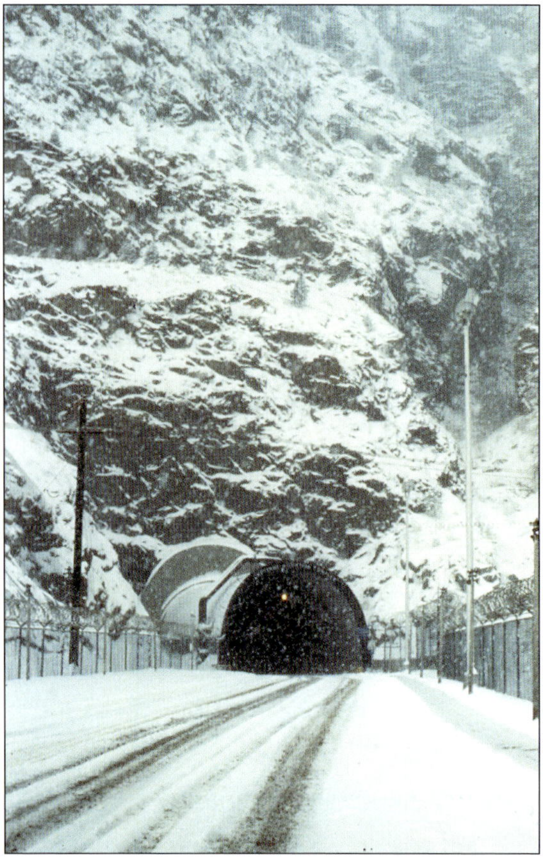

This is a snowy photograph of the north portal entrance to Cheyenne Mountain Complex. With the entrance to the mountain about 1,000 feet higher in elevation than Colorado Springs, the entrance gets a bit more snow than the city.

Celebrities often visit Cheyenne Mountain for a VIP tour and a chance to meet and thank the troops. Here, drivers from the National Hot Rod Association pose in front of the north portal in 2012. Pictured from left to right are Alexis DeJoria, Jack Beckman, Courtney Force, and Melanie Troxel.

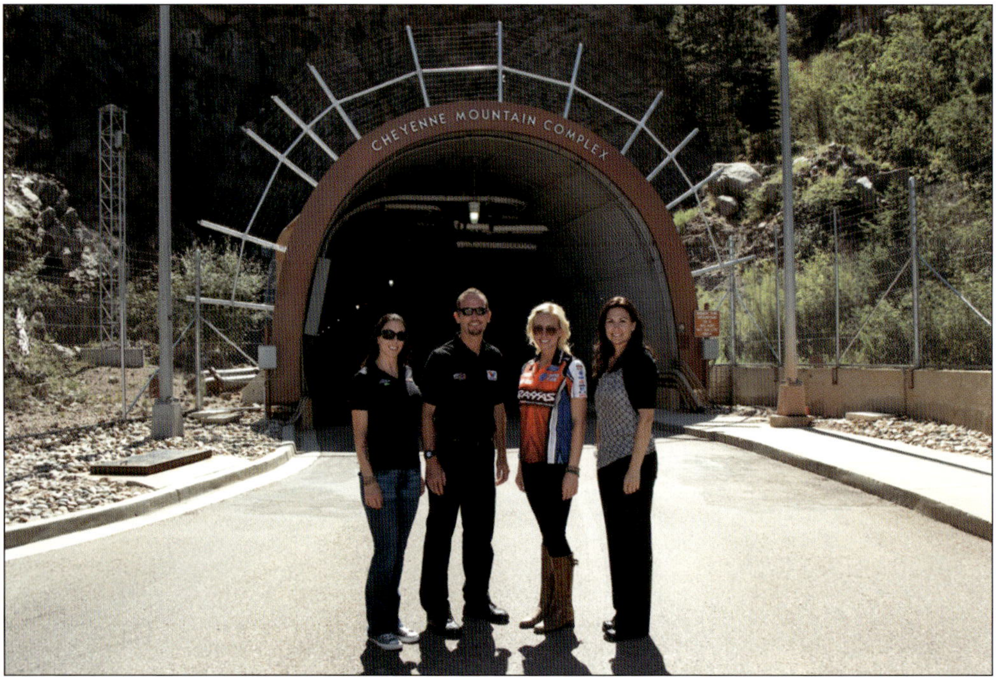

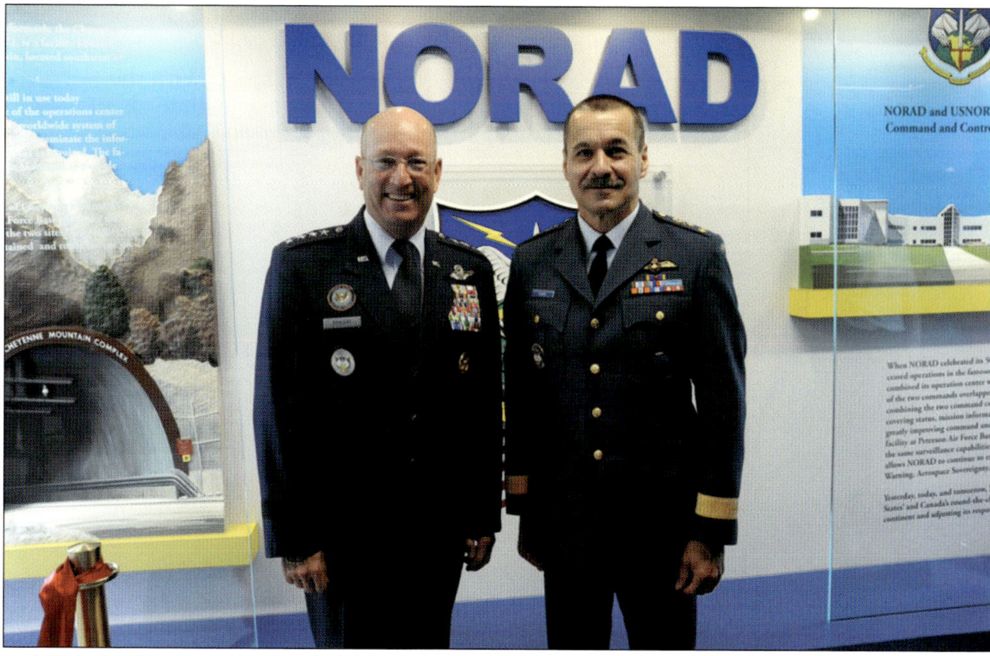

In 2004, the Pentagon honored NORAD and USNORTHCOM with the opening of a permanent display. Canadian Gen. Gene Renuart (left), NORAD commander, and Canadian Lt.-Gen. Marcel Duval, NORAD deputy commander, pose in front of the display after the ceremonial opening.

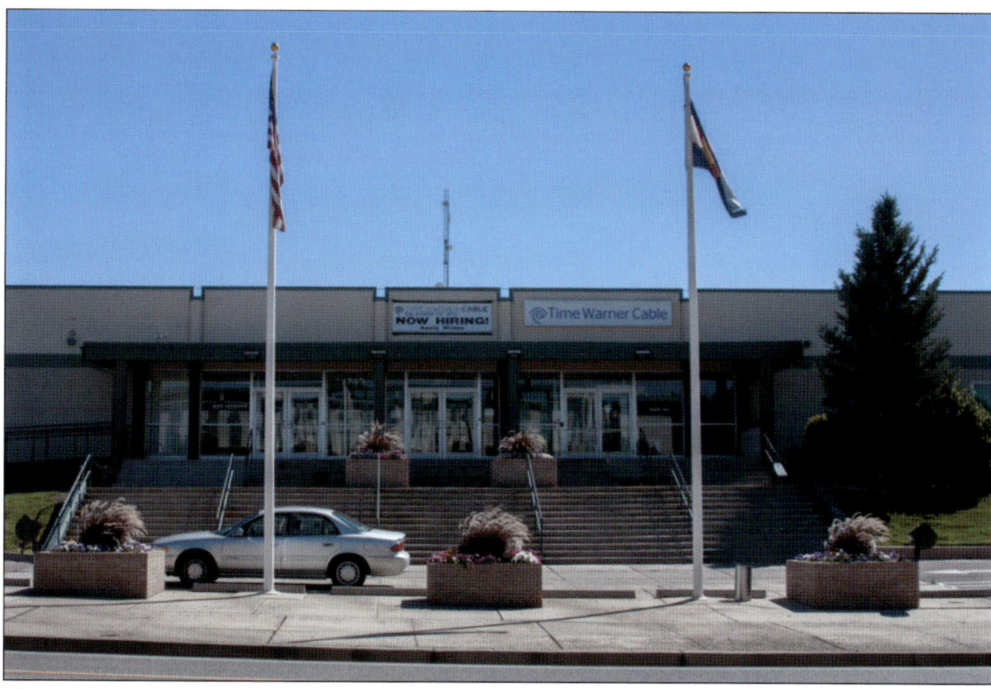

This is a present-day view of the entrance of the Chidlaw Building in downtown Colorado Springs. The former headquarters is now an office building. Heavily changed inside, the exterior is the same as it was when NORAD departed the facility in the mid-1970s.

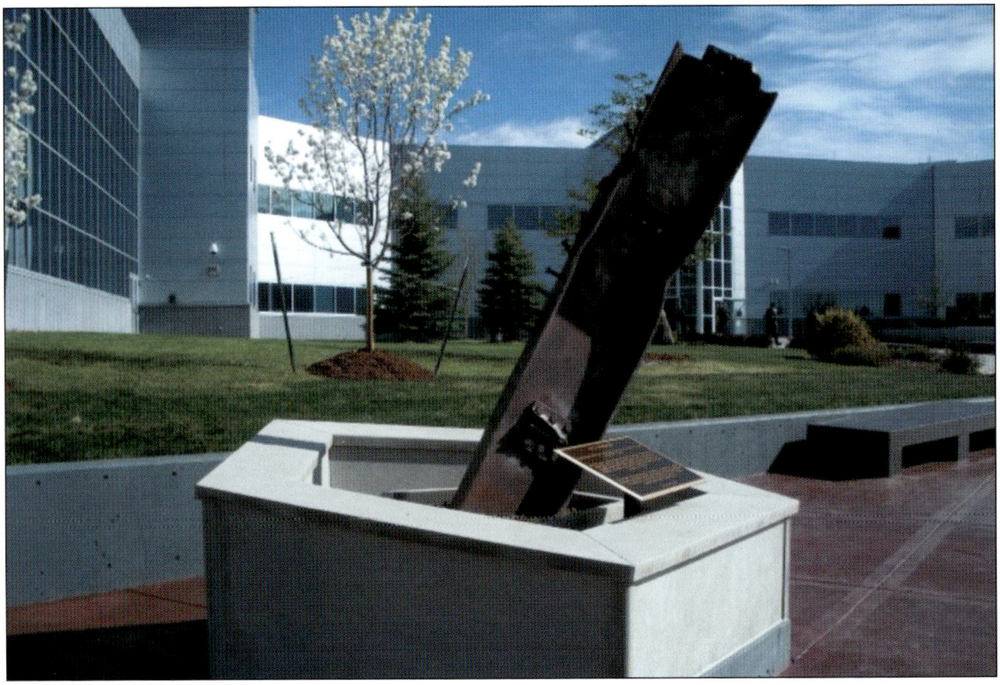

In May 2010, Gen. Gene Renuart dedicated the 9/11 Memorial in front of the NORAD-USNORTHCOM Headquarters. The steel girder is from the World Trade Center complex, and it faces toward New York City. The dirt in the pentagonal container is from the Pennsylvania crash site of United Flight 93. (Author's collection.)

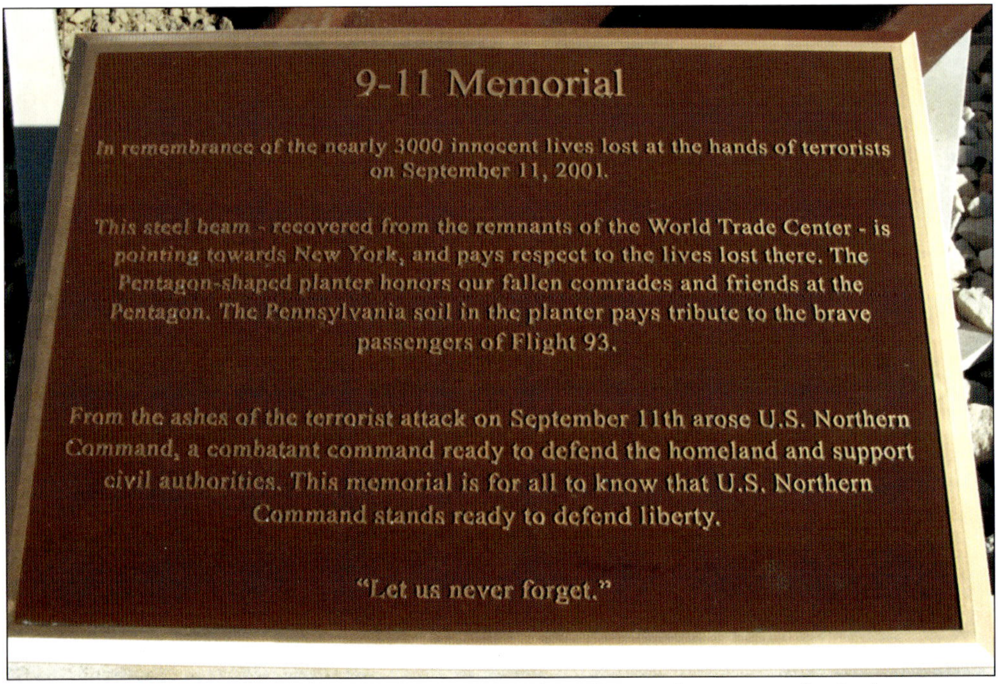

Every day, the men and women of the two commands walk past this memorial, which serves as a reminder of the enormity of their mission of protecting North America. (Author's collection.)

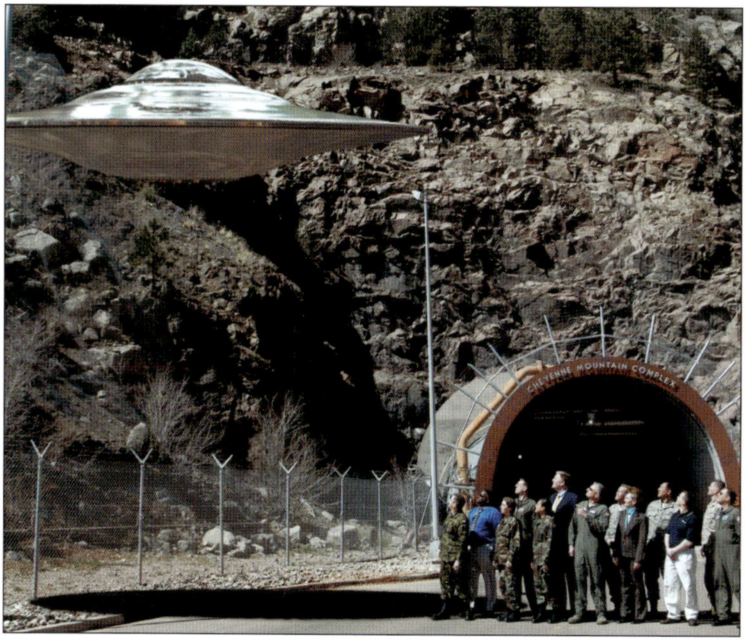

The lore of Cheyenne Mountain AFS has always intrigued people about what actually goes on inside the top secret facility. One of the interesting legends is that Cheyenne Mountain is where the United States stores UFOs, in collusion with Nevada's famous Area 51. This staged photograph is a favorite of conspiracy theorists—or is it staged?

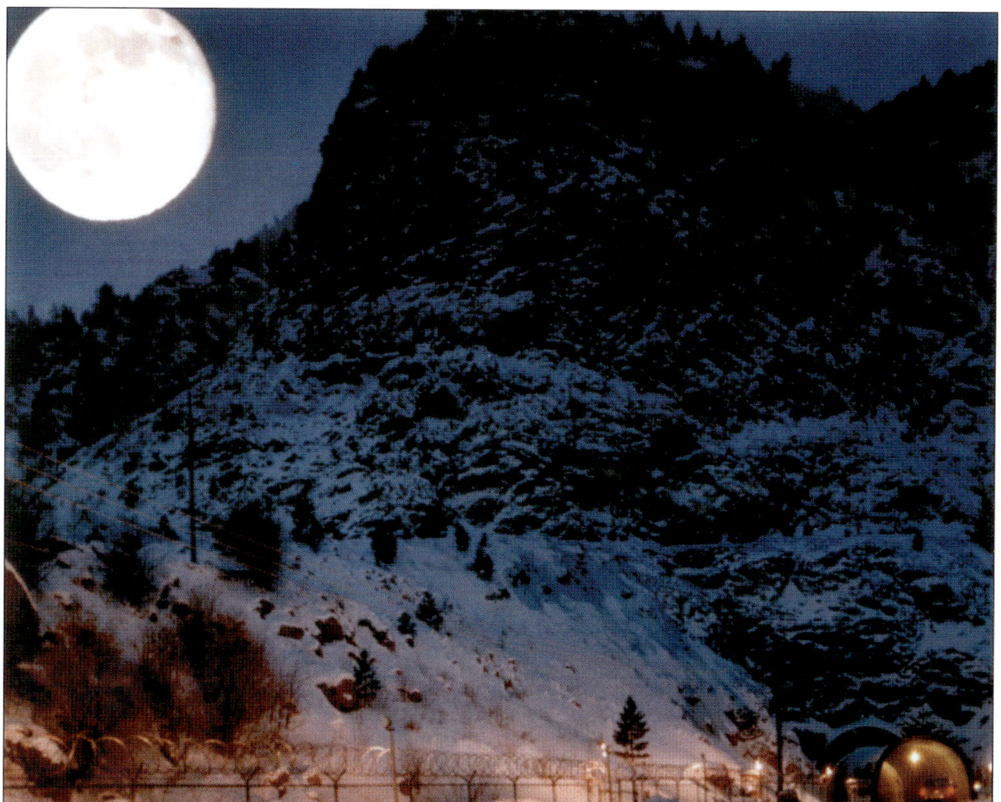

This stunning wintery photograph shows the full moon just about to go behind Cheyenne Mountain. With its location nestled in the Front Range of the Colorado Rocky Mountains, some spectacular shots have been taken of Cheyenne Mountain and its surrounding area.

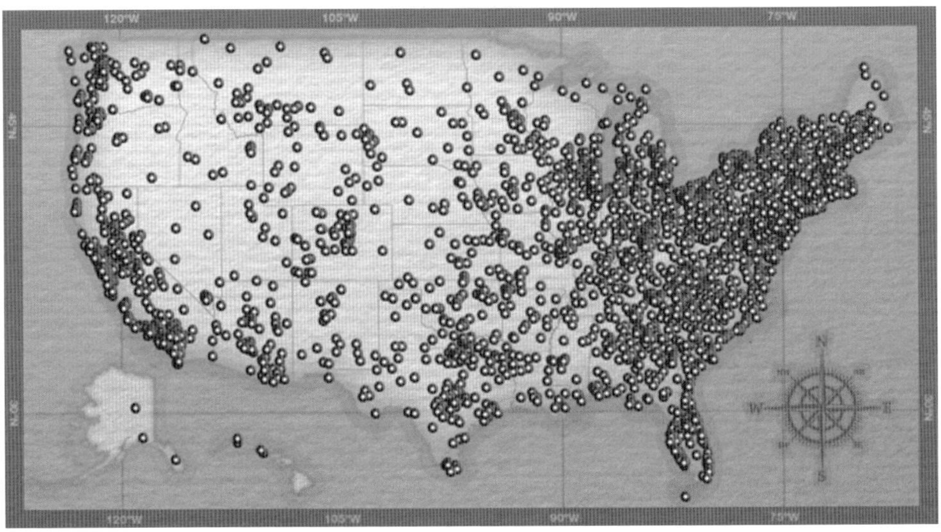